P7-ENJ-427

THE ROGER FEDERER STORY

Quest For Perfection

RENÉ STAUFFER

New Chapter Press

Cover and interior design: Emily Brackett, Visible Logic

Originally published in Germany under the title "Das Tennis-Genie" by
Pendo Verlag. © Pendo Verlag GmbH & Co. KG, Munich and Zurich, 2006

Published across the world in English by New Chapter Press,
www.newchapterpressonline.com
ISBN 094-2257-391
978-094-2257-397

Printed in the United States of America

Contents

From The Author v
Prologue: Encounter with a 15-year-old. ix
Introduction: No One Expected Him. xiv

PART I

From Kempton Park to Basel 3
A Boy Discovers Tennis 8
Homesickness in Ecublens. 14
The Best of All Juniors 21
A Newcomer Climbs to the Top 30
New Coach, New Ways 35
Olympic Experiences 40
No Pain, No Gain 44
Uproar at the Davis Cup 49
The Man Who Beat Sampras 53
The Taxi Driver of Biel 57
Visit to the Top Ten 60
Drama in South Africa. 65
Red Dawn in China 70
The Grand Slam Block 74
A Magic Sunday. 79
A Cow for the Victor 86
Reaching for the Stars 91
Duels in Texas 95
An Abrupt End. 100
The Glittering Crowning 104
No. 1 109
Samson's Return 116

New York, New York 122

Setting Records Around the World. 125

The Other Australian 130

A True Champion. 137

Fresh Tracks on Clay 142

Three Men at the Champions Dinner 146

An Evening in Flushing Meadows 150

The Savior of Shanghai. 155

Chasing Ghosts 160

A Rivalry Is Born 163

Two New Friends: Woods and Sampras 169

The Perfect 10 175

PART II

The Person: Nice but Firm 183

The Player: Like a Chameleon 190

The Opponent: Just to be in his Shoes 197

The Entrepreneur: Sign of the Hippo 204

Everybody Wants Him: The Everyday Media Routine. 215

The Celebrated Man: The Media's View 220

The Ambasssador: On a Noble Mission 225

Timeline. 231

Quotes On Roger Federer. 239

Grand Slam Man 244

From The Publisher 245

List Of Press Sources For Quotations. 246

Index 247

From The Author

I made the decision to write a book about Roger Federer after Wimbledon in 2003, when he became Switzerland's first male Grand Slam champion. I had been covering Wimbledon for over twenty years and was well aware of the tremendous significance of this victory. I approached Roger and his parents with this idea, but they were of the opinion, however, that his story had only just begun and that it was too early to write a biography about a 22-year-old. I have to admit that they were right—but just a few years later, Federer's place in history became evident—in the circle of the all-time greats, next to players such as Björn Borg, Pete Sampras, Rod Laver or Fred Perry.

This book attempts to demonstrate how long and difficult Federer's way to the top has been, what was preventing him from developing his tremendous talent more quickly, how he finally managed to exploit his potential and how extraordinary his winning streaks in this competitive international sport have been. The book also puts a light on Federer's surroundings and the people who were vital in his quest for perfection. It may serve to illustrate how high the goals are that yet lie before him in his future career—such as the Grand Slam or the high-water mark of 14 Grand Slam titles. The fact that this is a major topic of discussion with the international media, players and experts is no coincidence.

As the proverb goes, a prophet is not without honor save in his own country. In the case of Federer, his accomplishments and talents as a sportsman, ambassador and role model of universal dimensions also generally seem to be more highly regarded by those outside the Swiss border. If some readers become more aware of what a godsend Federer has been for tennis and for sports in general, as an athlete as well as a human being, then this book has already accomplished very much.

In viewing the materials that I have gathered in folders, electronic archives and personal recollections of him over the past dozen years, the thought occurred to me over and over again that Roger Federer may be the athlete who has conducted the most interviews. There likely isn't any question that he hasn't been asked. Federer answers all of them again and again with admirable patience; he deals with us members of the media collegially and candidly. Again and again, he takes extra time for his countrymen even if he doesn't have to and even if almost everything has been said. With pleasure, I want to thank him for all of his collaborations with me through the years.

Working on this book, it has also become clear to me how much has happened to him and around him in such a short span of time—things that are worth repeating or recording—all the more so because sometimes important contexts only become visible at a greater distance. A feeling of astonishment always comes over me at how this ambitious, dissatisfied junior developed into one of the greatest figures in the sports world—particularly in light of the fact that his character has hardly changed. Aside from his athletic ambition, Roger Federer has remained a modest man who doesn't think that he's anybody special. If he does make unpopular decisions, then this is usually due to his realization that they are necessary in order to achieve his lofty career goals.

While Federer continues to write his history at breath-taking speed that will hopefully fill many more folders and archive files, I would like to thank some other people who helped me with this book. I especially want to mention Randy Walker, who I started to know and appreciate while he was working for the U.S. Tennis Association and who was the driving force in setting up the English version for New Chapter Press. He brought a lot of new enthusiasm into this work and I thoroughly enjoyed the process of updating and adapting the book.

I also want to thank Pendo publishing in Munich and Zurich who took the initiative and offered me an opportunity as a career change to write this book. I want to thank the many people I interviewed or who provided information, who were willing to share their recollections or their knowledge about Roger with me—especially his parents. I also want to mention the many international and Swiss colleagues on the tennis tour who have accompanied

Roger over the years, who have described and pointed out that what he has achieved is anything but average, especially for a small nation like Switzerland. Furthermore, I want to acknowledge the precious help of the media departments of the ATP with Nicola Arzani and Greg Sharko, an unfailing source of great stats and information, and of the ITF, above all Barbara Travers and Nick Imison.

I would also like to thank Tamedia AG, my boss, Fredy Wettstein, and the colleagues at the sports editorial office of the *Tages-Anzeiger* and the *Sonntags-Zeitung* who made it possible and helped me to accompany Federer's development in a journalistically diverse way and to hopefully do appropriate honor to his accomplishments. I would also like to thank my good friend Jürgen Kalwa in New York, who wrote a book about Tiger Woods, who supported me with important tips, as well as my sister Jeannine who was the first one to critically read this manuscript and provided me with valuable feedback. Last but not least, I would like to thank my wife, Eni, and our daughter Jessica. It wasn't easy for any of them to have me at home an entire winter —but mostly behind closed doors and in another world.

René Stauffer
Müllheim, Switzerland, May 2007

Encounter with a 15-year-old

It was September 11, 1996. I was on assignment for the *Tages-Anzeiger* and was supposed to write a story about the World Youth Cup, a sort of Davis Cup for juniors that was being played in Zurich, the location of our editorial office. I was skeptical. A story about a team tournament involving obscure 15 and 16-year-old tennis players—who would be interested in that? I viewed this assignment as a tiresome task, thanks to the Swiss Tennis Federation since they had charitably taken on the tournament for its 100-year anniversary. No, this certainly would not be an interesting assignment.

On this day, I met Roger Federer for the first time. He played on a far away court surrounded by wire mesh at a tennis and recreation facility called Guggach. Officials from the Swiss Tennis Federation told me that Federer was a pretty good player and that there was little to criticize except that he was sometimes very temperamental. He just turned 15 and was actually too young for this tournament, but his credentials were impressive—he had already won five Swiss national junior championship titles, was the best Swiss player in the 16-and-under age bracket and was already ranked No. 88 nationally.

On this day, he played against an Italian named Nohuel Fracassi, who since this encounter with Federer, I never heard from again. Fracassi was more than a year older, bigger and stronger than Federer and he had already won the first set when I arrived. The mood was reminiscent of an insignificant club tournament. There were three or four spectators, a referee and no ball boys. The players fetched the balls themselves. However, I was instantly fascinated by Federer's elegant style. I had already seen some players come and go in my fifteen years as a tennis journalist but it appeared to me that an extraordinary talent was coming of age here in front of me. He effortlessly put spins on balls so that the Italian—even on this slow clay court—would often just watch the ball fly past him for winners. With hardly a sound, he stroked winning shots from his black racquet, moved fast and gracefully. His strokes were harmonious and technically brilliant.

His tactics were also quite unusual. There were no similarities to the safe and consistent "Swedish School" of baseline tennis that was very common back then and usually resulted in promised success on clay courts. Federer would have nothing of that. He looked to end points quickly at every opportunity. He appeared to have mastered every stroke, which was quite unusual for juniors in his age group. He dominated with his serve and his forehand, but his powerful one-handed backhand and the occasional volley also looked like something taken from a tennis textbook.

Roger Federer was a diamond in the rough, no doubt. I was astonished and wondered why nobody had yet seen him or written about him. Was it perhaps because the media had so often prematurely written in superlatives about talented young players only to discover later that they did not measure up to the task of international tennis? Not every Swiss tennis player could be a new Heinz Günthardt, Jakob Hlasek or a Marc Rosset, perhaps the three best Swiss men's players ever. Perhaps because hardly anybody was scouting for new talent in Switzerland since our little country was already over-proportionately well-represented in professional tennis with Rosset, the 1992 Olympic champion, and the up-and-coming 15-year-old Martina Hingis, already a Wimbledon doubles champion and a semifinalist in singles at the US Open.

But perhaps the reason was also that Federer's athletic maturity stood in stark contrast to his behavior. He was a hot-head. On this September afternoon, his temper exploded even from the smallest mistakes. On several occasions, he threw his racquet across the court in anger and disgust. He constantly berated himself. "Duubel!" or "Idiot!" he exclaimed when one of his balls narrowly missed the line. He sometimes even criticized himself aloud when he actually won points but was dissatisfied with his stroke.

He didn't seem to notice what was going on around him. It was only him, the ball, the racquet—and his fuming temper—nothing else. Being so high-strung, he had to fight more with himself than with his opponent across the net this day. This dual struggle pushed him to the limit and I assumed he would lose despite his technical superiority. I was wrong. Federer won the match 3-6, 6-3, 6-1.

I found out later that Federer already won a hard-fought, three-set match the day before against a tenacious young Australian player by the name of Lleyton Hewitt, with Federer fighting off a match point to win by a 4-6, 7-6, 6-4 margin. This Federer-Hewitt match occurred in front of a crowd of 30 people who purchased tickets for the day—plus the four people who bought a tournament series ticket for all sessions. Nobody could have known that these two players would become two of the greatest players—both earning the No. 1 ranking and going on to compete on the greatest stages of the sport in packed stadiums and in front of millions of television viewers around the world.

I wanted to know more about Federer and asked him for an interview. He surprised me once again as he sat across from me at a wooden table in the gym locker room. I feared that the young man would be reserved and taciturn in the presence of an unfamiliar reporter from a national newspaper and he would hardly be able to say anything useful or quotable. But this was not the case. Federer spoke flowingly and confidently with a mischievous smile. He explained that his idol was Pete Sampras and that he had been training for a year at the Swiss National Tennis Center at Ecublens on Lake Geneva. He also said that he probably was among the 30 or 40 best in his age class in the world and that he wanted to become a top professional but still had to improve his game—and his attitude.

"I know that I can't always complain and shout because that hurts me and makes me play worse," he said. "I hardly forgive myself on any mistakes although they're normal." He looked in the distance and said almost to himself—"One should just be able to play a perfect game."

Playing a perfect game—that's what motivated him. He didn't want to just defeat opponents and win trophies, even if he liked the idea of becoming rich and famous or both, as he admitted. For him, instinctively, the journey was the reward and the journey involved hitting and placing balls with his racquet as perfectly as possible. He seemed to be obsessed with this, which would explain why he could become frustrated even after winning points. He didn't want to dominate his opponent in this rectangle with the net that fascinated him—he wanted to dominate the ball that he both hated and loved.

Federer had great expectations—too many at that time that he would have been able to achieve them. His emotions carried him away in this conflict between expectations and reality. He seemed to sense his great potential and that he was capable of doing great things—but he was not yet able to transform his talents into reality.

His unusual attitude towards perfection had a positive side effect in that he did not consider his opponents as rivals who wanted to rob the butter from his bread, as the sometimes reclusive Jimmy Connors used to say. His opponents were more companions on a common path. This attitude made him a popular and well-liked person in the locker room. He was social and someone you could joke around with. For Federer, tennis was not an individual sport with opponents who needed to be intimidated, but a common leisure activity with like-minded colleagues who, as part of a big team, were pursuing the same goal.

He became terribly annoyed at his own mistakes but he had the capacity to question things, to observe things from a distance and to put them in the correct perspective after his emotions had abated. He was also willing to admit weaknesses. "I don't like to train and I also always play badly in training," he casually observed during this interview. "I'm twice as good in the matches."

This sentence surprised me as well. While many players choked under pressure, he apparently maintained a winning mentality. This strength that abounded in the most important matches and game situations really drove many opponents to distraction and enabled Federer to escape from apparently hopeless situations. It also helped Federer establish one of the most unbelievable records in sports history—24 consecutive victories in professional singles finals between July of 2003 and November of 2005—double the record held by John McEnroe and Björn Borg.

Federer's triumphs at this World Youth Cup were in vain. The Swiss team, lacking a strong second singles player and an experienced doubles team, finished the tournament in defeat in 15th place. Roger Federer won but the Swiss lost—a scenario that was to repeat itself many times over years later at the actual Davis Cup. The hot-head nonetheless received a compliment from the coach of the Australian team at the World Youth Cup, Darren Cahill, the former US Open semifinalist, who was in charge of Lleyton Hewitt at the time. "He's got everything he needs to succeed on tour later," said Cahill.

I was able to return to the office with enough material for a nice story. It was to be my first about Roger Federer—but it would not be the last. The story's title was "One Should Be Able To Play A Perfect Game."

INTRODUCTION
No One Expected Him

The saying that great things are preceded by their shadows applies to tennis like no other sport. From the immense number of ambitious, talented, mentored or pushed junior tennis players around the world looking for the way to the top, the real champions normally outshine the rest very early on.

I will never forget the day, for example, in the crowded press room at Wimbledon in 1984 when my German colleague, Klaus-Peter Witt, whom everybody called "KP," stormed up to me, grabbed me and dragged me away. "We've got him! We've got him!" he shouted. "The Red Bomber is here!"

KP led me through the whirling crowd of the Southeast corner of the All England Club to Court No. 13 where there was a great deal of commotion. People were standing tip-toed and craning their necks to get a glimpse of the court. A 16-year-old with red hair and blue eyes was in the process of outclassing American Blaine Willenborg. The red-head led 6-0, 6-0 and British journalists were frantically checking for the last time that a player at Wimbledon completed a match without losing a game. But the teenager relieved them of this task when he lost four games in the third set.

The guy was an unparalleled force of nature. He was a player who punished balls with his brutal serves and groundstrokes. His name was Boris Becker. Speaking about Becker, the German coach, Klaus Hofsaess, said that "he would eat a rat to improve his forehand." KP was enthused. Becker, who already negotiated his way through the Wimbledon qualifying tournament, also survived his second-round match in the main draw, defeating Nduka Odizor of Nigeria. In the third round, Becker was on Court No. 2—dubbed the "Graveyard of Champions"—facing American Bill Scanlon, when he stumbled and injured his ankle in the fourth set. Becker was down with a severe ligament injury and was carried from the court on a stretcher.

In the evening, KP and I were at the bar of the Gloucester Hotel Casino and asked Becker's coach, Gunther Bosch, how the boy was. Bosch spontaneously handed us a room key and said, "Ask him yourself."

We had been expecting to find an inconsolably beaten young man, but Becker was lying on the bed, watching television, oblivious of the large bandage on his leg. There was not a trace of whining or discouragement. "Look, that's me, that's me," he exclaimed in excitement as he pointed at the television screen that was showing the summary of the day at Wimbledon. KP and I looked at one another in agreement that if this German doesn't make it, then who will?

The next year, Boris Becker won the Wimbledon title at the age of 17, the youngest man to ever win the championship.

Like Becker, most great tennis champions first appeared on the tennis scene in a clap of thunder. Stefan Edberg from Sweden, the German's greatest rival, won the junior "Grand Slam" by combining the four biggest titles, the Australian Open, the French Open, Wimbledon and the US Open. John McEnroe stormed into the semifinals at Wimbledon in 1977 at age 18 as a qualifier and also made headlines because of his uncouth behavior and fiery Irish temperament. Björn Borg reached the Wimbledon quarterfinals in 1973 in his first attempt as a 17-year-old and one year later, he won the first of his six French Open titles and one year after that, in 1975, he led Sweden to its first Davis Cup title, winning all 12 of his singles matches during the championship run.

The list goes on. Pete Sampras was barely 19 years old and ranked No. 12 in the world when he won the US Open in Flushing Meadows in 1990, defeating Ivan Lendl, McEnroe and Andre Agassi in his final three matches. At just 17, Agassi was among the best two dozen players in the world due largely to his booming forehand. In 1982, Sweden's Mats Wilander won the French Open at 17 in his very first attempt at Roland Garros. In 2005, Rafael Nadal of Spain did the same in his first French Open, winning the title two days after turning 19.

The great women champions tend to break through at even younger ages. Steffi Graf, the most successful professional player with 22 singles titles at Grand Slam tournaments, already reached the top 100 in the world rankings by age 13. Tracy Austin, Andrea Jaeger, Monica Seles, Jennifer Capriati, Anna Kournikova, Martina Hingis, Maria Sharapova—all flourished in professional tennis at very early ages.

I heard about Martina Hingis for the first time when she was nine and appeared in the score columns of a little local newspaper as "Hingisova." She was a phenom, already touted world-wide as a potential great champion before she even played a match on the WTA Tour, similar to the stories of Capriati and Venus and Serena Williams.

When she was 12 years old, Hingis played in the French Open junior girls championships (for players 18-and-under), and there literally was a parade of players, coaches, media representatives and fans who wanted to catch a glimpse of this phenomenon. Mark McCormack, the founder and long-time director of the International Management Group (IMG), the world's largest sports agency, sat fascinated by the little girl in each of her matches through the tournament.

When Hingis won the title and was awarded her trophy and flowers on Court No. 2 at the end of the tournament, Bud Collins, the most widely-known American tennis commentator, *Boston Globe* tennis columnist and connoisseur of colorful slacks, sat at the edge of the court. "Hey, Stauffer," he shouted to me over the many rows of people. "Here's your meal ticket for the next twenty years!"

What Collins meant—and how right he proved to be—became evident to me with the passage of time. A single top player can fundamentally change a country's tennis scene—and also improve prospects for reporters. KP experienced this extreme change in Germany with Becker. For years, he dreamed of covering a top-10 ranked German player—one who was worth traveling the world, covering at all the major tournaments. Before Becker's Wimbledon victory, KP fought with his editors to cover more tennis. Now, his editors squeezed him like an orange and pressured him for more copy and larger stories. "I've already submitted 1,000 lines," he groaned in 1985 after Becker's historic victory at Wimbledon, "and they still don't have enough." How could I have known that this would happen to us years later in Switzerland?

Everything was different with Roger Federer. Although he qualified as an early talent, he was never considered one who could ever dominate the sport. Many who knew him from his youth are still amazed today at his development. "I never would have thought that he would become No. 1. He wasn't superman. He was just another competitor like everyone else," said Dany Schnyder, one of his biggest rivals in his youth. Professional player Michael Lammer from Zurich, a childhood companion of Federer, said, "You noticed that he was a great talent when he was 15 or 16, but it was not until he went to the top of the juniors at 17 that it first became clear that he had the stuff to become a top player."

People like Bud Collins never sat in the grandstands at Federer's junior matches, prognosticating his international career. It was remarkable that he was the world's best junior as a 17-year-old and the winner of the Wimbledon junior title in 1998. This, however, was no guarantee of becoming a top professional player.

A few years would pass before a wider public took notice of him around the world. In his early professional career, he was considered a super talented player, but one who appeared unlikely to live up to his potential. People thought he was destined to be an underachiever. For years he was dogged by the label "best player without a Grand Slam title."

Nobody expected greatness from Roger Federer—even in Switzerland. When he first appeared on the scene, he was overshadowed by the success of Hingis, who just became a major force in women's tennis. When he was on his way to becoming the world's best junior, Hingis, his senior by just 312 days, was already at her zenith. She won three of the four Grand Slam tournaments in 1997 and took center stage—especially in Switzerland. Why should one be at all concerned about Federer, a talented junior with an uncertain future, when Switzerland had the current No. 1 ranked woman in the world?

Even in Switzerland, there was very little talk about Federer as a future No. 1 player. In the land of alpine skiing, one was cautious about raising expectations. The exotic idea that a new Boris Becker or Pete Sampras could be coming of age between Lake Geneva and Lake Constance hardly crossed anybody's mind. However, this was not a disadvantage for the young player.

To the contrary, Federer could develop quietly and not be subjected to the pressures of expectations, from his parents and from the public.

Nonetheless, Federer grew up in a climate where professional tennis was quite pervasive. The Swiss Indoors, one of the most important ATP indoor tournaments, took place just a short stroll away from his ancestral home in the suburbs of Basel. Roger's mother Lynette was very involved in the tournament's organization and Roger himself was a ball boy at the event in 1994 and even had his picture taken with Jimmy Connors when he was a 13-year-old.

Swiss men's tennis had a short, but somewhat successful history in the days shortly before and after Federer's birth. Heinz Günthardt from Zurich, who was somewhat prematurely celebrated as the new Björn Borg after his triumphs as a junior in 1976, pioneered the way for Switzerland in the 1970's. At a time when hardly anybody could spell out the initials ATP (Association of Tennis Professionals), Günthardt won the junior tournaments at the French Open and Wimbledon as a 17-year-old. Although he did not meet expectations as a professional—due primarily to a chronic hip condition—he managed to achieve a first in Springfield, Mass., when he won his first ATP singles title and became the first player ever to win a tournament after losing in the qualifying rounds of the tournament. (Günthardt would enter the tournament that he would eventually win as a "lucky-loser"—only fortunate to gain entry into the tournament when player withdrawals allowed losers in the qualifying tournament to gain entry into the event.) Günthardt was a US Open quarterfinalist in 1985 and won doubles titles at both Wimbledon and the French Open. After his career, he served as Steffi Graf's coach and helped her win 12 of her 22 Grand Slam tournament titles.

Shortly after Günthardt's career ended in the mid 1980s, Swiss player Jakob Hlasek climbed to the No. 7 world ranking in 1989. After Hlasek, it was Marc Rosset, who won the gold medal in singles at the 1992 Olympic Games in Barcelona.

Rosset was an individual to whom Federer could not only look up to because of his stature, (Rosset is six foot, seven inches tall), but the man from Geneva was also a consistent top 20 player in the mid 1990's and, with Hlasek, led Switzerland to its only appearance in the Davis Cup final in 1992, where it lost to the United States. Rosset was one of the first to recognize Federer's potential. "He has everything he needs to become a top player—talent, ambition, a smart mouth and the necessary will to endure," he said. He was also willing to help Federer, who was 11 years his junior. He became Federer's mentor and Federer felt himself drawn to Rosset as well. "Perhaps because we're both jokers, honest, direct, impudent, vivacious and a little chaotic," said Federer.

However, Rosset's sympathy didn't go so far as to let Federer win right away when they faced each other on tour later. Their very first match came in the final match of the ATP event in Marseille in 2000, with Rosset winning in a third-set tie-break in the first-ever ATP singles final played between two players from Switzerland.

Even though Federer did not grow up in a great tennis country, Switzerland was also not a tennis "No Man's Land." Therefore, he saw no reason early on why a Swiss man could not make it to the upper reaches of the tennis world.

PART I

CHAPTER 1

From Kempton Park to Basel

The village of Berneck is situated in the northeastern corner of Switzerland in the St. Gall Rhine valley, where the Alpine foothills are kissed by the famed Foehn winds and the inhabitants speak a rough dialect of German. The people of this village feel a closer association to Austria and its Vorarlberg state—located just on the other side of the Rhine—than they do Switzerland's major cities of Zurich, Bern or Geneva. A few kilometers to the north, the Rhine flows into Lake Constance, where the waters comprise the borders between Switzerland, Austria and Germany.

Roger's father, Robert, grew up in Berneck as son of a textile worker and a housewife. At the age of 20, he left the area and followed the course of the Rhine and arrived in Basel, a border city in the triangle between Switzerland, Germany and France and where the Rhine forms a knee joint and flows north out of the country. Basel is where some of the world's most important chemical companies are headquartered and Robert Federer, a young chemical laboratory worker, found his first job at Ciba, one of the world's leading chemical companies.

After four years in Basel, Robert Federer was seized by wanderlust, and in 1970, he decided to emigrate and pull up stakes from Switzerland. It was a coincidence that he chose South Africa, but also due to formalities. Among other things, he could get an emigration visa with relative ease in the country dominated by Apartheid. It was also a coincidence that he found a new job with the same employer he had in Switzerland, Ciba. The chemical company, along with several other foreign companies, was located in Kempton Park, an extended suburb of Johannesburg near the international airport.

It was in Kempton Park where he met Lynette Durand, who came to work for Ciba as a secretary. Afrikaan was the spoken language on her family's farm—she had three siblings; her father was a foreman and her mother was a nurse—but Lynette went to an English school and her intention was to save money as quickly as possible and to travel to Europe. She preferred England, where her father was stationed during World War II.

Robert Federer is a modest and unpretentious man who usually remains in the background. He prefers to observe and listen quietly and then to steer things in the direction desired. He is small of stature with a prominent nose and he has a distinct mustache. He is athletic, strong, quick-witted, funny, cosmopolitan and easy-going. Nothing characterizes him better than his ringing laughter that draws his eyes into narrow slits and raises his bushy eyebrows. Despite his affability, he knows how to defend himself when crossed. He is realistic but decisive. A female portrait painter once described him as being "caustic, having the bite of a bear."

Lynette, the charming 18-year-old secretary with the piercing eyes, instantly made a favorable impression on Robert Federer when he saw her in the company cafeteria in 1970. They met and eventually became a couple. Robert took Lynette to the Swiss Club in Johannesburg to introduce her to his new hobby—tennis. The young woman, who used to play field hockey, was instantly enthused about the sport and began to play regularly. The couple had a wonderful time in South Africa—Apartheid hardly affected them.

Robert Federer cannot really explain why they moved to Switzerland in 1973. "You had this feeling of being a migratory bird," he said. Back in Basel, he often asked himself why they didn't stay in Africa, especially because his consort admitted to having difficulty with the confines of Switzerland and the narrow mentality of its people. "But one learned quickly to adjust," she said. The couple married and a daughter, Diana, was born in 1979. Twenty-months later, Lynette Federer then bore a son, on the morning of August 8, 1981 in Basel's canton hospital. He was named Roger because it could also be pronounced easily in English. Roger's parents, even in the first hours of his life, felt that one day it could be beneficial for their son to have a name that was easy to pronounce in English.

The name Federer was already familiar in Berneck before 1800, but it is actually an extremely uncommon clan name in Switzerland. The most famous Federer up to that point was Heinrich Federer, a priest turned poet who died in 1928. In 1966, on his 100th birthday, he was immortalized on a Swiss postage stamp.

In the 1970s, the Ciba Company that Robert and Lynette Federer continued to work for in Switzerland sponsored a tennis club in Allschwil, a suburb of Basel, and the Federer family soon became regular players. Lynette displayed a great talent for the sport with her greatest triumph coming when she was a member of the Swiss Inter-club senior championship team in 1995. She loved tennis so much that she soon became a junior tennis coach at the club. She later became involved in the tournament organization at the Swiss Indoors, the ATP tournament in Basel, working in the credential office.

Robert Federer was also a committed tennis enthusiast and was a regionally-ranked player. He and his wife would later more frequently hit the golf course, but at the time, tennis still came first. Lynette often took her son to the tennis courts. Young Roger was fascinated by balls at a very young age. "He wanted to play ball for hours on end—even at one-and-a-half years old," his mother recollected. His skill was plainly apparent: He could hardly walk but he managed to catch larger balls. Little Roger hit his first tennis ball over the net at three-and-a-half years old. At four, he could already hit twenty or thirty balls in a row. "He was unbelievably coordinated," his father gushed.

The Federer family was neither rich nor poor, just solid Swiss middle class. Roger grew up in a townhouse with a yard in a quiet neighborhood in Wasserhaus in Münchenstein, a suburb of Basel. Impulsive and ambitious, he was not an easy child. "Defeats were total disasters for him, even at board games," his father remembered. He was "a nice guy" in general "but when he didn't like something, he could get pretty aggressive." Dice and game board pieces sometimes flew through the living room.

Even as a little boy, his mother said, he always did as he pleased and attempted to push limits, whether it involved teachers at school or his parents at home or with sports. "He was very vibrant, a bundle of energy, and was sometimes very difficult," said Lynette. When forced to do something he didn't like, Roger reacted strongly. When bored, he questioned it or ignored it. When his father gave him instruction on the tennis court, Roger would not even look at him.

Roger was a popular boy, always friendly, not arrogant, well-behaved—and very athletic. He tried skiing, wrestling, swimming and skateboarding but it was sports that involved balls that especially fascinated him. He played soccer, handball, basketball, table tennis, tennis and, at home, he even played badminton over the neighbor's fence. He always had a ball with him, even on the way to school. One of his idols was Michael Jordan of the NBA's Chicago Bulls. He was outdoors every free minute he could muster. Work in the classroom that required concentration and sitting still wasn't his thing. He was not an ambitious student at school and his grades were mediocre.

Robert and Lynette were the ideal parents for a sports fanatic like Roger. They let him run free when he wanted to but didn't force him. "He had to keep moving, otherwise he became unbearable," Lynette said. She and her husband emphasized taking up various kinds of sports. They took him to a local soccer club called Concordia Basel at an early age so that he would learn to interact with teammates and become a team player.

His mother, however, declined giving her son tennis lessons. "I considered myself not to be competent enough and he would have just upset me anyway," she said. "He was very playful. He tried out every strange stroke and certainly never returned a ball normally. That is simply no fun for a mother."

For hours, Roger hit tennis balls against a wall, a garage door, in his room against a wall or even against the cupboard in the house. Pictures and dishes were not safe and his sister's room wasn't spared either. "Things would sometimes break," Roger admits today. Diana didn't have an easy time with her brother and was forced to put up with the antics of her rambunctious younger brother. "He would always come around shouting when I was with my friends or he would pick up the receiver when I was on the phone," Diana said. "He really was a little devil."

As is the case for siblings of the highly-talented, it wasn't easy for Diana to stand in her brother's shadow. Whenever the family went out together, Roger became more and more frequently the center of attention. Lynette took her aside once: "Diana, it's no different for you than for your mother," she told her daughter. "Many people talk to me but the topic is always your brother."

Diana, an aspiring nurse, only occasionally watched her brother's matches. For example, at the 2005 Masters Cup in Shanghai, she and her mother left the stadium in mid-match to go on a vacation to South Africa. Diana is proud of her brother but prefers not being in the limelight and doesn't assiduously follow every detail of his career. For example, when she watched Roger play Tomas Berdych of the Czech Republic at the Swiss Indoors in Basel in 2005, she had no idea that Berdych had surprisingly defeated her brother at the Athens Olympics one year earlier, dashing his dreams of an Olympic medal.

CHAPTER 2

A Boy Discovers Tennis

Roger Federer's first idol was Boris Becker. He was four years old when Becker won his first Wimbledon title in 1985 and Germany, subsequently, came down with collective tennis fever following the epic win by their native son. Roger cried bitterly in 1988 and in 1990 when Becker lost Wimbledon finals to Stefan Edberg. Federer the boy watched tennis matches on television for hours on end. His mother was amazed at the details he retained.

"I liked tennis the best of all sports," Roger said looking back. "It was always exciting and winning or losing was always in my hands." He quickly became the best in his age group just after entering school and was allowed to participate in special training sessions three times a week at a loose union of tennis clubs in Basel and its environs. It was at these special training sessions where he met Marco Chiudinelli, another talented youth a month younger than him also from Münchenstein. The two became friends and spent considerable time together off the tennis court.

After training, the two boys sometimes played squash with their tennis racquets and played table tennis and soccer against each other. Their parents both jogged and bicycled together. When a region-wide top tennis group was formed, Roger and Marco, both eight-years-old, became members of the group, despite playing at different clubs—Federer at the Old Boys Tennis Club, where training conditions were better for him than at the Ciba Tennis Club in Allschwil, and Chiudinelli at the Basel Lawn Tennis Club.

"It was pretty loud when we were in training," Chiudinelli recollected. "We talked more than we trained. Training didn't seem too important to us. We just wanted to have a good time and we goofed around a lot. One of us was frequently kicked off the court."

Federer and Chiudinelli soon became the black sheep of the group and their parents were angry to discover that one or the other was forced to sit on the sidelines and watch half of the practice sessions for disciplinary reasons.

"Roger lost to practically everybody in training," said Chiudinelli. "He was the only one that I beat, but the difference was enormous. When it came down to business, he could flip a switch and become a completely different person. I admired that about him. I could give him a thrashing in training but when we played at a tournament a day later, he gave me a thrashing. Even back then he was a real competitor."

The two eight-year-olds played against each other for the first time at an official event at a tournament called "The Bambino Cup" in Arlesheim. "Back then we only played one long set of up to nine games," Chiudinelli explained. "Things weren't going well for me at the beginning. I was behind 2-5 and I started to cry. We cried a lot back then even during the matches. Roger came up to me and tried to comfort me when we switched sides. He told me everything would be all right, and in fact, things did get better. I took the lead 7-6 and noticed that the tide had turned. Then he began to cry and I ran up to him to give him encouragement and things went better for him. It was the only time that I could beat him."

Roger trained with Adolf Kacovsky, a tennis coach at The Old Boys Tennis Club who everybody called "Seppli." Like many of his fellow Czechs during the "Prague Spring" in 1968, Kacovsky fled Czechoslovakia and the Russian tanks that rolled into the Czech capital to quell the rebellion. He arrived in Basel one year later, via Tunisia, where he was the club's head professional until 1996.

"I noticed right away that this guy was a natural talent," said Kacovsky of Federer. "He was born with a racquet in his hand." Federer was only given group lessons at first but soon received special one-on-one attention. "The club and I quickly noticed that he was enormously talented," Kacovsky said. "We began giving him private lessons that were partly funded by the club. Roger was a quick learner. When you wanted to teach him something new, he was able to pick it up after three or four tries, while others in the group needed weeks."

The star pupil was not only talented and in love with hitting the ball but also ambitious. Kacovsky recounted that Roger always said that he wanted to become the best in the world. "People just laughed at him, including me," he said. "I thought that he would perhaps become the best player in Switzerland or Europe but not the best in the world. He had it in his head and he worked at it."

However, Roger's tournament career at the club began with a fiasco. In his first tournament competition at the age of eight, he lost his first serious competition 6-0, 6-0, although, according to his own estimation, he didn't play all that badly. Not surprisingly, Federer cried after the loss.

"His opponent was much bigger," said Kacovsky. "He was also very nervous in his first game where the match really counted."

Roger constantly sought out people to practice with and if he found no one, he hit balls against the wall, over and over for hours. At age 11, the Swiss tennis magazine *Smash* first became interested in him. A small article appeared about the young Federer in October, 1992 after he reached the semifinals at the Basel Youth Cup, a gateway series to competitive tennis. Although Roger was improving rapidly, he still suffered many bitter defeats. Dany Schnyder, the younger brother of the later top women's player Patty Schnyder, became his arch rival and his biggest junior adversary. "I tried everything but it didn't make a difference," Roger recollected. "I always lost and lost decisively."

Schnyder, six months older than Roger, grew up in the neighboring village of Bottmingen and has fond recollections of his junior duels with Roger. "We played against each other 17 times between the ages of eight and 12," he said. "I won eight of the first nine matches but lost the last eight matches. Roger always played aggressively. I kept the ball in the court for the most part. Everything went wrong for him at the beginning. His gambles didn't pay off. That's probably why I won. But then suddenly his shots stayed in."

"I was surprised to see Roger suddenly storm to the top," said Schnyder, who eventually gave up his tennis career to pursue academics. "One noticed that he had good strokes at 11 or 12, but I never would have thought that he would become the No. 1 player in the world. I think what he's accomplished is great—but he's not an idol, a world star or a super hero for me. Whenever we see each other, he's still the same guy as when we first met."

Schnyder also corroborated the fact that Federer didn't take practice matches nearly as seriously as tournament matches. "When things counted, he could always rise to the occasion," he said. Roger himself was aware that his performances in practice matches had not dispelled all doubts. "I was conscientious but I didn't like to train," he said years later. "My parents always said, 'Start training better,' but I often had problems getting motivated. I was a match player."

Negative emotions also often took control of him on the court. "When things weren't going the way he wanted, he would curse and toss his racquet," Kacosvky explained. "It was so bad, I had to intervene sometimes."

"I was constantly cursing and tossing my racquet around," said Federer. "It was bad. My parents were embarrassed and they told me to stop it or they wouldn't come along with me to my tournaments anymore. I had to calm down but that was an extremely long process. I believe that I was looking for perfection too early."

In 1993 at the age of 11, Roger won his first Swiss national title, defeating Chiudinelli in Lucerne in the final of the Swiss 12-and-under indoor championships. Six months later, he defeated Schnyder in the final of the Swiss 12-and-under outdoor chamionships in Bellinzona. Both tournament victories were very important to the developing Federer. "I thought, 'Aha! I can compete,'" he said. "I can do it."

Michael Lammer from Zürich, a year younger than Federer, remembered at that time that Federer was still a work in progress. "You could see early on that he was a talent, but at this age, it's hard to say that a new star is being born," said Lammer. "At the beginning, he still had problems with his backhand because he played it single-handedly and he didn't have that much power. That's why he sliced a lot, but his forehand was complete by then."

Their duels, said Lammer, were explosive. "It was chaotic sometimes," he said. "We played about five or six times before we were 14-years-old. He was very emotional. Our games were very even but he gained strength at the decisive moment because he was instinctively doing the right thing. That's why I could never beat him."

Roger was still playing club soccer in addition to tennis, but the many practice sessions in the two sports were too hard to coordinate. So, at age 12, he decided to give up soccer and concentrate on tennis. The choice wasn't difficult for him although his soccer coaches also confirmed that he was a great talent. "I scored a few goals in soccer but I didn't do anything especially well," said Roger. "We won some regional tournaments but I had already won a national title in tennis."

His great talent lay not in his feet but in his right hand.

Roger's quest for perfection also led to his decision to give preference to tennis over soccer—not because he was a loner, but in the collective setting of a soccer team, Federer was simply too dependent upon his teammates. As a soccer player, he not only had to deal with his own imperfections but also with those of his fellow players. This wasn't for him in the long run. He had enough to do fuming over his own mistakes.

After his ninth birthday, Federer sometimes trained at the Old Boys Tennis Club with Peter Carter, a young assistant instructor. The Australian, who wanted everybody to call him Peter whether they were housewives or bank directors, was a sympathetic, serious man with straight, blonde hair that fell uncombed across his forehead. He had large blue eyes and a soft voice. He was born in 1964 in Nuriootpa, a small city with 40 wine producers in the Barossa Valley in South Australia. As a member of the Australian Sports Institute, he became a tennis professional but was not even a journeyman player, achieving a career-high ranking of No. 173.

In 1984, Carter played the Swiss satellite circuit, a tournament series at the lowest professional level, and despite not meeting with much success, his hiatus in Switzerland proved fateful. The Old Boys Tennis Club asked him if he wanted to play with on their national "league tennis" B-level club team. Carter agreed. Soon he was not only playing for the team, but was also active as club's coach and by the beginning of the 1990s, his workload was constantly increasing.

The Old Boys Tennis Club offered him a full-time coaching position in 1993 to build a mentoring program for the young tennis players. Carter accepted and he was now training a group that included a 12-year-old Federer. "Peter was not only an ideal coach for Roger but also a good friend," Seppli Kacovsky recollected. "He was also an excellent instructor and psychologist."

"When I first saw him," Carter once said of the future world No. 1, "Roger hardly came up to the net. His talent was instantly visible. Roger could do a lot with the ball and the racquet at a very young age. He was playful and especially wanted to have his fun." Federer, he said, was very natural and was coordinated in every respect. "He had a great feel for the ball and he always had a very good forehand," said Carter. "He learned with extraordinary speed and ease, including things that he had seen Boris Becker or Pete Sampras do on TV. He always made progress."

When Roger was 13, his dream became an obsession—he wanted to become the No. 1 player in Switzerland and then reach the top 100 in the world rankings. His playing level and ranking allowed him to play in international junior competitions. In the meantime, he was no longer as much a Boris Becker fan but became an enthusiast of Stefan Edberg, the Swedish rival of Becker.

The idea to send Roger to the Swiss National Tennis Center in the Swiss city of Ecublens came about in winter 1994/1995. His parents were satisfied with Peter Carter and the training conditions but the National Tennis Center mentoring program—or the "Tennis Etudes" program—was funded by the Swiss Tennis Federation and thus was financially attractive to the Federers.

Eight boys and four girls trained at the National Tennis Center on Lake Geneva, where qualified coaches were available to them. The students had the option of living with guest families and could attend public schools where they were exempt from certain subjects. One of the program's central figures was Pierre Paganini who, like Peter Carter, would play a central role in Federer's career. A former decathlon athlete and college-trained sports teacher, Paganini was the endurance trainer and administrative head at Ecublens.

When his parents asked Roger if he was interested going to Ecublens, he objected. However, they were even more astounded to later read their son's statement in a tennis magazine of his intention to graduate from the academy. In March of 1995, Federer went as one of 15 candidates to Lake Geneva to take the entrance examination that included a 12-minute run, an endurance test, demonstrations of his skills on the court and a test match. Federer quickly convinced Pierre Paganini and Christophe Freyss, the national coach, that he was worthy of entry. They informed him while he was still in Ecublens that he passed the entrance examination.

CHAPTER 3
Homesickness in Ecublens

Perhaps everything would have been different in the career of Roger Federer if the Christinet family in Ecublens had not existed. The family was always contacted by officials of the National Tennis Center when in need to house young talent. Two of the three children in the Christinet family had already left home so there was enough room in their house. Plus, the family did not want their youngest child, Vincent, to be alone. Roger became the second student of the mentoring program to be taken in by the family.

Roger, who had just turned 14, moved in with the Christinets after summer vacation in 1995. Although Ecublens is only three hours by train from Federer's home in Münchenstein, Roger found himself in a strange world. He described the first five months in Ecublens as some of the worst in his life and even used the word "hell."

"I just wasn't happy down there," he said. "I was away from my parents for weeks on end. I couldn't speak French and didn't have any friends. I found it difficult to get motivated and I was sad quite often."

Language was a major barrier. Thanks to his mother, Roger could speak some English but that didn't help him here. French was the spoken language in Lake Geneva—at school as well as on the tennis court. "When he arrived, he couldn't speak a word of French," said Cornelia Christinet, the lady of the house. "My son, who was almost Roger's age, couldn't speak a word of German." As a native born Swiss German, she at least could speak with the young guest in his native language, which she did from time to time. "We had a great time with him," she said. "He was so easy to get along with."

Roger won his first national 14-and-under title in July, but at Ecublens, he was the youngest boy in the program and his training partners were much stronger than he previously experienced. He had to gain respect first, but he was also homesick and called home often. He feverishly awaited Fridays when he could get on to a train and go home for the weekend to his family and his friends, like Marco Chiudinelli, who did not take the step to go to Ecublens. "I was always the best and the oldest, but now I was suddenly the youngest and the worst," Roger recollected. "I wanted to go back home. My parents helped me at the time and talked me into staying."

Lynette was convinced that a crucial reason why he didn't give up and move home was due to the fact that his parents never forced him to take the step of going to the National Tennis Center. "He made the decision himself and the consequences of it didn't become clear to him until later," she said. "He fought his way through because it was what he had wanted."

Cornelia Christinet noticed very little of Roger's homesickness. "If he cried, then it was only in his room," she said. "I only noticed that he telephoned a lot with his mother, every evening for an hour. It didn't bother me. That's normal at his age. He got along very well with his parents and it took a while for him to get used to living with a strange family."

At least he had the youngest member of the Christinet family, Vincent, who almost became a brother to him during his two years in Ecublens. "They were upstairs together every evening in the play room—rough-housing, horsing around," Cornelia remembered. "Roger soon no longer had the feeling of being in a strange family." Roger and Vincent cemented a friendship that continued into Federer's professional career. Years later, Roger invited Vincent to birthday parties or got him tickets for such events as Wimbledon or the Tennis Masters Cup in Shanghai.

His surrogate mother could hardly get him out of bed in the morning—"I sometimes had to wake him up 20 times," she exaggerated. It was usually so late by the time he was up and out of bed that he jumped into his clothes and hopped on his bike without eating breakfast. He peddled his bike back and forth between his guest family's home, school and the tennis center either in summer or winter. His eating habits were unique—he did not eat meat, preferring spaghetti or pizza—and enormous amounts of breakfast cereal. "He came back downstairs every hour to get a bowl full with milk," said Cornelia. "I thought it wasn't very healthy but I let him do it and his parents knew about it."

The first child that the Christinet family hosted was also very different than Roger. "With the first boy, his mother was always following him around, didn't let him catch his breath for a minute and was constantly badgering him. She called every day because of this or that, that he shouldn't forget his socks." This boy, Cornelia said, didn't make it very far in tennis.

It was completely different with the Federers. They were tolerant and understanding. "I learned a lot from them," said Cornelia. "From an educational point of view, they handled the situation perfectly. The mother of the first talented boy had great expectations—the mother! With Roger, he was the one that wanted to become a top player. His parents were there to provide the framework and to help him if necessary, but they never forced him to do anything. They let him go about his business and weren't overly protective. They had faith in him. They didn't scold him when something didn't work out with the coaches or at school. They talked to him and explained to him that coaches and teachers had their jobs to do as well."

Roger went to the La Planta secondary school in Ecublens and partially compensated for the lessons he missed because of training through tutoring sessions.

"He wasn't interested in much at school," said Annemarie Rüegg, the administrative director of the "Tennis Etudes." "He even fell asleep three or four times during lessons. Then the school called and said that this Roger Federer had to participate better. He had no ambition at school, just the goal of becoming a tennis professional. He often lacked discipline when it came to studying. He always had to be told—'That's just how it is.' You have to do this now—but he never moaned and groaned. I found out that he was homesick from his mother, with whom I had good contact."

Yves Allegro, three years older than Federer and one of the first graduates from the "Tennis Etudes," witnessed first-hand Federer's struggle with school and being away from home.

"He had enormous difficulties," he said. "There were problems with the language and with the coaches and he cried a great deal. He was really good at tennis and anybody could see he was very talented, but nobody imagined he would ever become the No. 1 player in the world. He wasn't even the best in his age group."

Roger's difficulties affected him adversely on the court with his results being rather mediocre. However, events in December showed that his competitive power was still present. At the Orange Bowl 14-and-under championships in Miami—one of the biggest junior tournaments in the world—Federer was forced to start play in the qualifying tournament. However, Federer won his three matches without losing a set and defeated three more opponents in the main draw of the tournament—among them David Martin, the best American player in this age group—before losing in the round of 16. Federer called his effort in Miami, "the most important triumph internationally to date."

In 1996, Federer won his fourth and fifth Swiss national titles—in the 16-and-under division. Roger's talent was on course again as he settled down and became accustomed to Ecublens. Shortly before his 15th birthday, he was allowed to play in the Swiss Interclub's top league—although just in the preliminary round. Peter Carter and Reto Staubli played on the team for the Old Boys Tennis Club, both of whom would accompany Federer on the professional tour years later.

Roger beat the crafty young Australian Lleyton Hewitt at the World Youth Cup in late summer and afterwards gained his first experiences in professional tennis at a Swiss satellite tournament. At the age of 15, he was ranked No. 86 in Switzerland and was promised additional financial support from the Swiss Tennis Federation.

His rush towards the top continued unimpeded in 1997 when he won both the indoor and outdoor Swiss national junior championships in the 18-and-under division. These titles marked his last national titles as Roger became more focused on the challenges of international tennis. Allegro, who fell victim to Federer during his final national junior triumphs, said he began to notice the enormous potential that lay dormant within the player. "When Roger was returning to Ecublens from a major international junior tournament in Prato, Italy, I asked him how it went and how did he play," Allegro said. "Roger said, 'Well. Thank you. I won.' I said, right, sure, but he had really won and, not only that, but without losing a set. I thought to myself if he can win at tournament like this at 16, he's really going to be a great player."

Allegro recalled another story during this time period that also impressed him and gave him the indication of where Federer was headed. "We had to fill out a form stating our goals. Everybody wrote: To someday be among the top 100 in the world, but Roger was the only one to write: To first be in the top 10 in the world and then become No. 1," he said. "From that point on, we viewed him in a different light."

Swiss Tennis made a big move in 1997. Ecublens served its purpose and the "House of Tennis"—the new Swiss National Tennis Center opened in Biel along the German-French language border within Switzerland. The National Tennis Center, the "Tennis Etudes" program as well as the association administration was united under one roof at this facility. There were courts with a variety of surfaces, a modern restaurant and a real players' lounge—a vast improvement over Ecublens.

At the same time, Swiss Tennis also expanded its training staff. Among the new members of the coaching staff was Peter Carter, Federer's coach from Basel. "He was brought in under the ulterior motive that he could be paired with Roger," Annemarie Rüegg admitted. "We saw the potential he had and wanted to provide him with individualized training." Federer also sometimes worked with another coach, Peter Lundgren, a former professional player from Sweden.

In the summer of 1997, at the age of 16, Roger Federer completed the mandatory nine years at school and decided to become a professional tennis player. With the exception of a few English and French lessons, he concentrated completely on the sport from this point forward. His parents were aware that this step was unpredictable and risky. "We had immense respect for the entire process," Robert Federer recalled. "Everybody was telling us how talented Roger was," his mother added. "But we wanted to see results. We made it very clear to Roger that we could not financially support him for ten years so that he could dangle around 400 in the world rankings." Although the parents' financial commitment to Roger's career was sustainable—due to the Swiss Tennis Federation's assistance with Roger—Lynette Federer increased her workload from 50 to 80 percent in order to ensure the family's financial security. Money, it would soon prove, would not become an issue for very long.

Now training in Biel, Roger no longer lived with a guest family and moved into an apartment with his good friend Allegro. "Roger's parents approached me and said that he would like to share an apartment with an older player and they asked me if I would be willing to do this," said Allegro. "This sounded financially interesting to me so Roger's and my parents went out looking for apartments together."

The 16-year-old and the 19-year-old teenagers moved into a two-bedroom apartment with a kitchen, a bathroom and a small terrace above a soccer field. "We often watched matches and gave live commentary," Allegro said. "It was a lot of fun. I usually did the cooking because I had more experience. Roger didn't have much initiative but he always helped if I asked him to. His room was usually somewhat messy and when he cleaned it up, it was just as chaotic two days later."

The young professionals, however, were completely focused on the sport. They otherwise passed the time watching television or playing electronic video games. "Roger was never a party guy," Allegro said. "I once read that he drank alcohol but that only happened very rarely." He played computer games sometimes until two in the morning but he never went out or went to parties.

Marco Chiudinelli, meanwhile, moved to Biel to further his tennis abilities and also became part of Federer's circle. "We were cyber world guys," said Chiudinelli. "We never felt attracted to parties and smoking or drinking didn't interest us. We preferred to hang out on the courts or at the Playstation."

Roger was still the same playful, fancy-free hot head whose temper sometimes exploded. "You often heard a yodeling, a liberating primal scream from the dressing room or the players' lounge," Annemarie Rüegg recalled. "You knew it was Roger. He needed to do this as a release. He was pretty loud but it wasn't unpleasant."

However, Roger became unpleasant if things weren't going well on the tennis court. His verbal outbursts were notorious and he often tossed his racquet. Roger personally recounted probably the most embarrassing story from his time in Biel. "There was a new curtain at the tennis center," he said. "They said that if someone were to wreck the curtain, they had to clean toilettes for a week. I looked at the curtain and thought that it was so thick that there was no way anybody could wreck it. Ten minutes later, I turned around and hurled my racquet at the curtain like a helicopter. It sliced through the curtain like a knife going through butter." Everybody stopped playing and stared at Roger. "No, I thought, that's impossible, the worst nightmare. I took my things and left. They would have thrown me out anyway." As punishment, Roger Federer, who hates nothing more than getting up early, had to help the grounds-keeper clean toilettes and the tennis court at an ungodly hour of the morning for an entire week.

In 1997, the Federer family was confronted with a momentous decision when Robert received an offer from his employers, Ciba, to take an executive position in Australia. Robert worked for three months each in Melbourne and Sydney on two occasions, and he and his family spent some extended holiday time in the country, visiting Queensland and the Great Barrier Reef. They enjoyed Australia and at first, the plan to move to Australia was an exciting proposition. However, skepticism grew as the consequences became clearer. The family decided finally to stay in Münchenstein. The Federers did not want to give up their circle of friends and they were uncertain if Roger would have the same opportunities to develop his tennis career as he had in Switzerland.

CHAPTER 4
The Best of All Juniors

The year 1998 began auspiciously for Roger Federer. He started the year winning the Victorian Junior Championships in Australia. He narrowly missed reaching the junior singles final at the Australian Open, botching a match point in losing to Sweden's Andreas Vinciguerra in the semifinals.

During the following spring and summer, he showed that he was a confirmed all-around player who could win on any surface. He was well ahead of any player in his age class internationally. He competed effortlessly at the highest level of international junior tennis—primarily against players who were one year to 18 months older than him. In the clay court season, he won the international junior title in Florence, Italy, but at Roland Garros in Paris, he was defeated in the first round.

At Wimbledon, Federer celebrated his greatest triumph to that point in his career. On July 5, he defeated Irakli Labadze from the Republic of Georgia 6-4, 6-4 to win the Wimbledon junior singles championship, becoming the first player to win the title from Switzerland since Heinz Günthardt in 1976. In fact, Federer did not lose a match for the week on the grass courts of southwest London as he also won the junior doubles title with Olivier Rochus from Belgium. "I felt satisfied but not overjoyed," said Federer, who was astonishingly unimpressed. But Peter Carter, who was almost always with him, was enthused. "Roger played with the concentration of a professional," he said. "Now he just has to improve his volleys."

A little chaos, however, followed the big victory. As a reward for winning the Wimbledon junior title, Federer received a wild card entry into the Swiss Open in Gstaad from tournament director Köbi Hermenjat. Federer received his first chance to play in an ATP tournament, even though he was not qualified to play since his world ranking stood at No. 702. Gstaad, the clay court tournament that traditionally takes place the week after Wimbledon, is played in a picturesque jet-set vacation area in the Bernese Alps. It is one of the oldest professional tournaments with a history dating back to 1915. It is loved by players and spectators alike because of its idyllic location in the little village with many chalets, the majestic Palace Hotel—whose courts previously hosted the tournament—and its postcard ambiance. Hermenjat was one of the most senior tournament directors on the ATP Tour and well-acquainted with everyone in the tennis world. He embodied a piece of tennis history. He was a ball boy for the tournament when he was 11 years old and had been the tournament director since 1965. Tennis legends such as John Newcombe, Tony Roche, Ilie Nastase, Ken Rosewall and Roy Emerson—after whom later the Centre Court was named—are all past champions of the Swiss Open.

Federer very reluctantly declined taking part in the traditional and prestigious Wimbledon Champions Dinner and left London that Sunday. He flew to Basel and continued by automobile to the Bernese Alps. It was well after midnight when he arrived at the luxury resort.

Federer's ATP tournament debut proved difficult. At Wimbledon, he played on grass courts and almost at sea level. In Gstaad, he found himself on slippery clay courts and at over 3,000 feet above sea level. At Wimbledon, the balls bounced low, but in the high air at Gstaad, the balls bounced high and fast. The clay surface also demanded a completely different running technique than on grass. At Wimbledon, he competed against inexperienced junior players. An array of world class players were in the draw at Gstaad. There was no doubt that the tournament was a few sizes too big for him. His purpose, however, was just to gather some experience and be presented, on this grander sporting stage, to a larger portion of the Swiss public.

Federer drew German Tommy Haas, ranked No. 41 in the world rankings, as his first-round opponent, scheduled to play on Tuesday, the second day of the tournament. On Monday, due to great demand, Federer held a press conference to discuss his Wimbledon junior success and his ATP debut. "I would have preferred to play on the Centre Court than on the secondary court," he said confidently of where the Gstaad tournament officials chose to schedule his match. There was so much interest in the Wimbledon junior champion that the thousand seats in the grandstands at Court No. 1 in Gstaad were not enough to accommodate the storm of spectators. As it turned out, Tommy Haas was not Federer's opponent. The German withdrew from the tournament a few minutes before match time due to stomach trouble. Lucas Arnold, a lucky loser from the qualifying tournament, was Federer's opponent. The Argentine clay court expert, ranked No. 88 in the world, defeated Federer 6-4, 6-4, but Arnold admitted that he was impressed by the 16-year-old, saying "he plays like Pete Sampras and he has a great serve."

Federer was disappointed but he had no reason to be crushed. "I competed very hard, but did not play well. If I had played well, I would have won," he said in an upbeat tone. "You have to do more running with the professionals than with the juniors and pros are not going to make as many mistakes."

Stéphane Oberer, the Swiss Davis Cup team captain, technical director of the Swiss Tennis Federation and Marc Rosset's long-time coach, also was in Gstaad and witnessed Federer's ATP match debut. Oberer recognized Federer's talent and pulled strings in the background to mentor him. "Roger was still playing like a junior," Oberer said in Gstaad. "Individual points were of little value to him but he has everything to become a champion one day. We just had to be careful not to burn him out. It wasn't important that he was strong for now but that he could realize his potential in four to six years."

Oberer gave Federer the opportunity to accompany the Davis Cup team as a practice partner, where he was able to train with the team in the first round against the Czech Republic in Zurich in April. Following the tournament in Gstaad, Federer again traveled with the team to La Coruna, Spain for the Davis Cup quarterfinal with Spain. Even though the Swiss didn't stand a chance against the Spanish Armada of Carlos Moya and Alex Corretja, the trip proved to be a valuable learning experience.

Federer wanted to finish the year as the No. 1 ranked junior in the world. After his triumph at Wimbledon, he was ranked No. 3 behind France's Julien Jeanpierre and the Chilean Fernando Gonzalez. Everybody knew that it was a major difference if he finished the year No. 1 against being ranked No. 2 or No. 3. As with professional tennis, the best junior players are over-proportionally rewarded—the No. 1 players get better contracts and more wild card entries into big tournaments. The wild card entries spared the select players from the difficultly and unpredictable nature of qualifying tournaments. Wild cards provided an opportunity for young players to compete in bigger tournaments that they would not be able to gain entry into due to their lower world rankings.

Federer bolstered his quest for the year-end No. 1 junior ranking with a semifinal showing at the European Championships in Klosters, Switzerland in the summer. At the US Open, he reached the junior singles final, where David Nalbandian of Argentina denied him a second straight junior Grand Slam title.

Yet, before the chase for the year-end No. 1 junior ranking reached its decisive phase, the unexpected happened. Federer achieved his first great breakthrough on the ATP Tour. With a ranking of No. 878, he traveled to Toulouse, France at the end of September and, to his own surprise, advanced through the qualifying rounds to progress into the main draw of the tournament. In only his second ATP tournament, the 17-year-old registered an upset victory over No. 45-ranked Guillaume Raoux of France—his first ATP match victory—allowing the Frenchman just four games. In the next round, Federer proved this win was not a fluke by defeating former Australian Davis Cup star Richard Fromberg 6-1, 7-6 (5). In the quarterfinals—his sixth match of the tournament including matches in the qualifying rounds—Federer lost to Jan Siemerink 7-6 (5), 6-2, with a throbbing thigh injury hampering him during the match. The Dutchman was ranked No. 20 and went on to win the tournament two days later, but Federer was also handsomely rewarded. He received a prize money check for $10,800 and passed 482 players in the world rankings in one tournament—moving to No. 396.

In recognition for his results in Toulouse, Federer received a wild card entry into the Swiss Indoors, Switzerland's biggest tournament, from tournament director Roger Brennwald. This tournament guaranteed him a prize money paycheck of at least $9,800. The tournament took place at St. Jakobshalle in Basel's south side, within walking distance of Federer's home in Münchenstein. This event, played originally in an inflatable dome in 1970, is one of the most important indoor tournaments in the world that almost every great player has played in. When a virtually unknown Czech player named Ivan Lendl defeated the legendary Björn Borg in the Swiss Indoor fi-

nal in 1980, it garnered major headlines around the world. The 34th and
final duel between John McEnroe and Jimmy Connors took place at the Swiss
Indoors in 1991. Future world No. 1 Jim Courier won his first ATP tourna-
ment in Basel in 1989. Stefan Edberg won the Swiss Indoors three times and
Ivan Lendl won the title twice. Borg, McEnroe, Boris Becker, Vitas Gerulaitis,
Goran Ivanisevic, Yannick Noah, Michael Stich, Pete Sampras and Guillermo
Vilas are also champions of the event.

For Roger Federer, the Swiss Indoors is like a Grand Slam tournament. The
St. Jakobshalle is the place of his dreams, like Centre Court at Wimbledon. In
1994, he was a ball boy at the event, grabbing balls for such players as Rosset,
Edberg and Wayne Ferreira, who won the title back then. Now, four years
later, he was a competitor in the event. His first-round match was against
none other than Andre Agassi. In his youthful hauteur, Federer boldly stated
"I know what I'm up against—as opposed to Agassi who has no idea who I am.
I am going to play to win."

But Agassi, the former No. 1 player ranked No. 8 at the time, was without
question a larger caliber opponent than what Federer faced in Toulouse. Agassi
allowed the hometown boy only five games in the 6-3, 6-2 defeat and said he
was not overly impressed by the Swiss public's new darling. "He proved his
talent and his instinct for the game a few times," the American said kindly.
"But for me it was an ideal first round where I didn't have to do all that much
and where I could get accustomed to the new conditions."

After appearances in big events in Toulouse and Basel, Federer next competed on the much lower level Swiss satellite circuit—and felt as if he were
in a bad movie. He just played before 9,000 spectators against Agassi, one
of the all-time greats, in front of a major television audience with all the
newspapers writing articles about him. Meanwhile, he just signed with the
world's largest sports agency, International Management Group, and was being supplied, like Pete Sampras, by brands such as Nike and Wilson. But now
he suddenly found himself in the eastern Swiss town of Küblis, in a gloomy
tennis stadium in a valley wedged in the Bündner Mountains. There were no
spectators, no line judges and no ball boys. He was not facing Andre Agassi,
but Armando Brunold, the No. 11 player in Switzerland, whom Federer by
now outclassed as the No. 6 player in the country.

The first-round match at the circuit's first tournament proved to be a culture shock for Federer and he reacted apathetically. His listlessness didn't escape tournament referee Claudio Grether. "He simply stood unmotivated and non-chalantly on the court and double-faulted twice each game," Grether explained. After Federer lost to Brunold 7-6, 6-2, Grether imposed a $100 fine against Federer because he violated the "best effort" rule stipulating that professional players must put forth their best efforts in every competition. "I could have disqualified him as well but then he would no longer have been able to compete in the rest of the circuit," Grether said. Federer silently received the verdict. With prize money earnings of only $87, Federer left Küblis with a $13.00 deficit. It would be the only professional tournament he played where he actually lost money.

But Federer learned his lesson. "The fine was justified," he admitted and he reacted in a way that showed his class. A week later, he won the second tournament on the circuit and went on to win the circuit's overall points title. His effort paid off and despite his initial setback, he moved passed 100 opponents in the world rankings, landing at No. 303. Not bad for somebody who just turned 17.

As the Orange Bowl in Florida approached in December, it became clear that Federer would have to win the event—one of the biggest tournaments on the junior tennis calendar—if he wanted to overtake France's Julien Jeanpierre—his senior by 17 months—and become the year-end No. 1 ranked junior in the world. The tournament took place in one of the most beautiful places on the tennis tour, The Tennis Center at Crandon Park on Key Biscayne—the island paradise within the shadow of downtown Miami. The second biggest tournament in the United States—the Sony Ericsson Open—is also held at the facility every March for which the grandstands at Centre Court are enlarged.

The tournament started off with a near disaster for Federer. After being just two points from defeat, he avoided a first-round upset bid by Raimonds Sproga of Latvia, winning by a 5-7, 7-6, 6-0 margin. By contrast, Jeanpierre was not as lucky and fell in the first round to Feliciano Lopez of Spain. The following day when Roger had the day off, another potential disaster presented itself. "We were condition training when Roger started horsing around," recollected Annemarie Rüegg, who accompanied the Swiss team to the Orange Bowl. "He was acting like a monkey while jump-roping and was jumping around like Tarzan. Suddenly he landed sideways on his foot and sprained it. It looked bad. He had a giant swelling on his foot. He was abruptly jolted from his silliness."

Another person in the same situation perhaps would have given up, abandoned his great goal, and pursued another one—but not him. "Roger Federer does not quit," he said years later—and the same was true already in 1998. He began treatment with accompanying physiotherapists and did everything to preserve his chances to achieve his goal. "I was amazed at his metamorphosis," said Rüegg. "Just before he was horsing around but now he was suddenly calm and serious. I noticed that he can be serious if he wants to be. He understood that it was a serious situation, that a lot was riding on the tournament, and that he had to concentrate all of his efforts on this one goal if he wanted to achieve it. I realized for the first time that he was a champion. He could do it."

Despite the handicap and with a bandaged foot, Roger won the next three matches without losing a set. In the semifinals, with the swelling in his foot virtually gone, Federer avenged his US Open loss to Nalbandian with a 6-4, 6-2 victory. In the final, Federer defeated another strong Argentine, Guillermo Coria, 7-5, 6-3. Federer won the Orange Bowl and left Miami with a bowl full of oranges—and bleached-blond hair after a spontaneous $250 hair-styling adventure.

On December 21, 1998, for the first time, the name "Federer" appeared in the No. 1 position on the International Tennis Federation's world junior rankings. "A great Christmas present," he said happily. However, Federer still endured one more week of uncertainty until his year-end No. 1 ranking was official. It wasn't until an upstart American junior named Andy Roddick defeated Jeanpierre in the semifinals of the last junior tournament of the year—the Yucatan Cup in Mexico—that Federer clinched the year-end No. 1 ranking.

At the end of his 1998 season, Federer sat for a comprehensive interview with *Tages-Anzeiger* in the lounge of the tennis facility in Diepoldsau during a Swiss satellite circuit. Curious players frequently drifted into the vicinity of the interview in an attempt to listen in to what was being discussed.

Some players friendly with Federer even made jestful comments during the serious interview.

It was clear to Roger Federer that his time as a professional tennis player was about to begin. He exceeded all expectations as a junior and there was no reason for him to spend any more time on the junior or the satellite circuits. He was on the threshold of the top 300 in the world rankings and Stéphane Oberer, the Swiss Davis Cup captain, unequivocally told him that he was counting on him for the Swiss Davis Cup team in the coming year.

Federer viewed this rapid development with calm. He himself was somewhat surprised by his success but he remained grounded and seemed pleasantly normal. "It's funny," he said. "When I come into a hotel, people say 'Hi, Mr. Federer.' Some people seem to be proud to be able to speak to me. I've noticed that the more well-known one becomes, the less one has to pay. Everybody wants to invite me and everybody wants to be nice to me just because I can play tennis well."

But he knows, he said, that these are not real friends. "I haven't changed much," he said. "I'm pretty well-known now in Switzerland but I don't have the feeling of being a star." When asked how to describe himself, he calmly answered. "I'm honest. I'm a cool type. I'm athletic and likeable, and pleasant, I think."

Federer now stood at 6'1" (1.86 meters) in height and weighed 175 lbs. (80 kilograms). This was too heavy, he believed. "I have a gut," he said. "I should do more for my stomach muscles." Sweets and snacks and eating properly became more of a priority. "I've just started to eat meat," he said. "Before I only ate sausage, hamburgers and such. Now I don't always have to be afraid to eat when I'm invited somewhere for a meal."

He said he was also proud that he was now able to better maintain his emotions on the court. An incident at the US Open proved to be somewhat of a turning point. He was provoked by some of the US Open's traditionally vocal fans. Federer could not keep his mouth shut and demolished a racquet in his frustrations. Federer kept his cool in the autumn tournaments—resulting in positive results. "I didn't get upset at either Toulouse or Basel. That was very solid," he said. "I never would have thought that it would have been possible, I don't know if this has something to do with the big stadiums. Perhaps I'm more ashamed when I lose control there."

He also engaged in fewer soliloquies during matches. "I often asked myself 'Why are you so stupid and get upset?' But when one plays well and doesn't get upset, that's the greatest feeling in the world." After all, he said, he's just a perfectionist. "I don't accept it when I miss easy balls even if it is normal and even if the professionals do it."

Peter Carter corroborated this mental progress; "He has to be more patient if he wants to be successful at the professional level."

Carter and Federer were constant companions, training and traveling week after week. This sometimes led to friction in their relationship. "If I'm on tour for a month just with Peter, we sometimes get on each other's nerves," Federer said. "Then I miss my friends or my girlfriend. That's why it's important for me to get along well with other juniors. I like it when other Swiss players and coaches are around. That's a change of pace I enjoy."

He looked ahead to his first full year on the professional tour with confidence and excitement. He no longer found any great weaknesses in his game. "I have slowly come to master all the strokes," he said. "I could perhaps volley better or improve my footwork, little things."

What did he have to worry about? He had, after all, defeated two top 50 players in Toulouse "That showed me that I could compete up there if I played well," he said. "Now I just have to work on making it run smoothly. Then getting to the top should take care of itself."

CHAPTER 5

A Newcomer Climbs to the Top

When the ATP issued its 1999 "Player Media Guide," Roger Federer was not featured among the 300 biographies in the book. As the year developed, this proved to be a mistake in planning. His first complete year as a professional brought him disappointments, setbacks and a difficult summer but it also placed him as the youngest player in the top 100 of the world rankings.

His status as the official International Tennis Federation world junior champion and Wimbledon junior boys' singles champion proved, as he had hoped, to be an ideal launching point into professional tennis. Altogether in 1999, he received eight wildcards for ATP tournaments over the course of the year, exempting him from playing in the qualifying rounds.

Young pros normally start by playing in satellite circuits or futures tournaments until they have sufficiently improved their rankings to play at the next level—the challenger tournaments. A ranking in the top 120 is usually required in order to play on the ATP Tour and at the four Grand Slam Tournaments—Melbourne, Paris, London and New York—and sometimes even that is not enough. Even top 100 players often have to participate in qualifying tournaments at the nine Tennis Masters Series tournaments—the most important events in tennis just below the Grand Slams—in order to win one of the last free places in the main draw.

The wildcards that Federer received immediately put him in the fast lane and spared him strenuous trips to satellite, futures and challenger events—but it also made him play much tougher opponents and made it much more difficult for him to win stretches of matches.

The wildcards into ATP events allowed him the chance to earn ATP ranking points and prize money. Even defeats at the French Open or Wimbledon meant respectable amounts of prize money. In addition to wild cards into

Swiss ATP events, Federer also received wildcards from the French Open and Wimbledon even though both events traditionally gave wildcards to players from their own countries. Because of the substantial prize money, Federer managed to acquire over $20,000 at both Paris and Wimbledon alone even though he lost in the first round of both events in 1999.

It became evident in his first professional year that his highest comfort level came at indoor tournaments. Federer played seven outdoor tournaments during his rookie year—losing in the first round each time. In addition, he was 0-2 in two outdoor Davis Cup matches against Belgium. He also failed to advance through the qualifying rounds into the main draw at the Australian Open and the US Open.

But Federer, the rookie, performed admirably at indoor events. He won six straight matches at the challenger tournament in Heilbronn, Germany immediately in January—three in the qualifying rounds and three en route to the semifinals. This effort immediately placed him into the top 250 players in the world. He registered his best victory of his young career in the beginning of February in Marseille when, ranked No. 243, he beat reigning French Open champion and world No. 5 Carlos Moya from Spain in the first round en route to the quarterfinals. He likewise qualified at the ATP event in Rotterdam, where he reached the quarterfinals and led world No. 2 Yevgeny Kafelnikov 3-1 in the third set before losing. Nonetheless, Federer was ranked among the world's top 130 players by the end of February.

Federer's roommate, Yves Allegro, realized at this time he would go far. "I said back then that he would make it into the top 10 or maybe even to No. 1, but many people laughed at me," Allegro said. "The way that Roger made the jump from the juniors to the professionals inside a few months was impressive. I was impressed about all the details that Roger picked up from watching players play on TV."

Before the outdoor season—and his series of first-round defeats—Federer achieved another career highlight in April—his Davis Cup debut. Switzerland was slated to play against Italy in a first-round match in Neuenburg, Switzerland. However, the Swiss team experienced some tumultuous months leading into the tie as Marc Rosset, the No. 1 Swiss player, quarreled and separated from his coach of 11 years, Stephane Oberer, and threatened to quit the Davis Cup if Oberer remained the captain of the Swiss team. Luckily, Oberer resigned at the beginning of February and was replaced shortly thereafter by Claudio Mezzadri, a former top-30 ranked Swiss player.

Federer's Davis Cup debut could not have been better. He decisively beat Italian No. 1 Davide Sanguinetti, ranked No. 48 in the world, 6-4, 6-7 (3), 6-3, 6-4 in his first match in the 3-2 win for the Swiss. "It was unfortunate that Federer was playing for the opponent," Italy's team captain, Paolo Bertolucci, said afterwards, "but it was fun to watch him. There are not many people in the world who can play tennis so well."

In July, the Swiss played Belgium in Brussels in the quarterfinals and Federer, not quite 18-years-old, found himself acting as the leader of the Swiss team in only his second match as a member of the team. The higher-ranked Rosset was with the team in Brussels, but was feeling ill during the week and, after much deliberation, declined to play singles in the tie. Federer was unable to carry the Swiss team on his back as he lost two marathon matches to Christophe van Garsse and Xavier Malisse in the Swiss loss.

At the time, Federer was an inconsistent player with the fascinating repertoire of strokes. He still had trouble concentrating and often couldn't find his way to winning matches, despite his technical superiority. This was especially the case in matches that exceeded three sets, where stamina, patience and tactical maturity—not brilliance—were required. He became irritated when the wind and weather altered playing conditions and when fans moved in the grandstands.

However, he consistently proved that he had everything it took to compete with the pros—indoors or outdoors—regardless of court surfaces. This proved to be the case on the clay courts at Roland Garros, where the 17-year-old made his main draw Grand Slam tournament debut as the youngest competitor in the men's field. In his first-round match, Federer drew Patrick Rafter, the Australian two-time US Open champion. He jumped out to win the first set against the world's No. 3-ranked player who then was at the peak of his career. However, the sun came out and the conditions became warmer and faster. The clay courts dried out and balls moved much faster through the court. The Australian's attacking serve-and-volley style seemed to run on automatic and he won in four sets.

"The young man from Switzerland could be one of the people who will shape the next ten years," the French sports newspaper *L'Equipe* wrote during the tournament. Rafter shared the same opinion. "The boy impressed me very much," he said. "If he works hard and has a good attitude, he could become an excellent player." Asked at a press conference what he was still lacking to beat such players, Federer said, "I just have to mature."

Four weeks later, Federer made his main draw debut at Wimbledon and faced the experienced Czech, Jiri Novak. It was only Federer's second appearance in the main draw of a Grand Slam tournament, but he once again showed that he could dominate a match over long stretches. It appeared he was on his way to a victory—leading Novak two sets to one—when his concentration began to fade and he became mired down in the first five-set match of his career. Federer's inexperience showed as he was unable to capitalize on eight break points in the deciding set—and lost.

After the string of seven first-round defeats in Key Biscayne, Monte Carlo, Paris, Queens, Wimbledon, Gstaad and Washington, D.C.—as well as the Davis Cup disappointment in Brussels—Federer lost in the qualifying rounds at ATP events in Long Island and the US Open in New York. Federer's crisis, however, suddenly vanished when the indoor season began in the fall of 1999.

With a first-round win over former Wimbledon and US Open finalist Cedric Pioline of France in Tashkent, Uzbekistan, Federer reached the top 100 in the world rankings, and at the age of 18, he was the youngest player within the group. He beat another seven opponents on the ATP Tour by the end of the year and reached his first career ATP semifinal in Vienna. He ended the year by winning the challenger tournament in Brest, France in his last tournament appearance in a challenger or satellite-level event. From this point forward, Federer only competed on the ATP Tour and in the Grand Slam events. It took him only about a year to transition from an inexperienced newcomer into an established professional.

His rookie season resulted in a 13-17 record in ATP Tour, Grand Slam and Davis Cup events, but his leap from No. 302 to No. 64 in the world rankings and his $223,859 in prize money was impressive for an 18-year-old rookie.

"I never would have expected to be ranked so high so quickly," he said. "My goal was crack the top 200 in the rankings."

For a while, he even had chances of ending the year ranked higher than Rosset and finishing as the top-ranked Swiss player. Not achieving this feat was not that troubling. After all, Roger Federer's goal was not just to become the No. 1 ranked Swiss player—he wanted to become No. 1 player in the world.

"This year, every match he played was like a final when he was a junior," Peter Carter concluded at the end of the season. "Against fellow junior players, he used to win almost every match, but now he lost many matches and also lost his confidence. But he learned a lot from his defeats." Carter was convinced that he could play well on any surface—outdoors and on clay courts. He just lacked experience. The goals he set for 2000 were rather modest. "It would be nice if I could place among the top 50," Roger said.

Before the end of 1999, Federer had to go back to a little-loved school classroom one last time—he spent three days at the "ATP Tour University" in Monte Carlo. During this training, Roger learned from the ATP what challenges top players could expect to face and how to deal with them. He later related that it was during these training sessions that he lost his fear of the media. "I was afraid of the press at first and I had expected that they would write bad things about me," he said. "Why should I talk to them, I thought. But then I realized that the media could also help us players to improve our images and we could help them to write good stories."

CHAPTER 6
New Coach, New Ways

The year 2000 began even better for Roger Federer than the previous year. At the opening event of the season in Adelaide, he finally experienced his first ATP match victory at an outdoor tournament, defeating Jens Knippschild of Germany in the first round, before losing to the Swede Thomas Enqvist. At the Australian Open, he beat former French champion Michael Chang en route to the third round before losing to Arnaud Clement of France. However, Federer continued to post his best results indoors. Playing indoors in Zurich against Australia in the first round of the Davis Cup, he defeated Mark Philippoussis and, with teammate Lorenzo Manta, topped Wayne Arthurs and Sandon Stolle, to give Switzerland a 2-1 lead. However, when in position to clinch the win for Switzerland, he narrowly lost to Lleyton Hewitt 6-2, 3-6, 7-6 (2), 6-1 as Australia defeated the Swiss 3-2.

Just eight days after his Davis Cup loss to Hewitt, Federer achieved a career milestone—his first ATP tournament final. He advanced into the championship match at the ATP event in Marseille, France, where he faced, of all people, his friend and countryman Marc Rosset in the final. At this time, Roger's world ranking was No. 67, which was 10 places better than the six-foot-seven-inch man from Geneva. However, despite winning the first set, Federer lost to Rosset on this day, falling by a narrow 2-6, 6-3, 7-6 (5) margin. Only 12 days later, nearly the same scenario repeated itself in London when Federer and Rosset squared off again—this time in the quarterfinals. Once again, Federer won the first set, but lost the match. As in Marseille, Federer watched as Rosset went on to win the tournament. The title ended up being the last ATP title for the 1992 Olympic champion.

Despite the defeats to Rosset, Federer cracked the top 50 in the world rankings. Having achieved his goal already for the season, he now quickly set his sights on reaching the top 25.

On Easter Sunday in April, a fax drifted into major newsrooms in Switzerland, without a sender name and with the terse headline: "Press Communiqué Tennis." The 22-line press release was somewhat awkwardly written and began: "Roger Federer has decided to go his own way. Beginning October, 1, 2000, he will be working with his current Swiss Tennis Federation coach Peter Lundgren. The separation from Swiss Tennis is taking place after many years of cooperation and on the best terms." This statement was followed by kind sentiments of gratitude to the Swiss Tennis Federation and especially Peter Carter, who, the press release said, led him to the No. 1 world junior ranking in 1998 and then to a top 50 world ranking. "This ranking made it possible for me to stand on my own two feet and I have therefore decided to take an independent course," Federer said in the statement.

The official separation from the guidance of the Swiss Tennis Federation made sense for Federer because it provided him with a more flexible environment that was adjusted to his own needs. However, the fact that Federer decided to work with Lundgren and not Carter, whom he knew better and with whom he had worked together much longer, came as a surprise to most. Federer could not really explain the reasons for the choice.

"It was a toss-up," he said. "Both of them are nice, funny guys." His inner, gut feelings made the decision. "And they were more in favor of Peter Lundgren," he said.

Carter didn't hide his disappointment but he reacted magnanimously. He immediately relinquished supervision of the 18-year-old to the Swede and rededicated himself as the Swiss Tennis Federation's coach to other players.

As it turned out, Federer now had a coach who was completely compatible with him. The stocky 35-year-old Swede, with the long blond hair that made him look like a Viking, could be both strict and demanding. He was easygoing by nature, always positive and quick with a joke. He also was well-versed in the ways of professional tennis from his days playing the circuit himself. He played against most of Federer's new opponents, played in all the major tournaments around the world and competed on the Centre Courts at all the major venues. He was a familiar, popular and respected figure on the tennis scene.

Lundgren's accomplishments also deserved merit. In his professional career that ended in 1994, he earned over a million dollars in prize money and chalked up many spectacular achievements, including victories over Pete Sampras, Andre Agassi, Mats Wilander, Ivan Lendl, Michael Chang and Pat Cash. "But I also lost to many unknowns," he noted in his modest way when asked. Lundgren triumphed at three tour events—Cologne, Rye Brook, N.Y., and San Francisco—and in the mid 1980's, he fought his way to No. 25 in the world rankings. However, for much of his career, his ranking hovered in between No. 50 and No. 80 in the world. Lundgren was sometimes mistaken for Björn Borg because of his hair but his style of playing was completely different from the Swedish legend—aggressive and on the offensive, sometimes from the baseline, sometimes at net.

Lundgren, who lived with his girlfriend and their two children near Goteborg, viewed his profession as a vocation. "I am a coach because I know most about tennis and I want to pass along this knowledge," he explained. He said that he made many mistakes himself during his career and wanted to prevent them from happening to Federer under the motto—a wise man not only learns from his own but from others' mistakes. Federer admitted that Lundgren possessed a character like his own. "He always did it the hard way," he said. "When someone told him not to throw his racquet, he turned around and smashed two of them right away, just like I did earlier."

Before coming to work for the Swiss Tennis Federation in 1997, Lundgren worked in such places as Germany, Sweden and, in 1996, he worked with the top Chilean player, Marcelo Rios. The usually sulky and unshaven Chilean with the long dark hair was one of the least popular players on the tour. He was considered to be irritable and stubborn. "Those were the longest eight months of my life," Lundgren admitted. In contrast, his work with Federer, for which he signed on for 40 weeks of the year, was almost heaven.

The Swede attested to the teenager's limitless potential. He believed that Federer was already among the top 300 or 400 players in the world even at age 16 and that Federer, who was 18 by then, "can be No. 1, but it's a long road. I was No. 25 in the world but a long ways away from his level. This guy is something special. He's from another planet." Sven Gröneveld from the Netherlands, also a Swiss Tennis Federation coach, likewise had euphoric praise for Federer. "Roger can achieve anything that he wants," he said. "He can win Grand Slam tournaments and be No. 1 in the world. He can take it to a higher level whenever necessary. When he's in the zone—his zone—then he's one of the most difficult players to beat on the tour."

Lundgren quickly realized the main thing they had to work on with his young charge. "Roger has to be able to win in an ugly way," he said. "He is an artist and when his strokes don't work, he becomes irritated and loses his concentration. He can do anything with the ball but sometimes he has to learn how to simplify his game." His volley was also a weakness. "He hated volleys when we started working together," said Lundgren. "He played as if sharks were lurking at the net in the service box. We drove off the sharks by training a lot."

The beginning of the new Federer-Lundgren partnership came in the middle of the clay court season. It was a bleak time for Federer. He lost in the first round of the clay court events in Monte Carlo, Barcelona, Rome, Hamburg and St. Polten. Entering the French Open, Federer's career clay court record on the ATP Tour and Davis Cup was 0-11. Lundgren attributed the losing streak to faulty seasonal planning. Before the beginning of clay court season, Roger went to the River Oaks Invitational exhibition tournament in Houston, leaving him too little time to prepare in Europe.

The black dearth on the red clay court surface finally ended for Federer in Paris. He won his first profesional match on a clay court, defeating Wayne Arthurs of Australia 7-6 (4), 6-3, 1-6, 6-3. After a second-round win over Jan-Michael Gambill of the United States, Federer defeated countryman Michael Kratochvil from Bern in a suspenseful five-setter determined by an 8-6 final set. The victory over Kratochvil put Federer into the round of 16 of a Grand Slam tournament for the first time. It was a strong result to be in the fourth round of a two-week Grand Slam tournament, played over a two-week period with 128 players competing in the main draw. Although Federer lost his next match to Spain's Alex Corretja, one of the best clay court players in the world, Lundgren was very satisfied with the result. "Corretja played a great match but Roger was still able to hang in there for two hours," he said. "This experience will give him strength and self-confidence."

His new confidence, however, didn't immediately reveal itself. Two weeks after his match with Corretja, Federer lost in the first round of Wimbledon to former world No. 1 Yevgeny Kafelnikov of Russia. Federer, was still encouraged. "I didn't play very well but it wasn't too shabby," he explained and went on to gush about the atmosphere at his favorite tournament. While Federer had not yet won a main draw match at Wimbledon in his two visits, he said confidentally that just as he had won the junior tournament at the All England Club in 1998, he would someday win the men's singles title. Some journalists looked at one another and shook their heads.

Federer's summer following Wimbledon was disappointing. His first-round loss at Wimbledon was the first of five straight first-round tournament defeats. His streak stopped at the US Open, where his third-round showing did little to improve his match record. At this point in his career, Federer lost in the first round of 21 of his first 38 ATP tournaments. But Federer's discouraging tournament results did not blunt his enthusiasm for his next tournament destination—the 2000 Olympic Games in Sydney, Australia. On and off the court, Federer's life was about to change.

CHAPTER 7
Olympic Experiences

The Swiss Olympic tennis team was in shatters at the start of the Sydney Games. Martina Hingis and Patty Schnyder both withdrew from the women's competition at the last minute. Marc Rosset, the 1992 Olympic champion, was also a late withdrawal, costing Federer an opportunity to play Olympic doubles. The Swiss Olympic Committee was furious. Tennis players were depicted as pampered and spoiled athletes who didn't appreciate the true value of the Olympic Games.

The Swiss tennis team shared living quarters, socialized and dined with fellow Olympians from the Swiss archery, judo and wrestling teams in the Olympic Village, where Federer had the privilege of occupying a single room. "That was the best event I ever attended," Federer said years later as he embellished his long-time fascination of the Olympic Games. The contrast to the monotony of life in the hotels could hardly be bigger. The Opening Ceremonies, the interaction with athletes from other sports, the atmosphere in the Olympic Village and the feeling of belonging also made an impression on Mirka Vavrinec, a member of Switzerland's women's Olympic tennis team. "The Olympics are fantastic, unbelievably beautiful, unparalleled," Vavrinec gushed of the Olympic experience courtside following a practice session. She also had nice things to say about Federer, the youthful star of the Swiss team, who was three years her junior—"I had no idea he was so funny."

Mirka was born an only child in Bojnice, in the Slovakian part of Czechoslovakia in 1978. Her parents fled the Communist country with her when she was two-years-old to make a new life for themselves in the Swiss border city of Kreuzlingen on Lake Constance. Her father, Miroslav, a former javelin thrower, and his wife, Drahomira, ran a jewelry shop. In the fall of 1987, when Mirka was nine, Miroslav took his family to nearby Filderstadt,

Germany where Martina Navratilova happened to be competing in a WTA Tour event.

The Czech-born Navratilova dominated women's tennis and, like the Vavrinecs, defected from Czechoslovakia. When in Filderstadt, she warmly greeted the Vavrinec family. "We got to stay a few days with her," Mirka said of the trip. Navratilova asked her if she played tennis. Mirka said no, "I do ballet." The eight-time Wimbledon champion (she would go on to win her ninth title in 1990) advised her to try tennis. She said that Mirka's good physique and athletic talent would serve her well on the tennis courts. Navratilova put out feelers and asked the former top Czech player living in Switzerland, Jiri Granat, if he could test and coach the girl.

Navratilova's instincts were correct. Mirka immediately showcased great skills with a tennis racquet. But not only that, she also had grit and endurance. Tennis instructor Murat Gürler, who tutored her in her early years, recalled that she was "completely into it" when it came to tennis. Mirka told the Swiss tennis magazine *Smash* in 1994, after winning the Swiss juniors' title for 18-year-olds at the age of 15, "Tennis is my life, but it certainly can't be easy to work with me because I can be really stubborn."

Her ambition and her uncompromising nature were tremendous. In 1993, following a tournament in the city of Maribor in Slovenia, she convinced her coach to take her to a tournament in Croatia. The trip required travel through a part of Croatia where there was still fighting in the Balkan civil war. The two passed through destroyed villages, tanks and burned cars. She was afraid, but her ambition was greater.

Mirka ranked among the top 300 in the world by the time she was 17. A protracted heel injury in 1996 kept her off the circuit for months, causing her ranking to fall over 300 places. She valiantly fought back to No. 262 in the rankings by the end of 1997 and looked euphorically to the future. "I really want to place in the top 30 in the world rankings," she said.

Mirka meanwhile obtained a Swiss passport. The only connections she still had to her native land were a few relatives still living in Slovakia as well as the confused mix of German and Slovakian spoken at home. She maintained loose ties to Navratilova and was fortunate to find a patron, the Swiss industrialist Walter Ruf, who helped her to survive financially on the women's tennis circuit.

Thanks to her ambition and her endurance—as well as to her backhand that some even considered the best in the world—Mirka cracked the top 100 in the world rankings for the first time in 2000. She luckily received a wild-card entry to play at the Olympic Games in Sydney, even though her ranking did not qualify her to play.

While Mirka won only two games in her first-round match against eventual silver medalist Elena Dementieva of Russia, Federer began to rack up victory after victory. Benefiting from an Olympic men's field without Andre Agassi and Pete Sampras, and upset losses by US Open champion Marat Safin, Tim Henman and Michael Chang in his half of the draw, Federer won four straight matches and found himself in the semifinals. It was his best result of his career to date and surprisingly, it came at an outdoor event

At age 19, Federer was in position to become the youngest Olympic gold medalist in modern tennis. However, he played cautiously against the German Tommy Haas, ranked No. 48 (12 places behind Federer) in the semifinals and decisively lost. He did, however, still have a chance to win the bronze medal, but instead of registering a lifetime achievement of winning an Olympic medal, Federer suffered one of his greatest disappointments, losing to Arnaud DiPasquale of France, ranked No. 61 in the world. Despite being up 3-0 in the first-set tie-break, Federer lost seven of the next nine points to lose the tie-break 7-5. In the second set, Federer fought off a match point in the tie-break at 6-7 and won the tie-break two points later. Federer broke DiPasquale, who began suffering from cramps, to take a 2-1 lead in the final set, but the Frenchmen rallied to win the two-and-half-hour match 6-7 (5), 7-6 (7), 6-3.

"Considering how the match was going, I should never have lost," Federer said, hardly able to hold back the tears. "I really wanted to be standing on the podium. Now I have nothing to take home except my pride."

But Federer, who had recently said "I would choose tennis over a girlfriend" would leave Sydney with more than his pride. His friendship with Mirka blossomed into romance. Mirka said at first she wasn't aware that he had taken a romantic interest in her. "He didn't kiss me until the last day of the Olympic Games," she admitted.

They parted ways for now. She followed the women's tour to Japan and then to Europe. However, the relationship became more intense over the next few months. The public still had to wait a long time until stories and official pictures of the new "dream couple" surfaced. When a newspaper disregarded Federer's request to please keep his new relationship under wraps, he reacted angrily. "I don't think that this has to come out in public," he complained. "I spoke with my girlfriend and she didn't want this exposed either, because then we would both just have to talk about our relationship and not about our tennis anymore."

Mirka's career, however, didn't work out as hoped. She managed to reach the third round of a Grand Slam tournament at the 2001 US Open, losing to future world No. 1 Justine Henin-Hardenne, but the price she had to pay for her victories was high. Like her Swiss colleague, Martina Hingis, Mirka encountered problems with her feet—despite several operations and rest. Her career-high ranking was achieved on Sept. 10, 2001 when she ranked No. 76 in the world, but a torn ligament in her right foot prevented her from further improving and forced her into a hiatus that lasted for months.

The 2001 US Open was her last great success on the tennis tour—with the exception of the Hopman Cup in Perth in January of 2002 where she was able to celebrate a victory over Argentina alongside her boyfriend. Shortly afterwards, at the age of 24, she played her last match on the WTA Tour in Budapest. She was forced to have another operation and was once again on crutches. It was still quite some time until she finally realized that her career was really finished. Her record as a professional concluded with 202 victories and 159 defeats—including the lower-level challenger and satellite events—with overall earnings of $260,832.

The abrupt and premature end of her career cast her into a depression. "It's not easy when you do something you like your entire life and then have to quit it from one day to the next," she said later in an interview at Wimbledon. "I fell into a deep hole. The most difficult part was when I was home for eight months and couldn't do anything. I had a lot of time to think and watch tennis on television. Roger was my greatest support back then. He gave my tennis life back to me. When he wins, it's as if I win as well."

CHAPTER 8
No Pain, No Gain

Roger Federer was still the youngest player in the top 100 of the ATP rankings at the end of the 2000 season and was rapidly working his way to the top. However, when it came to winning his first ATP singles title, it seemed as though he was jinxed. No matter how well he played, he just couldn't break through and win his first title. By contrast, Lleyton Hewitt, who was just five months older than Federer, already won six titles in his career, including four alone in 2000. Hewitt also ranked No. 6 in the world rankings and was firmly established as a consistent top 10 player.

Hewitt's style was different and simpler. He was fast and was one of the greatest warriors on the court—fighting tooth and nail for every point and wearing his opponents down with his steady baseline play. He intimidated opponents with fist pumps and his signature yell-out of "C'mon!"

While Hewitt was winning in a relatively non-dazzling way, the opposite was usually the case for Federer. He charmed the spectators with dynamic displays of the most diverse strokes and with his virtuoso onslaught. He seemed to possess infinite potential—but he nonetheless repeatedly lost to inferior opponents. He seemed like somebody who had the winning lottery ticket but didn't know what to do with all his money. "He has so much potential that it sometimes confuses even himself," said John McEnroe, himself, a one-time artist with the tennis ball.

Federer's time finally seemed to come in October of 2000 in Basel, his hometown. He overcame a match point in defeating Hewitt for the first time in his career in the semifinals, winning by the narrowest of margins—8-6 in the decisive third-set tie-break. "That was one of my most unbelievable matches," the local matador said exuberantly of one of his early marquee wins. But Federer was not able to carry the momentum through to the title, losing a hard-fought final to No. 6 seed Thomas Enqvist of Sweden.

The final-round showing in Basel placed Federer among the top 25 ranked players in the world. But mental and physical exhaustion from the long season set in and Federer won just three matches in his final four tournaments and finished the 2000 season ranked No. 29. For the first time, he failed to achieve his goals for the season—winning his first title and finishing the year in the top 25 of the rankings.

Federer's 2000 season—his second as a professional—taught him the bitter lesson that spectacular strokes and talent by themselves weren't enough to win tournaments and get to the top. He had to work on his physical fitness. Although fitness training was something he didn't particularly like, he hired a fitness coach, Pierre Paganini, an old acquaintance from his time with the Swiss Tennis Federation at Ecublens, to join Lundgren as part of his team. Training with the 43-year-old Paganini 100 days a year proved to be a stroke of luck.

"He is the best fitness trainer you can imagine," said Lundgren of Paganini. The bald, bespectacled man was a former soccer player as well as a smart, professional and unobtrusive worker—and he quickly deduced what Federer was lacking. "Athletically, he had great shortcomings. There was enormous potential for improvement, especially in legwork and body building," Paganini recalled. "His problem was that his enormous talent allowed him to cover up his athletic shortcomings." At the same time, however, he also had to defend his position in the world rankings and he could not afford to just work on basic conditioning. "I had a time table of three years to bring him up to the best physical condition."

Paganini's goal, however, was not to transform Federer into a muscle-man. "A tennis player is not a sprinter, a marathon runner or a shot-put thrower," he said. "But he does have to have something from all of them and he does have to be able to summon all of these qualities when playing." Because Federer was a creative player who often improvised many different shots during a match, he had to be able to execute many different movements, unlike a player like Hewitt, who tended to play the same style and hit the same type of shots repeatedly. Paganini worked with Federer to achieve a "coordinated creativity," high precision movements and the ability to muster top athletic performance after four hours of play. "Roger couldn't be permitted to choose the wrong tactic for physical reasons," Paganini said.

Every day brought fresh challenges for Paganini to keep the young firebrand's morale high. "Roger is not a workaholic that you can hit 3,000 backhands to and he hits them and feels good doing it. Training has to be fun for Roger," said Lundgren.

"He wants to work hard but he needs a lot of variety," Paganini said. "He has to see that an exercise is useful to him. He is an artist. If you motivate him, then he turns into a training animal."

In Biel in December of 2000, Federer received a two-week preview of what his new training work would entail. Paganini developed special exercises for him that he termed "integrated fitness training." Federer, for example, ran on the side of the court until he was exhausted and then immediately ran back onto the court to play tennis. "The natural reflexes and all the bad habits that are the hardest to break kick in when one is in an exhausted state," Paganini said, explaining his method. "And then the coach goes to work on them."

While many tennis players only concentrated on building fitness in December, the only tournament-free month of the year, Federer punctually worked on his fitness training the entire year. Paganini was immediately enthused by the professional dedication shown by his protégé. "He was really motivated for such exercises and this surprised me," he said. "But he is, after all, a natural athlete." Paganini, who called Federer "naturally coordinated," said Federer accepted the fact that fitness work and practicing would not always be fun. "He noticed that he was there to acquire something that would later serve him on the tennis court."

Paganini's three-year plan proved successful. "Today, Roger can reach a maximum speed of 20 km/h (12 mph), which means that he can keep up with a regional sprinter for the first 30 meters," he recollected in 2003. Federer could run 3,300 meters in 12 minutes, 9,300 meters in 40 minutes and he could press 150 kg (330 lbs) while doing knee-bends. This was an immense improvement from before.

Federer found it easy to motivate himself for these goal-oriented training sessions because they broke up the routine. "Just a little bit of change does me a lot of good," he said. "Once I'm out on the court, I don't have any problem getting motivated. If I want to be No. 1, I have to give my all in training." Thanks to Paganini, he understood why he was training so hard. He quickly noticed that his improved fitness was helping him to increase his self-confidence. "I feel mentally really good because I know that I am physically prepared and that I can compete," he said after the first extended training session with Paganini.

Lundgren expected a lot from Federer in 2001, his first full season as Federer's private coach. He was convinced that "if he plays like he did last fall in Sydney, Vienna or in Basel, he'll be in the top 15." He even dared to speculate that "he could have his first title very soon."

At the start of the season, Federer and Martina Hingis won the Hopman Cup in Perth. It was not an especially significant event but it was, after all, the International Tennis Federation's sanctioned world mixed tennis tournament. He reached the third round of the Australian Open—avenging his Olympic loss to DiPasquale in the first round before losing to eventual finalist Arnaud Clement. February, however, became the best month of his career to date. At the indoor event in Milan, Italy after the Australian Open, Federer defeated Olympic Champion Yevgeny Kafelnikov for the first time in his career in the semifinals to reach his third career ATP singles final. Federer seized the opportunity and, with his parents in the stands cheering him on, he finally won his first ATP singles title, defeating No. 53-ranked Julien Boutter of France 6-4, 6-7 (7), 6-4.

Lundgren was correct. A milestone was achieved. "The relief is enormous," Federer said. "I've had to wait a long time for this moment. It should get easier from here on out." But the excursion to Milan didn't end very happily for Roger's father. In his excitement, he locked his car keys inside the car and had to smash in the car window to retrieve them.

A week later, another career milestone was achieved for the 19-year-old as he returned to Basel for Davis Cup duty against the United States. There was no stopping Federer. He beat Todd Martin and Jan-Michael Gambill in two breath-taking performances in singles, and in between, paired with Lorenzo Manta to defeat the American team of Gambill and Justin Gimelstob in doubles. With his three match victories in the 3-2 Swiss defeat of the USA, he joined Raul Ramirez, Neale Fraser, Nicola Pietrangeli, Frank Sedgman, Henri Cochet and Laurie Doherty as the seventh and the youngest player to win three live matches in a Davis Cup tie against the United States. "It's like a dream," said Federer, who shed tears of joy after his match-clinching victory over Gambill.

The Americans, by contrast, were stunned. "You'd have to be blind not to see that he's got a great future in store for him," said Gambill. U.S. Captain Patrick McEnroe didn't try to make any excuses although he was missing his two strongest players, Andre Agassi and Pete Sampras, in this match. "We knew that Federer would be tough but we didn't expect this," he said. "Whenever he got hold of the ball, the point was his."

February would bring even more success for Federer. The week after his single-handed defeat of the U.S. Davis Cup team, he reached the semifinals in Marseille where his 10-match winning streak was ended by Kafelnikov. The next week, he reached his fourth career singles final, losing to Nicolas Escude of France in a third-set tie-break in the final of Rotterdam. The ATP chose him their "Player of the Month" and effusively praised in their official press communication, "The Federer Express has arrived!" A playful warning was also issued in the press release stating that Federer, "has been blessed with so much talent that it almost seems unfair to his opponents."

CHAPTER 9

Uproar at the Davis Cup

Davis Cup captains are among the most publicly visible personalities in tennis. During often tension-filled Davis Cup weeks, they become the most important figures for players who are used to their own rituals and routines. Since Davis Cup rules—in effect since 1900—allow each team captain to remain on the court to coach and converse with players during matches, Davis Cup captains become even more important during these often dramatic, pressure-filled nationalistic matches than a coach on the regular tour. Since Davis Cup captains must hail from the country they are representing, the number of candidates to choose from is often limited and friction, power struggles and dismissals occur very often.

This phenomenon is well-known in Switzerland's Davis Cup history. In 1992, when Marc Rosset led the team to its only appearance in the Davis Cup Final, the captain, Roland Stadler, was suddenly relived of his duties. When asked what a Davis Cup captain actually does, Austrian Thomas Muster, referring to the difficult balancing act, said that he must "hold the towel, hold the water and shut up."

Federer's near single-handed effort against the United States in Basel temporarily relieved any tension in the Swiss Davis Cup camp, but nonetheless trouble was still brewing in the Swiss team. The unrest stemmed from a decision at the end of 1999, when the Swiss Tennis Federation replaced the popular team captain and director Claudio Mezzadri with Jakob Hlasek, a former top 10 player. The players clearly favored Mezzadri and they felt that it was an affront that Hlasek, the association's favorite, was being forced upon them. Not only that, but Hlasek's five-year contract gave him broad authority.

The Swiss Tennis Federation knew that hiring Hlasek had hidden dangers but it underestimated the consequences of its move. With Rosset as the ringleader, the Swiss players threatened to boycott Switzerland's home match against Australia in 2000, but they backed down at the last minute. At that time, Federer was forced to remain neutral in the controversy as he was contractually obligated to play Davis Cup in exchange for the Swiss Tennis Federation financially supporting him on the tour. But now, following his separation from Swiss Tennis, he was free and could choose if he wanted to play or not.

On the eve of the Olympic Games in Sydney, Switzerland's Davis Cup manager René Stammbach managed to coax a commitment out of Federer to play Davis Cup for Switzerland in 2001 under Hlasek. To sweeten the deal, Federer received an offer allowing Peter Lundgren to be integrated into the team. In addition, Stammbach offered to review the situation at the end of the year and comply with Federer's wishes if his relationship with Hlasek did not improve.

The strained relationship between Federer and Hlasek was difficult to determine. The chemistry between the two just didn't work. Hlasek was a no-nonsense, mechanical worker who valued discipline and wanted to keep the Davis Cup team under his thumb as much as possible. Federer, on the other hand, was an artist who liked to be surrounded by people who were looking for a change of pace, team spirit and fun. Under Hlasek, Federer was deprived of this environment, which made it even more astonishing that Federer played so well under Hlasek up until this point.

The situation escalated dramatically in April of 2001 in the quarterfinals against France in the Swiss city of Neuchatel. On the first day, Rosset and Arnaud Clement opened the series and engaged in an epic five-set struggle that lasted almost six hours, with the fifth set alone lasting two-and-a-half-hours. Despite serving for the match, Rosset faltered and lost to the Frenchman 15-13 in the fifth set. The match consisted of 72 games and at the time was the longest Davis Cup match since tie-breaks were instituted in 1989

Following the marathon match, the unexpected happened. Federer played France's No. 2 player, Nicolas Escude, who was ranked lower than him, but repeated his success in Rotterdam over the Swiss No. 1 in a four-set win to give France the 2-0 lead. Following the match—at nearly midnight due to the length of the Rosset-Clement match—Federer spoke to the media with a grim look on his face at the post-match press conference. When asked of his lackluster performance, he did not hold anything back. "The truth is that it's no longer working out with Jakob Hlasek," he said. "I felt that on the court. We've been having problems with each other for a long time but this time, it just didn't work. It wasn't any fun being on the court." Federer said that he needed someone sitting in the coach's chair who he could talk to, with whom he got along with and with whom he could have fun. "That isn't the case with Jakob."

Federer's emotional outburst revealed the less familiar, uncompromising side of his personality—like a proud lion reacting passionately when things were not going his way. But the question still remained—how had Federer performed so well in previous matches against Australia, Belarus and the United States with Hlasek sitting courtside by his side? There was speculation that he was not happy with the fact that the relationship between Rosset and Hlasek improved and that he was jealous that Rosset was stealing the limelight from him. Roger's match with Escude took place after the epic Rosset-Clement match and most journalists were busy writing and analyzing about that match rather than focus on Federer. Weary spectators left the stadium soon after the Rosset match having seen enough tennis for the day.

Switzerland had never come from 0-2 behind to win a Davis Cup match, but Federer led the unexpected effort. With Manta, he helped the Swiss to victory in the doubles, by a 9-7 in the fifth margin over Fabrice Santoro and Cedric Pioline. In the first reverse singles match on Sunday, Federer tied the match at 2-2, defeating Clement in four sets. The impossible comeback from 0-2 appeared on its way to happening. In the deciding fifth and final match, George Bastl, who replaced the exhausted Rosset, reached match point against Escude. During a long rally from the baseline, a spectator shouted—in the belief that Escude's ball had landed out. The ball landed in and Bastl, distracted by the shout, made the error and went on to lose the match 8-6 in the fifth set. The Swiss lost to the French 3-2 after having played 23 sets over 21 hours.

Shortly afterwards, Federer dispatched a statement to the Swiss Tennis Federation in which he confirmed that he would no longer play under Hlasek. A few weeks later, the contract between Hlasek and Swiss Tennis—that would have been valid through 2005—was terminated. Australian Peter Carter, Federer's coach from his junior years, succeeded Hlasek as the director of the team, while it was determined that players not involved in the matches would assume the "official" role as team captain.

Hlasek had to go—even though he amassed an impressive record as captain. Against Australia, the Swiss were one set from victory, and against France, they were one point from reaching the semifinals. Belarus and the United States were soundly defeated. Hlasek was at the wrong place at the wrong time—or, as viewed from another perspective, Roger Federer had Swiss professional tennis under his complete control by the age of 19.

CHAPTER 10
The Man Who Beat Sampras

Wimbledon was always Roger Federer's favorite tournament. Even though he won the junior title in 1998, Federer had yet to win a match in the main draw of the tournament prior to the 2001 edition of The Championships. He was, however, full of confidence based on the best start to a year in his career and his best showing to date in the clay-court season. He reached the quarterfinals of Monte Carlo and defeated world No. 2 Marat Safin en route to the third round of the Italian Open. At the French Open, he achieved his best result in a Grand Slam tournament to date reaching the quarterfinals before losing to eventual finalist Alex Corretja. As Wimbledon began, Federer was ranked No. 15 in the world, and in the ATP Champions Race, that ranks players based on their year-to-date results, Federer stood at No. 7.

Federer's third start at Wimbledon finally brought him his first main draw victory—a 6-2, 6-3, 6-2 win over Belgium's Christophe Rochus—the older brother of Olivier Rochus, Federer's doubles partner during his junior Wimbledon boy's doubles title in 1998. In the second round, Federer escaped defeat in an unusual five-set win over another Belgian Xavier Malisse. After blowing a two-sets-to-love lead, Federer trailed by a service break in the fifth set before Malisse received a point penalty for insulting a line-judge and faltered, giving Federer the 6-3, 7-5, 3-6, 4-6, 6-3 victory, despite Malisse winning more points and registering more service breaks than the man from Basel. In the third round, Federer easily defeated Sweden's Jonas Bjorkman, but fell several times during the victory on the slippery grass, causing a painful groin injury that required pain-killers to dull the discomfort.

The round of 16 matches at Wimbledon in 2001 occurred on Monday, July 2, an unseasonably warm day in England. It was a very special day for Federer as he stepped on the grass of Wimbledon's Centre Court for the first time. Centre Court is the Sistine Chapel of the sport and the place where all of his earlier idols established their fame. In addition, his debut match on Centre Court was not against just anybody. For the first time, Federer faced Pete Sampras, the king of grass court tennis and the king of Wimbledon. The 29-year-old American's record at Wimbledon was staggering. He won seven of the last eight titles and lost only one of his previous 57 matches at Church Road—in 1996 in the quarterfinals to eventual champion Richard Krajicek of the Netherlands. He held a 31-match winning streak at Wimbledon entering his match with Federer.

Sampras was Federer's third favorite player growing up—behind Becker and Edberg. The finest chapter in Sampras' storied tennis career occurred at Wimbledon just 12 months earlier. With his fiancée—the actress Bridget Wilson—in the stands, along with his parents Sam and Georgia (which was extremely rare), Sampras defeated Patrick Rafter of Australia in the men's singles final to win his seventh Wimbledon title and his 13th Grand Slam tournament victory, breaking the all-time men's record he shared with Roy Emerson.

However, the 2001 season was far from successful for Sampras. He reached only one singles final and his ranking slipped to No. 6. But with his record and history at the All England Club, Sampras made it clear—"At Wimbledon, I'm still the man to beat." Sampras was at a point in his career where he was concentrating completely on the Grand Slam tournaments—especially Wimbledon. The No. 1 ranking, which Sampras held at the end of each year from 1993 to 1998—an ATP record—was no longer a top priority to him.

Against Federer in this round of 16 match, some people sensed something was in the air and that Sampras' streak of 31 matches could end. Federer was in shape, his self confidence was high and, at this point in his career, he had many professional experiences to draw upon from in his 58 previous ATP-level events. Said John McEnroe, "Federer has to stand up and show what he can really do." Federer himself asserted that he could beat Sampras even at Wimbledon. "I am not going to play to win a set or just to look good," he said. "I am going to play to win." Peter Lundgren, always the optimistic coach, also encouraged Federer's confidence. "Every streak has to come to an end sometime," he said. "Even for Sampras."

Federer grandly paraded onto Centre Court for the first time—his broad shoulders thrown back and his face expressionless as if he had always played there. He played the best match of his career to date. "I sometimes looked over at the other side of the net, wondering if it were real or just a wonderful dream," he said later. After three hours and 41 minutes of play, he slammed a forehand return of serve for a winner on match point to close out a 7-6 (7), 5-7, 6-4, 6-7 (2), 7-5 victory. At 7:20 pm local time, Federer sank to his knees and fell over on his side and gushed tears of joy. For Federer, it was a dream come true but for Sampras, it was a dream broken. His chance to match Björn Borg's five successive Wimbledon titles was ruined and at his age, the window of opportunity was closed.

Federer's upset created a global sports sensation. "Please make note of 2 July, 2001 in your calendars," *The Times* of London wrote. "It was the day when everything changed at Wimbledon." The British tabloid newspaper *Sun* hauled up heavier artillery: "Pistol Pete was gunned down. Federer played the match of his life. He not only broke Sampras' serve but his will."

Sampras, though bitterly disappointed, nonetheless reacted with dignity. He regretted the two break point opportunities in the fifth set that would have allowed him to serve out the match at 5-4. He also praised his conqueror as he had seldom praised anybody else previously. "I lost to a really, really good player who delivered a brilliant performance," said Sampras. "Federer is one of the most unusual players on the tour. Maybe he can make it all the way."

After a seemingly endless parade of interviews following his victory, Federer retired to his rented home on nearby Lingfield Road, where he lived during the fortnight with Lundgren. Like many players, he rented an apartment near the All England Club during the tournament in order to avoid the stressful journey between the club and the hotels in downtown London. It also had the advantage that you could wait out Wimbledon's traditionally frequent rain delays at home rather than in the locker room or players' lounge. Federer didn't sleep well following his epic victory and couldn't escape all the hoopla the following day. Even though he wore a brimmed hat and sun glasses on the way to practice, he was still recognized and mobbed by fans and media. After all, his next opponent on Wednesday was the British favorite and Wimbledon hopeful Tim Henman. The British media relentlessly questioned the man who vanquished Sampras about everything in his life and some journalists went off in search of scandalous stories and childhood photographs.

In contrast to the match with Sampras, the balls did not bounce Federer's way against Henman. He did not play poorly, but his concentration suffered in the crucial moments and he failed to capitalize on key opportunities in two tie-breaks. Federer's third career match with Henman resulted in his third defeat, as the Brit, cheered on by more than 15,000 fans on Centre Court, defeated Federer 7-5, 7-6 (6), 2-6, 7-6 (6).

Roger Federer was not going to be the Wimbledon champion, but neither was Henman. The Brit lost in the semifinals to Croatia's Goran Ivanisevic, who then defeated Rafter in an epic final decided by a 9-7 fifth-set.

CHAPTER 11

The Taxi Driver of Biel

Injuries are as much part of tennis as are annoying double faults and tiresome trips around the world. Tendons and joints are subject to considerable stress every day for hours on end because of the many abrupt changes players make in direction. This continues throughout the year as tournament conditions constantly change—from hard courts to clay to grass courts to indoors and outdoors. Federer's colleague, five-time Grand Slam tournament winner Martina Hingis, dropped off the pro tour at age 22 due to chronic pain in her feet that required two foot operations.

Up to this point, Federer fortunately avoided any major injuries. Even the groin problem that plagued him since his match against Björkman at Wimbledon didn't seem too serious. After all, he defeated Sampras in the next round. But after Wimbledon, Federer made the mistake of competing in the Swiss Open at Gstaad. He lost easily in the first round to Ivan Ljubicic, and in the process, proceeded to injure his hip muscle and developed shin splints. He had to rest for seven weeks and miss the tournaments in Montreal, Cincinnati and Indianapolis.

Federer celebrated his 20th birthday on August 8, 2001 far away from the tennis world. He underwent physical therapy and recovered from his injuries in Biel, which still served as his training base. He found a fellow patient in Michael Lammer, a rival from his junior years, who was also injured. Lammer, who also graduated from "Tennis Etudes" and was preparing for his college exams, was on crutches due to a torn ligament in his leg. Federer could at least still drive and he offered his services to his colleague. "Roger was really helpful and played taxi driver for me," Lammer recalled. "He waited for me at the train station, drove me to school and picked me up again and then we went together to physical therapy at the sports school in Magglingen."

The two injured tennis players, who won an international junior doubles title together many years earlier, took a two-room apartment near the National Tennis Center. Federer had his own room while Lammer slept in the living room. "It was cramped, almost too cramped, without many amenities," said Lammer, who became Federer's roommate for almost two years. "Mirka showed up a lot when Roger was there. She cleaned, cooked and saw to it that it was reasonably tidy." Federer, he said, liked to horse around back then but he always was more mature for his age. "We drank a beer or two but never to excess," said Lammer. "He had other priorities." The man who upset Pete Sampras at Wimbledon, however, could still enjoy himself until all hours of the night on his Sony PlayStation.

When Federer returned to the tour at the end of August at the US Open, his time off made his game a bit rusty and, after the brilliant performance over Sampras at Wimbledon, expectations were now much higher every time he stepped onto the court. His goal was to qualify for the season-ending Tennis Masters Cup in Sydney, reserved for the top eight players. Following his summer layoff, he fell to No. 9 in the year-long Champions Race that determined entry into the Masters Cup.

At Flushing Meadows, Federer reached the round of 16 where, unfortunately, he was soundly beaten by Andre Agassi. The rhythm and self-confidence that carried him from victory to victory at the beginning of the year were gone and the usual comfort of the indoor tennis season provided little to build on. The fall season saw Federer lose his opening round matches in Moscow, Stuttgart and Paris—all in three sets to players ranked below him. The surroundings of home carried him to his fifth career ATP final in Basel, where victory in his native city still proved elusive in a 6-3, 6-4, 6-2 loss to Tim Henman.

Federer's breakout year ended in disappointment. He finished the year ranked No. 13 in the world and missed qualifying for the Tennis Masters Cup. Lleyton Hewitt now stood more than ever in the limelight. The Australian won his first Grand Slam title at the US Open and was also celebrated as the champion of the Tennis Masters Cup in Sydney en route to finishing the year as the No. 1 player in the world.

It was clear to Pierre Paganini that Federer's time spent resting and recovering from his injuries was the reason he missed qualifying for the Masters.

Not only did Roger have to drop out of three important summer hard court tournaments in August due to his shin splints, but he also missed out on important fitness training. Paganini said that because Federer's entire body had been affected, complete rest had been necessary. The consequences of this were all the more discernible. "Federer had difficulties in the fall finding his rhythm," Paganini said. "But injuries are part of the job. Other players suffer injuries as well. The important thing is that Roger acted very professionally during the recuperation."

CHAPTER 12

Visit to the Top 10

Roger Federer experienced a colorful collage of victories and defeats in 2002, his fourth year on the professional tour. At the start of the year, the 20-year-old won his second career ATP singles title in Sydney—site of his Olympic successes in 2000. The victory immediately cast him as a dangerous outside threat to win the Australian Open. After winning his first three matches in Melbourne in straight sets, he battled German Tommy Haas in the round of 16. He led two sets to one and held a match point in the fifth set, only to fall by a 7-6 (3), 4-6, 3-6, 6-4, 8-6 margin. Another Grand Slam tournament was lost.

In February, for the first time in his professional career, Federer came into a tournament as the defending champion in Milan. Davide Sanguinetti of Italy, however, prevented Federer from repeating as champion, defeating the man from Basel 7-6 (2), 4-6, 6-1 in the final. In Davis Cup in Moscow against the Russians—Peter Carter's debut as the Swiss captain—Federer delivered another glittering performance. He dominated Marat Safin and Yevgeny Kafelnikov—both top 10 players competing in their hometown—on a clay court in Olympic Stadium with former Russian President Boris Yeltsin in attendance. Neither player won a set from Federer and, in six total sets, the duo won a mere 16 games combined. Nonetheless, Russia won the other three matches of the tie and defeated the Swiss 3-2. In Key Biscayne, Federer defeated Hewitt en route to the final—his first at a Tennis Masters Series level tournament—only to again lose to Andre Agassi, nine years his senior.

The clay court season began somewhat ominously. In Monte Carlo, he won only three games against David Nalbandian in the second round, while in Rome, he fell to the much-lower-ranked Italian, Andrea Gaudenzi, in the first round. Rome was the first tournament Federer played with his new Wilson 6.0 racquet. He changed to the new model—with a five percent larger hitting zone—in an effort to hit fewer balls off the frame and reduce the number of unforced errors.

Federer's visit to Hamburg, Germany proved to be more surprising. In two previous appearances at the tradition-rich Masters Series tournament, Federer had yet to win a match, with his loss to Franco Squillari in the first round the year before being a bitter low point. Playing on a side court against the Argentinean left-hander, Federer badly lost his temper and smashed and destroyed his racquet in the 6-3, 6-4 first-round loss. The incident made Federer take stock of his on-court temper. He decided this behavior had to stop.

In 2002, Federer began his campaign in Hamburg with little attention or fanfare and he himself had no great expectations. He simply hoped to survive the first round. After he won a first-round match against Nicolas Lapentti of Ecuador, Federer felt liberated. For once, he competed without pressure and played with nothing to lose. After two more straight-set wins over Bohdan Ulihrach of the Czech Republic and Adrian Voinea of Romania, Federer reached the quarterfinals, where he squared off against three-time French Open champion Gustavo Kuerten. Federer—playing what Lundgren called at the time the best clay court match he had ever played—defeated the Brazilian 6-0, 1-6, 6-2. "The way he played in the first set, that was a breeze" said Lundgren. "When he plays like that, nobody can beat him."

Max Mirnyi of Belarus, a friend of Federer's whom he often invited to practice with him in Switzerland, didn't stand a chance in the semifinals—losing 6-4, 6-4. In the final, Federer had no trouble defeating Safin, winning the best-of-five set match 6-1, 6-3, 6-4. The tournament win was his third as a professional, his first in a Tennis Masters Series event—and by far his greatest accomplishment of his career to date.

"He was too good," Safin said stoically. "I never stood a chance."

Proud of his accomplishment, Federer again could not hold back tears of joy. "That was super tennis, definitely the best game of my life," he said of his final-round destruction of Safin. Federer then treated the journalists to glasses of Champagne and said, "I absolutely must have a video of this match that I can play over and over again to boost my self-confidence."

Federer knew one of the spoils of winning in Hamburg—for the first time in his career, his name appeared in the top 10 of the world rankings. He moved from No. 14 to No. 8 and, in the year-to-date Champions Race, he moved to No. 2. Federer achieved another career milestone. "A feeling like this makes tennis much more fun," he said, joyfully anticipating the Grand Slam tournaments in Paris and London. Lundgren was even more radiant than usual. "I'm certain that he'll be in shape at the French Open," he said. "His self-confidence now is really great. He's definitely among the favorites in Paris."

Federer was considered the hottest player on the ATP Tour on the eve of both the French Open and Wimbledon. He arrived in Paris with hero-like status and viewed himself as a dangerous dark horse threat to win both titles. Prior to his first-round match with Morocco's Hicham Arazi in Paris, Federer said he was hoping not to expend too much energy. He fulfilled this goal, but not exactly in the way he planned. On a cool, drizzly Tuesday on tiny Court No. 2, Federer faced Arazi who, after a miserable clay court season, was only ranked No. 45 in the world. But Federer committed 58 unforced errors in 95 minutes of play and decisively lost 6-3, 6-2, 6-4. It was a debacle. He complained about the slipperiness of the court, the rainy, dreary weather, about being fatigued after Hamburg, and praised Arazi. In short—he was confused.

He now had plenty of time to prepare for the grass courts at Wimbledon, where he defeated Pete Sampras the year before. British bookies ranked Federer behind Hewitt, Safin, Agassi and Henman as the fifth most likely player to win the Wimbledon title. To John McEnroe, Federer was *the* favorite and boldly predicted he would win the tournament. Former Wimbledon finalist MaliVai Washington said to ESPN that "it is only a matter of time until Federer wins his first Grand Slam tournament. The real question is how many Grand Slam tournaments will he win?"

Prior to the start of The Championships, the ATP organized a telephone press conference with Federer for the international press. "I feel that my chances of winning the tournament are good," he explained on the call, while he attempted to refute the theory that he could not come to terms with being the favorite. "I feel better when I'm the favorite and I know that I can win the tournament. It helps me not to be the outsider. That's why I'm playing better this year than in previous years."

But Federer was also aware of the fact that he still didn't have a Grand Slam title, and that many were expecting him to win one—and soon. Federer, himself, felt burdened by the expectations, but more from the expectations that he placed upon himself to break through and win a Grand Slam tournament title. His impatience grew with each missed opportunity. He placed an enormous amount of pressure to break through and win either Wimbledon or the US Open in 2002.

In the first round at Wimbledon, Federer drew Croatian teenager Mario Ancic. Federer had no idea who he was and didn't find out much about him before their match. Prior to the 2002 Wimbledon Championships, the 18-year-old Ancic primarily played junior events and only advanced into the Wimbledon main draw through the qualifying tournament. He was ranked No. 154 in the world and stood at nearly six feet, six inches tall. The 2001 Wimbledon Champion Goran Ivanisevic, who like Ancic hailed from the Croatian coastal city of Split, even gave his young countryman tips on how to play Federer. Wimbledon was Ancic's Grand Slam tournament debut and his first match was played on Centre Court of all places, against Federer, the man who one year earlier defeated one of Wimbledon's greatest champions on the very same court.

Roger's father Robert, who seldom watched his son play live, traveled to Wimbledon to watch his son. Sitting in the bleachers at Centre Court, he anticipated peacefully watching a routine first-round victory for his son on this pleasant, warm and dry afternoon. He couldn't believe his eyes. Like in Paris, Roger unceremoniously lost in the tournament's opening round without winning a set. He was unrecognizable compared to the previous year's heroics and only scored one ace against the young Ancic in the 6-3, 7-6 (2), 6-3 loss.

Federer was shocked. As in Paris, he couldn't understand why he played so poorly. "I normally like to compliment young players," he said, "but the way I performed today, I can't really judge Ancic." Federer was forced to witness the top-ranked Hewitt, who was not considered to be a grass court specialist, go on to beat David Nalbandian in the final to become the first Australian Wimbledon champion since Pat Cash in 1987.

By contrast, Federer dropped out of the top 10 by virtue of his Wimbledon performance. Two weeks later at the Swiss Open in Gstaad, Federer experienced another unexpected defeat at the hands of Radek Stepanek of the Czech Republic in the second round. His crisis was incomprehensible. "He's not himself on the court anymore," said Lundgren. "Technically, there's nothing wrong with his game. It's in his head. He feels the pressure." For the moment, Federer lost his entire creativity, his entire joy in playing tennis and his self-confidence. "I allowed myself to become too dragged down mentally and I thought I couldn't play tennis anymore," he said later. But his greatest setback still lay before him and it would come from a completely unexpected direction.

CHAPTER 13
Drama in South Africa

South Africa was always a special place for Roger Federer. He held a South African passport since birth and became endeared to his mother's native country. He routinely traveled there with his family when he was little. "South Africa is a haven for him away from the world of tennis to find fresh inspiration," his mother explained once. "It has a certain openness to it. You grow up with a lot of space in South Africa, which is something different compared to the narrowness of a mountain landscape. South Africans are more open, less complicated. Roger had taken on these characteristics."

Meanwhile, Federer acquired a valuable piece of property along the picturesque Garden Route on the western coast of South Africa at the luxurious Pezula Resort. After the exhausting 2000 season, Federer vacationed in South Africa, where he went on safari with his godfather, Arthur Dubach, a work colleague of Federer's father during his work days in South Africa. They even experienced a rare site for tourists—a group of leopards killing and eating a gazelle.

In the early afternoon on August 2, 2002, the announcement came over the Swiss news agency Sportinformation—"Davis Cup Captain Carter Killed In Car Crash." According to the story, the accident occurred in South Africa where he was vacationing with his wife Silvia. There was no further information. The bad news was then updated with the report that a second man died in the accident.

What really transpired during this belated honeymoon between Peter and his wife was not immediately known. Carter was driving in a Land Rover in the vicinity of the Krueger National Park on August 1, Switzerland's national holiday. The accident occurred in the Phalaborwa area, about 450 km north of Johannesburg. The vehicle where Carter was a passenger and which friends and his wife were apparently following, was reported to have gone out of control due to a defective tire. The car then crashed into a river bed and rolled over.

The news reports were contradictory. At first, it was announced that Carter died in the evening and later that both passengers were killed instantly. According to initial reports, it was Carter who was driving at the wheel. Later, it was reported that a friend of Carter's was driving the car and later that a native South African was behind the wheel. The Limpopo police spokesperson in South Africa then issued the statement: "Carter and the driver, a South African, were killed instantly when the roof of their vehicle was crushed in."

Silvia Carter explained what really happened. "My husband was in the car with a very good friend of ours. We were driving ahead of them and they were following behind us. The vehicle did not have a defective tire. Our friend had to swerve to avoid a minibus that was heading directly at them. Such risky passing maneuvers are unfortunately a daily occurrence in South Africa. In order to avoid a frontal collision, he pulled off onto the 'accident lane.' The fateful thing was that a bridge was coming and they had to pull back onto the tarred lane. The speed as well as the difference in surfaces—the natural surface and the tarred surface—that the wheels had to deal with spun the Land Rover. It broke through the bridge railing and landed about three meters below on its roof."

Federer received the shocking news courtside at the Tennis Masters Series event in Toronto. He was never so upset in his life. Carter was a good friend and the most important coach in his career.

Although Federer lost already in the first round in Toronto, but was still playing in the doubles tournament partnering with Wayne Ferreira, ironically, a South African. The mood was grim for the third-round doubles match, which Federer and Ferreira lost to Joshua Eagle and Sandon Stolle. Federer played the match wearing a black armband in honor of Carter. His eyes were red. He nonetheless announced after the doubles loss that he was prepared to give an interview. "We spent a lot of time together, since I was a boy," Federer said of his relationship with Carter. "I saw him everyday when I was a boy. It's terrible...He died so young and unexpectedly." Federer said that the two always had a connection and they were born under the same Zodiac sign—he was born on August 8, the coach one day later. "Peter was very calm but he was also funny with a typical Australian sense of humor. I can never thank him enough for everything that he gave to me. Thanks to him I have my entire technique and coolness."

Carter watched Federer play for the first time when Roger was a kid in the 1990's and exuberantly told his parents in the Barossa Valley in Australia that he had discovered a gigantic talent who could go a long way. He worked with him for all but two years until 2000 and led him to his storied success in the world junior ranks as well as to a top 50 world ranking. After Federer chose Lundgren as his private coach, Carter remained a coach with the Swiss Tennis Federation and took up responsibilities in promoting new talent in men's tennis. He married Silvia von Arx from Basel in May of 2001.

Carter was the players' favored choice as Davis Cup team captain for a long time. However, when his wife suffered from lymph node cancer, Carter put his coaching duties on hold until Silvia's recovery was certain. Since Carter was not a Swiss citizen with a Swiss passport, he was not permitted, as Davis Cup captain, to sit with the players on the court or assume the role as the "official" Davis Cup captain. However, the International Tennis Federation, agreed to recognize him as a Swiss citizen and as the official Davis Cup captain as soon as he acquired a resident permit, which he was scheduled to receive in September of 2003. Carter led the team only once, in February of 2002 in Moscow.

Federer left Toronto for Cincinnati where, like in Paris, Wimbledon and Toronto, he lost in the first round. He couldn't concentrate. He no longer had confidence in his game and tennis was no longer fun. His thoughts were with Peter Carter. "When something like this happens," he said, "you see how really unimportant tennis is." He pulled the emergency brake. He withdrew from the doubles event in Cincinnati and pulled out of the next week's event in Washington, D.C., and flew home to Switzerland.

The funeral took place on August 14, 2002 on a warm summer's day in the Leonhard Church in Basel. About 200 people were in attendance to bid farewell, among them many familiar faces in the tennis world. Carter's friend from his youth, Darren Cahill, who was now coaching Andre Agassi, was also present. The simple ceremony, accompanied by music, was conducted by the same clergyman who married the Carters a year before. Silvia Carter gave a brief, touching speech, as did a friend who came from Australia, Davis Cup physiotherapist Caius Schmid and Christine Ungricht, the President of Swiss Tennis. "He was such a great person," she said. "Why him? Why does it always happen to the best?"

Federer's parents were also inconsolable. Carter formed a link to their son over the years. He informed them about everything concerning Roger when they were traveling together. "It was the first death Roger had to deal with and it was a deep shock for him," his mother said. "But it has also made him stronger."

Federer left the church with a sense of grief that he never before experienced in his life. "Any defeat in tennis is nothing compared to such a moment," he explained weeks afterwards. "I usually try and avoid sad events like this. It was the first time that I'd been to a funeral. I can't say that it did me good but I was close to him in thought once again and I could say goodbye in a dignified setting. I feel somewhat better now, especially in matters concerning tennis."

Although Federer lost in the first round of five of his last eight events, he no longer viewed his athletic position in such a negative light. He pointed out that he had expended little energy since his victory in Hamburg in May and was still physically fresh for the rest of the season. "You also have to see the positive things despite the defeats," he said. "I played a great deal at the beginning of the season and now I've had time to rest. All the energy that I now have will help me at the end of this year or in the coming year."

After reaching the round of 16 at the US Open for the second straight year, Federer only had one thing in mind—the up-coming Davis Cup match in Morocco. "We simply have to win there—for Peter," he said. The empty spot left by the fallen team captain was filled during Casablanca's late summer by Peter Lundgren. The task faced by the Swiss at the modern tennis facility in al-Amal proved difficult. The North Africans had two dangerous clay court specialists at their disposal—Hicham Arazi, against whom Federer lost at the French Open earlier in the year, as well as Younes El Aynaoui, who was among the top 20 players in the world. "I believe the Moroccans are the favorites because of their home advantage," Federer said.

Michel Kratochvil lost the opening match of the series to El Aynaoui, but then another Federer Davis Cup spectacle ensued. He easily defeated

Arazi—and then El Aynaoui—by identical 6-3, 6-2, 6-1 scores and also was the dominant figure in the doubles victory to lead Switzerland to the 3-2 win.

"Perfect from beginning to end," Lundgren described Federer's performance. There was huge feeling of relief in the Swiss camp after the victory. Wild cheering reverberated through the halls and doors as the victorious team retired to the locker room. Federer said the victory was important but "the fact that I played so well was only a bonus." Not surprisingly, he dedicated the success to Carter. "I thought about him today even more than I usually do."

The strong result at the US Open and his spectacular performance in Casablanca erased all of Federer's doubt and demons. His grieving for Carter slowly receded and his self-confidence returned. "The fact that I could keep Switzerland in the Davis Cup World Group through my victory gives me a lot of momentum," Federer said before the indoor season. Physically, he was still fresh due to many early-round defeats over the summer and his motivation for the final six weeks of the season was high. The goal was clinch a spot for the first time in the year-end Tennis Masters Cup in Shanghai, China as one of the eight best players for the year.

The undertaking was going to be difficult. Federer was ranked No. 10 in the year-to-date ATP Champions Race but he had to place at least in the top seven to guarantee a spot in Shanghai. In Moscow, Federer reached the quarterfinals, where for the first time, he was defeated by Safin. Eight days later in Vienna, a tournament where he always played some of his best tennis, Federer once again held a trophy over his head. In the semifinals, Federer defeated Carlos Moya 6-2, 6-3 in a match where Federer played so well that Lundgren talked of it for months. In the final, he defeated Jiri Novak of the Czech Republic and a rival for one of the final spots in the Shanghai field, by a 6-4, 6-1, 3-6, 6-4 margin. It was his first trophy since Carter's death and his thoughts were once again with his Australian friend and coach. "I dedicate this title to him," he said with glistening eyes at the award ceremony.

CHAPTER 14
Red Dawn in China

Roger Federer's title in Vienna represented a big step towards qualifying for the Tennis Masters Cup in China. Federer passed Albert Costa, Andy Roddick and Tommy Haas in Champions Race to rank No. 7 after his victory along the banks of the Danube. His ATP ranking, based on the 52-week results, also rose to a career-high No. 7—the career-high ranking that his countryman Jakob Hlasek achieved in 1989. After a quarterfinal finish at the Tennis Masters Series event in Madrid, Federer moved to No. 6 in the rankings—marking the highest ATP ranking ever achieved by a Swiss player. His trip to China was well within reach, but now he wanted to finally win "his" tournament—the Swiss Indoors in Basel. After finishing runner-up the last two years, Federer seemed poised to finally capture his hometown tournament. In the quarterfinals, Federer faced Roddick for the first time in his career and defeated the 19-year-old American 7-6 (5), 6-1 in an exciting match that lasted until midnight. In the semifinals, the brawny David Nalbandian, Federer's rival from junior days, spoiled Roger's hometown title dreams, winning a 6-7 (2), 7-5, 6-3 decision after trailing 7-6, 3-1.

The final ATP event of the year is the Tennis Masters Series in Paris, played at the Palais Omnisports de Paris-Bercy, a majestic entertainment arena located on the north bank of the Seine featuring manicured grass-covered sides on its outside walls. The event usually decides the final qualifiers for the year-end Tennis Masters Cup and 2002 was no different. Federer officially booked his ticket for Shanghai when Tim Henman lost in the third round to Nicolas Escude and Federer straight-setted Tommy Haas to reach the quarterfinals. With his goal achieved, Federer's quarterfinal with Hewitt lacked the tension of his previous matches, and he lost to the world No. 1 in straight sets.

Federer traveled to Shanghai in November of 2002 as the No. 6 ranked player in the world. At age 21, he was the youngest player in the Tennis Masters Cup field, had nothing to lose as a first-time qualifier and therefore, he was duly relaxed during the event. "Everything after this will be an encore," he said. The Tennis Masters Cup took place in one of five gigantic exhibition halls that were reminiscent of airplane hangars in the Pudong district of Shanghai, a faceless area between the airport and downtown.

For Federer, his trip to the Tennis Masters Cup in China was unique. "This is no ordinary tournament; it's an adventure," he said juggling tennis balls in front of his hotel and parading up and down along the edge of a four-lane main road in a publicity photo shoot for photographers. He was playing in the Far East for the first time and immediately felt comfortable in his new surroundings. He enjoyed the unique atmosphere of the 11,500 square meter Expo-Hall, whose 10,000 spectators turned the place into an electric atmosphere.

The Tennis Masters Cup was the biggest, the most expensive and the most widely-covered professional sports event in China at the time. For most Chinese, tennis was relatively unknown. It was an undiscovered sport that they didn't yet really understand. Whenever players double-faulted, the spectators would scream. Enthusiastic Chinese journalists would pose the strangest questions in press conferences. "Why are you always smiling, Mistel Fedelel? Because you are in such good shape?" a Chinese reporter asked Federer in broken English. Following another match, French Open Champion Albert Costa was asked by a Chinese scribe, "You always used to eat bananas when changing sides. Why not today? Perhaps because you don't like Chinese bananas?"

Federer, the Masters rookie who came to China with his mother Lynette and girlfriend Mirka, basked in the preferential treatment accorded to each of the eight participants. "I feel special here with the entire hullabaloo and the many body guards," he said. "They read your every desire from your lips. It's fortunate that there are so few players here." At Shanghai, it became even more clear that Federer possessed a certain star quality and that he wasn't blinded by the limelight. He loved the attention and flourished in it.

The Tennis Masters Cup is a round-robin event with the eight qualifying players paired in two round-robin groups of four. In his group, Federer ranked

Andre Agassi as the favorite and himself and Juan Carlos Ferrero of Spain as the leading contenders for the No. 2 position. Federer's assessment quickly proved to be wrong. Federer beat Ferrero in his opening round-robin match and then defeated Jiri Novak for a 2-0 round robin record. Federer then clinched his round-robin flight when Agassi lost to both Novak and Ferrero. No longer with a chance of making the semifinals, Agassi hastily left China in disappointment, using a hip injury as the reason for his withdrawal.

In the semifinals, Federer faced Hewitt, who already clinched the year-end No. 1 ranking for a second year in a row. The Australian barely qualified for the semifinals and benefited from Carlos Moya winning a three-hour meaningless match over fellow Spaniard Costa, where a Costa victory would have him reach the semifinals rather than Hewitt. Although Federer lost five of the last seven matches with Hewitt, he reasoned his chances of beating him and winning the first big championship of his career were very attainable.

Federer started his semifinal with Hewitt in furious fashion, taking a 3-0 and a 5-2 first-set lead, but Hewitt ran and fought as if his life were at stake. Hewitt fought off five set points and rallied for a 6-5 lead. Serving for the set, Hewitt staved off another five break points, before capturing the first set 7-5. Federer, however, was not ready to surrender. The second set turned into a wild back-and-forth struggle. Hewitt served for the match at 5-4 and held match point, but Federer broke back for 5-5. After holding serve for 6-5, Federer evened the match by breaking Hewitt's serve, connecting on his fourth set point of the game.

The Chinese fans went wild—out of their seats, screaming and cheering. In the commentary booth high above the stadium, Heinz Günthardt and Stefan Bürer, the Swiss TV commentary team, described the tension and fast-paced action to the audience back in Switzerland, where it was Saturday morning and many people postponed their weekend shopping to watch the dramatic match with their new sports hero.

As the match extended into a third hour, the breaks seemed to fall in favor of Federer. Leading 4-3 in the final set, Federer held two break points to put him in the position to serve for the match. Both opportunities, however, were lost and Hewitt held for 4-4. Hewitt then subsequently broke Federer's serve the next game to serve for the match at 5-4. The Australian reached his second match point—and shockingly double-faulted. Federer then broke Hewitt's serve to square the match at 5-5. Serving with new balls in the next game, Federer committed two consecutive double-faults to allow Hewitt to break him back and gained another opportunity to serve for the match. It took Hewitt another four match points before he finally corralled Federer and advanced to the final with an epic 7-5, 5-7, 7-5 victory. Following the match, Hall of Fame journalist Bud Collins walked into the press room and asked his fellow scribes, "Have you ever seen a better match?"

In the craziest match of his career to date, Federer was aware that he let victory escape from his grasp. "I have no one to blame but myself," he said to a small group of Swiss journalists who traveled to China. "Luck wasn't on my side. I blew a big opportunity. That hurts." A vacation in Phuket, Thailand helped heal the wounds.

CHAPTER 15
The Grand Slam Block

Roger Federer's declared goal for 2003 was, as before, to win a Grand Slam tournament. He finally wanted to rid himself of the moniker as the best player in tennis without a Grand Slam title. In his 14 career Grand Slam tournament appearances, his best results were two modest quarterfinal finishes—both achieved in 2001.

Coach Peter Lundgren still displayed an unshakable belief in Federer. He constantly repeated the mantra in his sonorous voice that Federer required more time than others to fully develop. "He has an unbelievable repertoire and he needs more time with his game for all the pieces to come together," he said, declaring that the goal to be achieved for the 2003 season was to reach the top four in the world rankings. "Roger is on the right path and shouldn't listen to what others are saying. He's like a bird that is learning how to fly. As soon as he reaches his maximum flying altitude, he'll be hard to beat. He is now beating all the players he is supposed to be beating. There isn't much of a difference between being ranked No. 1, No. 5 and No. 10."

Pleasant words and nice thoughts—but what else was Peter Lundgren supposed to say?

More disturbing than the initial, unexpected defeats to Jan-Michael Gambill in Doha and Franco Squillari in Sydney was the reappearance of the pains in his groin that just didn't want to go away. Federer was forced to rest and not practice for two days and his status for the Australian Open was in doubt. In addition, his late season surge and appearance in the Tennis Masters Cup in China late in 2002 diminished the already paltry tennis off-season. The season's first Grand Slam tournament came much too early in the tennis season, especially for those who competed in the year-end Tennis Masters Cup. "There isn't enough time to prepare," said Federer.

The Czech Pavel Kovac was a member of Federer's entourage as a physiotherapist since the past summer. He was a taciturn, burly man completely devoted to serving Federer. The wear and tear of the tennis circuit made Kovac and his services very important to Federer's future success. Kovac managed to stop Federer's pain just in time for him to post at the Australian Open. In his first three matches, Federer did not lose a set. Expectations rose, especially when two of his rivals in his half of the draw—Lleyton Hewitt and Marat Safin—were eliminated from the tournament—Hewitt losing to Younes El Aynaoui and Marat Safin withdrawing with injury prior to his third-round match with Rainer Schuettler. In the round of 16, Federer faced David Nalbandian for the third time in his professional career—and for a third time—he was defeated. Federer seemed dazed against Nalbandian and struggled with the Argentinean's backhand and strong counter-attack in the 6-4, 3-6, 6-1, 1-6, 6-3 loss. Another opportunity to win a Grand Slam tournament disappeared. Federer was completely devastated.

Away from the pressures of Grand Slam tournament play, Federer flourished and continued his winning ways. He won 16 of his next 17 matches—including two singles victories in Davis Cup against the Netherlands, where the Swiss, led by new captain Marc Rosset, defeated the Dutch 3-2. He then won his sixth and seventh career ATP titles in Marseille and Dubai. For the third consecutive year, the ATP named him the "Player of the Month" for February. While Federer experienced disappointments on the major stages of the Tennis Masters Series events in Indian Wells and Key Biscayne, he again demonstrated his strength in Davis Cup, registering all three points for Switzerland in its 3-2 upset of France in Toulouse. So excited was Federer at leading the Swiss into the Davis Cup semifinals, he uncharacteristically celebrated at a disco in the French city, dancing and partying until the wee hours of the morning.

Federer's success continued into the start of the clay court season as he won the title in Munich and also reached the final of the Italian Open, losing unexpectedly to Felix Mantilla of Spain. The result, however, still propelled him into the conversation as being a favorite to win the French Open.

"I feel much better this year than the year before when I first was in the top 10," he explained in one of the many interviews before the French Open. "It was a new situation for me back then. I've gotten used to it in the meantime."

He admitted to feeling the pressure from the public. "The entire world keeps reminding me that I am supposed to win a Grand Slam tournament and be No. 1 in the world. That's not fair because it's not that easy," he said. He then stated defiantly that "whoever wants to beat me will have to work hard for it. I don't want to lose in the first round at Roland Garros again."

On a summery Monday afternoon in Paris, Federer's first match at the 2003 French Open took place on Court Philippe Chatrier, the center court named after the Frenchman who was a past president of the International Tennis Federation. His opponent was an unknown Peruvian Luis Horna, whom Federer beat earlier in the year in Key Biscayne. Horna, ranked No. 88 in the world, had yet to win a match at a Grand Slam tournament. Federer took an early 5-3 lead in the first set, but began to show his insecurity and nerves when, during a routine rush to the net, he slipped and fell to the ground, only to mutter to himself and show negative emotions. Despite his lead, he seemed discouraged and, quite unusually, often glanced desperately at Peter Lundgren. Federer lost his service break advantage and despite holding a set point in the tie-break, he surrendered the first set by an 8-6 tie-break. The match immediately turned into a drama for Federer. He seemed frustrated, apathetic and didn't show any belief that he could win. He appeared mentally absent, missing even the easiest shots. He tallied 82 unforced errors in the 7-6 (6), 6-2, 7-6 (3) first-round loss.

The tournament was shockingly finished before it even really began. Federer, the fallen favorite, appeared in the overcrowded interview room with his head bowed low. "I don't know how long I'll need to get over this defeat," he said. "A day, a week, a year—or my entire career."

Federer became the ridicule of the tournament. France's sports newspaper L'Equipe ran a headline the next day translated as, "Shipwrecked In Quiet Waters" and published a cartoon in which a steam ship named "Roland Garros" steams away, leaving Federer behind in quiet waters. Florida's Palm Beach Post described him as the "Phil Mickelson of Tennis," comparing Federer to the American golfer who failed to win any of the major tournaments despite his great talent and many opportunities. "Federer has all the strokes but no Grand Slam trophy. He carries the dog tags of the best tennis player who has never won a major competition."

The loss undeniably confirmed Federer's reputation as a Grand Slam loser. He showed that he was a player who could not pull out a match even though he was not playing his best tennis—a characteristic that most champion tennis players exhibited, most notably in the present by Lleyton Hewitt, who could win a match on guts and determination alone. Since his victory over Sampras at Wimbledon in 2001, Federer was 0-4 in matches at the French Open and Wimbledon—the last three matches without even winning a set. His last five Grand Slam tournaments ended in defeat at the hands of much lower-ranked players

What could one say in his defense? Federer was now five years into his ATP career and approached his 22nd birthday. He won six ATP singles titles, excelled in Davis Cup play and time and again insisted he was capable of achieving greatness. He was considered one of the bigger stars in tennis and climbed to No. 5 in the world rankings. But outside of the title in Hamburg, all of the tournaments he won were smaller events and even the German Open was not a Grand Slam tournament. Federer failed routinely in the arenas where it was decided if a player was a champion or not. The once pre-cocious maverick simply could not bring his tremendous potential to bear at the Grand Slams. When looking at the successes of his idols, rivals or earlier great players, he couldn't help but feel envy. At his age, Becker, Borg, Courier, Edberg and Sampras as well as Hewitt, Safin and many others had already long since won their first Grand Slam titles. Federer, however, had not even reached the semifinals at a Grand Slam tournament. The experts were unanimous in their opinions that Federer was mature enough athletically to break through a win his first title. But athletic brilliance alone was not sufficient enough and Federer was still searching for the key to real success.

An analysis would seem to indicate that a mental block was preventing him from winning. He felt under pressure to such a degree at the Grand Slam tournaments that he couldn't concentrate on the moment, especially in the early rounds. This was a basic rule for success. The pressure came from all sides—but mostly from himself. He hadn't yet learned that these tournaments couldn't be won in the first week but they certainly could be lost. With some luck, he could have already won a Grand Slam title—in 2001, for example, after upsetting Sampras. Everything would have looked different.

After his loss to Horna, Federer seemed to be the loneliest man in tennis. He was a man alone braving the stormy tempest. How could he have known that this defeat was to be his last such one-sided Grand Slam defeat in a very, very long time? How could he have known that this painful experience was necessary in order to become the hardened, keen-sighted but yet modest champion who would have the tennis world at his feet?

Federer described what really happened when he faced Horna in Paris months later. "I was simply not prepared mentally," he said. "I put myself under too much pressure. After losing the first set, I couldn't get back into the match. I had the feeling that it was impossible, that I was no longer in control of the situation. After the first set, I said to myself, 'Even if I survive this round, I still have to play six more rounds to win this tournament.' That almost drove me insane. I put myself under such pressure that I couldn't play anymore."

After the match, he said that he was overwhelmed with questions about the how and why. "But at that moment, I didn't really feel like talking about it. I was too disappointed. I wanted to do nothing else but take eight days vacation and then start my preparations for the grass tournament in Halle. I didn't want to think about Roland Garros—I wanted to forget it. I didn't want to analyze what happened because I knew that I had simply failed mentally. I didn't accept it by any means."

CHAPTER 16
A Magic Sunday

Two weeks after his ill-fated appearance against Luis Horna at the 2003 French Open, Roger Federer was back on his saddle. The loss to Horna seemed like a surreal dream, but Federer's fortunes quickly changed for the better. He reached the final of fashion entrepreneur Gerry Weber's fancy pre-Wimbledon grass court tournament in Halle, Germany, where he faced Germany's Nicolas Kiefer. Despite losing all three previous matches with Kiefer, Federer gave him no quarter and won his fourth title of the year—and his first on grass since he won the junior title at Wimbledon in 1998. "Prospects for Wimbledon are good," he said after his win in Halle. "I know that I am going to England as the favorite and I am ready to win a big title. My chances on grass are better than on clay."

In contrast to 2002, when he resided in a luxurious house, Federer, on Peter Lundgren's advice, rented a small simple three-room apartment at 10 Lake Road in Wimbledon Village for the 2003 tournament. Federer lived in the modest apartment with Lundgren, his girlfriend Mirka Vavrinec and Pavel Kovac, his physiotherapist, who had to sleep in the living room because of the cramped conditions. Federer arrived early on the grounds of the All England Club, consciously keeping a low profile. He gave only obligatory interviews, didn't read any newspapers and didn't compete in doubles in order to concentrate only on the singles competition. "It wasn't easy keeping him away from everyone because the telephone was constantly ringing. Everybody wanted something from him," said Mirka, who meanwhile had officially taken over his management, organizing his appointments and travel schedule. Despite his dismal Grand Slam tournament record, most betting offices in Britain considered Federer one of the favorites to win the title at 5:1 odds—behind Andre Agassi and Andy Roddick.

Thanks to his good preparations and an improved attitude, Federer finally entered a Grand Slam tournament in positive and comfortable frame of mind. By contrast, defending champion Lleyton Hewitt was out of sorts and lost in the first round to the six-foot-10 inch Croatian Ivo Karlovic.

Federer fought his way into the round of 16 with the loss of only one set to American Mardy Fish in the third round. In the traditional Monday playing of the round of 16 matches at Wimbledon, Federer faced Spaniard Feliciano Lopez on the cramped and notorious Court No. 2—dubbed the "Graveyard of Champions" due to its turbulent history of many of the all-time greats losing matches to unheralded challengers. The Spanish left-hander was ranked No. 52 in the world and certainly did not enjoy the fame of Sampras, whom Federer defeated two years ago in the same round.

The Swiss player took it easy on the weekend prior to his round of 16 match. He trained for just an hour and felt rested and in top form. Then, suddenly, in the warm-up of his match with Lopez, he felt a stabbing pain in his lower back after hitting a practice serve. "I thought, my God, what's this? I couldn't move anymore. Everything had seized up," he explained later. He began his match with Lopez without his usual dynamic. After the second game of the match, he sat down in his chair, even though it was not a changeover, and called for the trainer.

Anxious minutes ticked away. While he was being treated with a heat cream by the trainer during his injury timeout, he lay on the grass turf and looked up at the sky in desperation. "I thought about giving up," he said. "But then I hoped for a miracle or that the next black cloud would bring rain again." His wish for rain did not come true, but a minor miracle did happen. Federer was able to continue play and went on to win a hard-fought, but straight-set 7-6 (5), 6-4, 6-4 victory. He had no idea how he did it and couldn't believe his luck. "Lopez had plenty of opportunities to beat me in three sets or drag out the match," he said. Federer said he began to feel better as time passed—and thanks to the pain killers as well as the increasing temperatures that loosened the muscles in his back. "It also helped that we were playing on a grass court and that Lopez was constantly looking to win the quick point," Federer said. He also admitted later that the pain was so strong that it not only adversely affected his serve and return but he could hardly sit during changeovers.

It was already certain before the quarterfinals that there would be a first-time Grand Slam tournament champion for the seventh year in a row. Following Hewitt's defeat, French Open Champion Juan Carlos Ferrero as well as No. 1 seed Andre Agassi were eliminated. Mark Philippoussis, the unseeded Australian, dealt Agassi 46 aces in his five-set upset victory in the round of 16.

On Tuesday, a day of rest in the men's tournament, Federer was still in pain. "I am going to compete for sure," he reassured Swiss journalists over the phone. But that evening, Dutch journalists hinted that Federer's opponent, Sjeng Schalken, probably couldn't compete as they reported that their countryman was at the hospital with a severe bruise and was having his foot X-rayed.

Rain gave Schalken some respite. The match was scheduled for Centre Court on Wednesday, but, due to the rain, was now scheduled for Thursday on Court No. 2. "Even with an injection, if I played on Wednesday, I would have had to throw in the towel after two games at the most," Schalken said. It rained on Thursday as well, delaying the match by another three hours, but Federer was healthy once again and a negotiated a relatively routine 6-3, 6-4, 6-4 victory over the No. 12-ranked Dutchman. Federer committed only eight unforced errors in a strong quarterfinal display played before half-empty grandstands.

To Federer's relief, he was in the semifinals of a Grand Slam for the first time and joined Marc Rosset as the second man from Switzerland to reach the final four of a major tennis tournament (Rosset lost to Michael Stich in the semifinals of the 1996 French Open.) Federer's semifinal match had the feel of a pre-determined final as fans and experts alike anointed the winner of his semifinal with Andy Roddick as the eventual winner of the Wimbledon title. Roddick was unbeaten on grass courts in his last 10 matches and was ranked No. 6 in the world. The other semifinal featured No. 14-ranked Sebastian Grosjean of France and Australia's Mark Philippoussis, ranked No. 48.

Roddick was considered the heir apparent to the American tennis throne held by Agassi and Sampras. He was the darling of the American tennis media and favored among them to defeat Federer—even though he lost all three previous matches with his Swiss rival. Federer seemed unimpressed by this— "He'll hardly be able to serve 200 aces."

The match didn't go as many had expected. Federer irritated Roddick by returning his serves, often clocked at over 135 miles per hour, as if it were standing still. Although the American trailed most of the first set, he held a set point at 6-5 in the first-set tie-break, which he squandered by hitting his trusty forehand into the net. It would be Roddick's only opportunity against Federer all afternoon.

Federer won what was by far his best match of the tournament. His serve was unshakable and only faced break point twice in his 7-6 (6), 6-3, 6-3 victory. Federer was in a Grand Slam final for the first time. As he left Centre Court, he received a standing ovation by the fans who watched his brilliant shotmaking display. "The spectators had no other choice than to give a standing ovation," London's *Daily Telegraph* wrote the following day. "The tennis played by Federer that swept Roddick, favored by many, from the court, was as inspired and flawless as it could only be on grass."

Roddick, who is more well-known for his powerful serve, only registered four aces in the match against Federer's 17. Federer ranked his performance as one of the best of his career, "I don't think I played a perfect match but it was definitely a very good match," said Federer.

Lundgren couldn't remember a time when Federer played so well. Roddick was at a loss. "I don't know if there's anybody out there more talented," said Roddick. "There's not much he doesn't have. He's a great athlete. He's so quick out there."

Federer proved that he could finally rise to the occasion in a big match in the later rounds of a Grand Slam tournament. This was his trademark as a junior player, but had yet to demonstrate the ability on the biggest stages of professional tennis.

However, the biggest match of his career still lay ahead—the Wimbledon final. His opponent was Philippoussis, who also won his semifinal in straight sets, defeating Grosjean 7-6, 6-3, 6-3 (the same score as the Federer-Roddick match). The Australian was once a top 10 player who reached the US Open final in 1998, losing to countryman Patrick Rafter. Philippoussis was known as much for his collection of expensive sports cars, fast motorcycles and his appetite for beautiful women as his tennis as his career took a turn for the worse with injuries and distractions. Following a third knee operation, Philippoussis was confined temporarily to a wheelchair but worked his way back to a No. 48 world ranking.

One of the few who believed in Philippoussis before the final was Pat Cash, the Wimbledon champion in 1987. "He can return better than Roddick and if he continues to serve as he has been, he'll win," Cash said. But the fellow Australian was mistaken. It would not be the only false prediction Cash would have regarding Federer's career.

Federer appeared loose and optimistic when he walked into the Wimbledon interview room on Saturday, the day before the final, wearing jeans and a T-shirt after his practice. "It will be a completely different match compared to the one with Roddick," he said. "Philippoussis charges the net after the serve and his serves are shallower. I'll have to stand closer to the baseline and return differently. I can't just block the serve like I did with Roddick. I'll have to try to return the balls at his feet so that he'll have difficult returns to play."

Federer's preparations and tactic proved to be ideal. The physically superior Philippoussis, nicknamed "Scud," began the final in fine form and scored 18 points directly off his serve in the first set, of which seven were aces. He attempted to intimidate Federer with stinging returns, but Federer was not impressed and didn't show the slightest vulnerability. In the first set tie-break, Philippoussis hit an ill-timed double fault to give Federer two set-points at 6-4. Two points later, a Federer ace gave him the first set.

From this point forward, the man from Basel dominated almost at leisure and played at an even a higher level than he did against Roddick in the semifinals. He did not face a break point in the entire match and, like the Roddick match, out-aced his stronger serving opponent (21 aces against 14 for Philippoussis). All the while, Federer kept a clear head, even though the match became more complicated. In the third set, with a two-sets-to-love lead, he reached 15-40 on Philippoussis serve at 5-5—points that had the character of match points. Federer was unable to handle a Philippoussis serve on the first break point, and on the second break point, he missed a forehand beyond the baseline by the narrowest of margins that would have given him the crucial service break. It was like a soccer player who missed a penalty shot in the final minute of play without a goalie in the net.

Federer recovered immediately from the lost opportunity, forcing a tie-break which he attacked with abandon quickly winning six of the first seven points. Federer stared at five match points to win the Wimbledon title. "You can see on TV that I was shaking my head," he explained later. "It's crazy, I thought. I'm so close. I had always dreamed about this. It went quickly after this, 6-2, 6-3. I served and knew that if I don't do it now, I'll be eternally sad." But he did it. On his third match point, Philippoussis returned his serve into the net. "Game, set and match Federer," said Chair Umpire Gerry Armstrong. "Seven-six, six-two, seven-six."

Federer, on his way to the net, sank to his knees, raised his arms, looked skywards and then to Peter Lundgren, Mirka Vavrinec and Pavel Kovac. They jumped up from the grandstands and fell into each others' arms. Federer shook hands with his opponent and the chair umpire, waved to the public, held his left hand in front of his face and stepped back to his chair where he began crying. He cried profusely when Alan Mills, the referee, congratulated him and held him by both shoulders. He looked skywards once again, stood up and waved once again to an audience who gave him a standing ovation. He sat back on his chair. The tears continued to flow.

Hardly a minute elapsed since the last point of the match, but, to Federer, seconds turned into minutes. "I was relieved, exhausted, overwhelmed with emotions," he said. "I thought I was on my knees longer than I really was." As the award ceremony was prepared, a dignified, almost pious calm settled over Centre Court. According to exact protocol, the Duke of Kent presented Federer with the 47 cm high "Challenge Cup," the gold-plated silver trophy with two handles and the miniature pineapple on the top that had been used since 1887—certainly the most beautiful and important trophy in tennis. He raised the trophy high but didn't yet have the heart to kiss it. It was still too early. The original trophy would remain in Wimbledon. Federer would be allowed to take home a 22 cm high replica.

In the official on-court champion's interview with Sue Barker of Britain's BBC television, Federer still was unable to control his emotions and his voice. He lost control of himself when the former British top player asked him if he knew that many of his friends came from Basel to watch the final. His voice broke—"Thanks to everybody...It's great..." The tears flowed once again.

Federer suddenly belonged to an exclusive circle in his sport. Having also won the junior title at Wimbledon five years earlier, Federer became the 4th player to win both junior and gentleman's singles titles at the All England Club, joining Björn Borg, Stefan Edberg and Pat Cash. When he left Centre Court following the photo sessions and victory laps, he walked into the entranceway of the club and found that his name had already been engraved on the 2003 silver championship plate located on the wall to the right.

CHAPTER 17
A Cow for the Victor

Roger Federer's sessions with the media following his victory in the 2003 Wimbledon final lasted more than two hours—longer, in fact, than the actual match. He rushed from one interview to the next and answered the same questions over and over—'How did you feel immediately after match point? How did you feel after you received the trophy? "I only knew that if I won, I would fall onto the grass and that I would enjoy it," he said. "I also thought, hopefully, I won't cry."

He always believed he was able to win a Grand Slam tournament. "The many successes I had at the smaller tournaments helped my self-confidence and made me more convinced that I could do it," he said. During the match, he said, he thought about the *Alinghi*, the Swiss racing yacht that unexpectedly won the America's Cup. "I remembered how the Swiss were ahead 3-0 and they just sailed away. 1 thought to myself after the second set, 'Just sail away now.'"

Five years earlier as Wimbledon junior champion, Federer missed the traditional Wimbledon Champions Dinner due to his urgent trip to Gstaad to play his first ATP tournament. This year, Gstaad would wait. He showed up at the Champions Dinner in the Savoy Hotel in evening formal wear along with Serena Williams, the women's singles champion, as well as Martina Navratilova and Leander Paes, the mixed doubles champions. Federer attended the event with his girlfriend Mirka Vavrinec, coach Peter Lundgren and mother Lynette and once again charmed the dignified members of the All England Club with his brief speech. "I am proud to have joined your club now," he said. "It would give me pleasure to hit a few balls around at leisure. Whoever would like to play me should simply give me a call."

After only three hours of sleep, Federer's media interview sessions continued the next morning. The pebble covered driveway in front of his apartment in Wimbledon Village was quickly transformed into a makeshift media center. Various television stations showed up—BBC, Sky TV, CNN, ITV, Swiss Television—as well as journalists from all around the world.

While almost every minute of his time was accounted for, Federer found time to give a special interview with *Tages-Anzeiger* that had been arranged for days through Mirka in the event that Roger won Wimbledon. When being interviewed while sitting in the little lawn in front of the house, Federer seemed jovial but not euphoric. He seemed able to comprehend the significance of his triumph. "The time has come because I have proven it to everybody. If my career were to end today, that would almost be O.K," he said. He knew that before winning Wimbledon, he was just a super tennis player, but now he was a star. "Winners and losers have so much but so little in common. Real champions are those who raise the trophy at the end. The winners stay. The losers go."

That's why the burden that fell away from him at the moment of victory was so immense, he said. "After the awards ceremony, I went into the locker room and couldn't move anymore. I was completely exhausted. My muscles were so tense from the pressure that I was thinking during the match that if I were to win, I would get a cramp. That's hard to imagine."

He now hoped that July 6, 2003 would mark a turning point in his career. "I know how to win major titles now and that I can do it again," he said. Federer admitted that he chose not to dedicate the victory to Peter Carter alone, since he wasn't sure if he would win any other Grand Slam titles. "That would have been unfair to the others," he said. "The title should be for everybody, but especially for me. Peter Carter naturally is included in this circle. If he were still here, we would have thrown a big party. I hope he was watching me from somewhere."

Lundgren was delirious with joy and couldn't stop laughing. "My emotions were unreal," he said. "I can hardly describe them even if I saw this victory coming because he is such a good player." He pointed out that he was the first Swede since Björn Borg's coach Lennart Bergelin to lead a player to victory at Wimbledon. Mirka explained that she always sensed how much Roger wanted to win this title. "It was a childhood dream for him," she said. "He didn't seem nervous before the final. I think that he slept the night before the final better than he ever had."

Much of the focus of most of British newspapers the morning after the final focused not on the result and the accomplishment of Federer, but on his tears and emotions. This, however, was not surprising as for two weeks, Federer paraded over the grass with a poker face, in stoic tranquility, seemingly undaunted by anything—not even by the searing back pain during his match against Feliciano Lopez. Some photographers already complained that Federer was not showing any emotion—that pictures of him all looked the same, like one tennis ball looked exactly like the other. But now, in the moment of triumph, he let the stoic mask fall off his face and expose a side that many didn't know or even suspected him to possess.

The *Daily Mirror* ran the headline "Roger the Blubberer," and even more respected newspapers, such as the *Independent* and the *Daily Telegraph*, showed enlarged pictures on their front pages of the Wimbledon champion crying while holding the trophy. It bothered Roger a little to see his tears so prominently displayed. But he wasn't ashamed. He usually didn't care what the media wrote about him but at this moment, he cared even less.

Federer-fever had long ago broken out in Switzerland. A sizable group of fans and supporters assembled in his old club, the Old Boys Tennis Club, to watch the final, including Seppli Kacovsky, Federer's first coach. The Swiss newspaper *Blick* wrote about the "tears for the ages" shed by "King Roger I." The television audience in Switzerland was quite impressive as 613,000 Swiss viewers tuned in to watch the event live—a number corresponding to 61.6 percent of the viewer market. Federer's fans celebrated his victory throughout Switzerland.

Honoring his commitment to compete in the Swiss Open in Gstaad the week after Wimbledon was very important to him. It was in Gstaad five years ago that he competed in his first ATP tournament thanks to a wildcard. Federer's loyalty to the event persisted. When it became clear that the new Wimbledon champion was actually going to compete in the small clay court tournament in Gstaad, the event received media credential applications from an additional 40 news outlets.

At 6:11 pm local time in Gstaad on Monday, July 7, Federer's private jet arrived in the small Swiss mountain town. He was met at the airport with Champagne and was allowed to choose between two suites in the Hotel Bellevue: The Suite Etoile or the Tower Room. He chose the one with a view of the stars.

The next surprise waiting for him on Tuesday weighed a mere 800 kg. Five hours prior to his first singles match on Tuesday, he was welcomed at Gstaad's Centre Court by 6,000 fans at the "Official Greeting for the Wimbledon Champion"—where he was presented with his next gift, a dairy cow named Juliette. The cow was a present from the tournament organizers led by Jacques Hermenjat, who assured Federer that he could leave the animal on the mountain and enjoy its cheese any time he wanted. Juliette, who would later give birth to a calf, now belonged to Federer. Juliette became a major topic of conversation between Federer and the media for much of the rest of the year. He would even pay her a visit the following winter, as protocol demanded.

Federer continued to ride the wave of his success in the mountains of Switzerland and it carried him farther than ever before at the Swiss Open. He reached the final of the event for the first time, where he ran out of gas in a five-set struggle with No. 10-ranked Jiri Novak. It would be his last defeat in a tournament final for a very long time.

Federer's time spent in the Bernese Alps helped him come to grips with the significance of his Grand Slam victory. He had no choice but to face the general public in the small luxury resort where everything was within walking-distance. Federer realized he was now a superstar—and it didn't bother him in the least. It was his wish, after all, to go all the way to the top and now he was prepared to deal with the consequences. "A Wimbledon victory changes your entire career, your entire life, your inner world," he admitted. "People look at you much differently. I would always want to win my first Grand Slam title at Wimbledon. That's where it all began. The all-white clothing, the grass—it's simply a classic."

It was not until he was on vacation when he could reflect on the Wimbledon title in peace and quiet. He then fully realized how his life had changed. "I was lying on the beach in Sardinia with the sun beating down on my stomach and I said to myself, 'So now you're a Wimbledon champion. Nobody can ever take that away from you," he said later. "At the time, I was in a funk on the court, in a kind of trance that I could hardly remember anything about afterwards. I was in the famous 'zone'. Suddenly everything was running on automatic. I had the feeling that I couldn't do anything wrong. It was a wonderful thing that I could play at such a high level in two of the most important matches of my career. That will give me confidence and inspiration for the months and years to come."

CHAPTER 18
Reaching for the Stars

With a Grand Slam title finally on his resume, Roger Federer focused on his next major career goal—securing the No. 1 world ranking. When he left London after his Wimbledon triumph, Federer was ranked No. 3 in the world behind 33-year-old Andre Agassi and French Open Champion Juan Carlos Ferrero. Federer said that until this time, it was premature to focus on or discuss the No. 1 ranking. "It was just too early," he said. "I knew that I first needed a good Grand Slam result. I've achieved that. Now I know that I have a chance to become No. 1 in the coming years."

Federer's initial opportunities to ascend to the No. 1 ranking materialized much earlier than expected. The day after his 22nd birthday, he was just one victory away from the top ranking in Montreal when he faced Andy Roddick in the semifinals of the Canadian Open. Federer was undefeated in four previous duels with the young American and his straight-set win in the semifinals of Wimbledon were fresh memories for both players. Despite a 4-2 lead in the final set, Federer seemed tense and uneasy. Ten double-faults eventually did him in and his chance for No. 1 disappeared in a 6-4, 3-6, 7-6 (3) loss to Roddick. "I was so nervous that I was shaking all over," he admitted later.

A week later in Cincinnati, Federer could clinch the No. 1 ranking by reaching the semifinals, but was defeated in the second round by David Nalbandian.

The US Open, the final Grand Slam tournament of the year, presented another opportunity for him to seize the top spot. As the tournament began, Federer seemed in the best position to capture the No. 1 ranking as he was the player with the least amount of points to defend from the previous year among the contenders for the No. 1 ranking. He survived the first three rounds without being seriously challenged, but in the round of 16, once again, his opponent was none other than Nalbandian.

Media and tennis insiders tagged the Argentinean as the arch-nemisis of Federer. The two players played four times as professionals, with Nalbandian winning all four times. Federer, however, rejected the idea that Nalbandian was the player he feared the most.

"That bothers me because I've never said that and I don't see it that way either," he told reporters almost defiantly in New York. "I've never lost to him decisively and I've even beaten him in the juniors."

The second week of the US Open became an ordeal as rain created a scheduling chaos. The round of 16 matches that were scheduled for the second Tuesday of the event did not start until 3 pm on Thursday. After four hours of play and two more interruptions due to rain, Federer had—for the fifth time in five professional matches—succumbed to Nalbandian 3-6, 7-6 (1), 6-4, 6-3. The Argentinean was still a mystery to him.

"I find it difficult understanding why I take the lead or fall behind," Federer said after the loss. "I knew that I had to play aggressively. But I just don't know how much I should risk when serving against him. He gets to many balls quickly and is great at reading my game. I don't know what to make of him." Federer could only watch from a distance as Nalbandian reached the semifinals, where he lost a heart-breaking five-setter to Roddick after leading two-sets-to-love and holding a match point. Roddick went on to win the championship, defeating Juan Carlos Ferrero, who assumed the No. 1 ranking by virtue of his runner-up showing. The American wept after his first Grand Slam title just as Federer had two months earlier at Wimbledon. Roddick won the tournaments in Montreal and Cincinnati earlier in the summer and moved to No. 2 in the world rankings.

Melbourne and the Davis Cup semifinal against Australia was next on Federer's agenda. At the suggestion of both Federer and Lleyton Hewitt, both the Swiss and Australian teams dedicated the match as a memorial for Peter Carter. A silver bowl was ordered and presented to Carter's parents during the matches.

After Hewitt opened the series with an easy win over Michel Kratochvil, Federer defeated Philippoussis 6-3, 6-4, 7-6 (3) in a rematch of the Wimbledon final. In the pivotal doubles rubber, Federer and the aging Marc Rosset were defeated in five-sets by Wayne Arthurs and Todd Woodbridge, giving Australia the important 2-1 advantage after the second day of play. Switzerland had to sweep the final two singles matches in order to reach the Davis Cup final.

Federer and Hewitt took to the Rod Laver Arena on a cool Sunday to open up the final day of play and Federer leisurely dominated Hewitt and stared at his 11th consecutive Davis Cup singles victory leading 7-5, 6-2, 5-3. With Federer two points from victory, the tide turned. A brief lull in Federer's performance was enough for Hewitt, carried by 12,000 spectators, to fight his way back into the match.

After winning the third set in a tie-break and the fourth set 7-5, the match was tied at two-sets apiece. The temperatures were so cold at the start of the fifth set that many of the Swiss journalists could barely take notes on the match their fingers were so stiff and frigid. Christine Ungricht, the President of Swiss Tennis, complained to the Swiss media that she felt the Australians had intentionally left the retractable roof of the Laver Arena open to give Hewitt an advantage in the colder conditions. "They want to give Federer hypothermia," she said. "What they're doing is not against the rules but I'm going to complain anyways."

Hewitt's momentum was too difficult for Federer to overcome and the Aussie won the epic match 5-7, 2-6, 7-6 (4), 7-5, 6-1, allowing Australia to reach the Davis Cup final. Hewitt's chest swelled with pride as he explained that he thought constantly of Pat Cash's comeback from a two-sets-to-love deficit against Mikael Pernfors of Sweden during the 1986 Davis Cup Final. Federer, who didn't show up in the interview room until two hours after the defeat, meekly said: "I couldn't be more frustrated." The flight back to Europe was torture for him. Every time he awoke, his body and his soul ached.

Federer no longer held great hopes of becoming No. 1 in the world for 2003. "Roddick and Ferrero deserved to be ranked in front of me," he said before the start of the indoor season. "Ferrero is the best clay court player and Roddick is the best hard-court player. This fall, I simply want to prove that I'm the best indoor player." He had no such luck. Although he defeated Carlos Moya in the final of Vienna to successfully defend a title for the first time in his career, the remainder of the fall season did not produce the results he desired.

After he lost Ferrero in the semifinals of Madrid, Federer once again failed to fulfill his boyhood dream of winning the title in his hometown of Basel. In the biggest tournament in his country, Federer was only a shadow of himself due to back problems and lost in the second round to Ivan Ljubicic. The next tournament in Paris likewise did not contribute to Federer being crowned the king of indoor tennis, losing for the fifth time and six meetings to Tim Henman of Britain in the quarterfinals. Henman, together with Hewitt and Nalbandian, became part of the small circle of his Federer's nemeses.

CHAPTER 19
Duels in Texas

In 2003, Roger Federer won six tournaments on all different surfaces—indoors in Marseille and Vienna, hard courts in Dubai, clay in Munich and grass in Halle and at Wimbledon. However, a gap in his resume was the absence of a tournament title in North America. Of the 21 tournaments he played on the North American continent since he turned professional, 10 ended in the first round. On only one occasion—in Key Biscayne in 2002—did he manage to make his way into a singles final. He wasn't even able to muscle his way as far as the quarterfinals at the US Open or at the big events in Cincinnati or Indian Wells.

Entering the 2003 year-end Tennis Masters Cup, which moved from Shanghai to Houston, Texas, Federer was perceived as just one of the players in the field—void of the usual fanfare of a Wimbledon champion. Said Bud Collins, the famed *Boston Globe* tennis columnist, "If you want to be famous in the United States, you have to win here."

Federer was well aware of his poor record in North America, but blamed his lack of major success on the fact that he only played the major North American events. These events featured all of the top players and, thus, were more difficult to win, especially with a minimal amount of training time on the American hard courts. "The players who live in the USA have an advantage because they can prepare better," he said. "But then again we Europeans hold the advantage in Europe." For Federer, the training conditions in the United States were less than ideal for him—the amount of practice and proper preparation time was reduced due to travel and the weather conditions were more extreme than in Europe. For a fine technician like Federer, these details made a difference between marked success and failure—especially considering that under ideal conditions, Federer reached the finals in seven of his last

12 tournaments he played in his home base of Europe. Overall, 15 of his 18 finals to date were played in Europe.

Federer also still considered himself to be an indoor specialist—half of his tournament final appearances were at indoor events. In North America, however, indoor tournaments are scarce, pay less and do not have the prestige of those in Europe. In fact, he was yet to play an indoor event in the United States, which made it even more disappointing for him that the Tennis Masters Cup, traditionally an indoor event, was played outdoors in Houston.

In contrast to his first visit to the Tennis Masters Cup in Shanghai the year before, where everything was organized down to the last detail, Federer was disappointed by the conditions at Houston's Westside Tennis Club, located in the middle of a residential area with 46 courts, featuring all four Grand Slam court surfaces. For starters, the surface of the court slanted downwards from the line judge's chair and was so uneven that balls took unpredictable bounces. The new—and apparently hastily built—stadium court could only seat some 7,000 people—a capacity that was small for a tournament of this stature. Since the event in Houston featured—for the first time in almost 20 years—the year-end singles and doubles championships at the same site, Federer and his fellow competitors found there was not enough space in the dressing rooms or on the practice courts to properly prepare and practice. At one point during his stay in Houston, Federer was forced to practice with Lundgren on a court that didn't even have a net!

Federer's luck of the draw did nothing to improve his mood. He was placed in the "Blue Group" of the round-robin event, where he was joined by Juan Carlos Ferrero, Andre Agassi, and...David Nalbandian. It would be a difficult challenge for Federer, who lost three of the last five matches against Ferrero, was winless against Agassi in three previous matches and was 0-5 in career matches with Nalbandian.

In the pre-event media round-table interviews, Federer was not reserved in expressing his criticism of the tournament. He confidently and objectively stated that he did not believe it was right that the event be played outdoors. He was also not shy in discussing the less than perfect conditions—stating his opinion that the stadium was too small and the court surface—with its slant—was not up to the standard of a Tennis Masters

Cup. His criticisms were consistent—whether he was asked in English, French or German.

His comments had repercussions. Shortly after the sessions with the media, Federer was abruptly approached and spoken to by a gray-haired man, who had not even properly introduced himself before confronting the Wimbledon champion. The man was Jim McIngvale, followed closely by his wife Linda, the owners of the Westside Tennis Club. McIngvale, who was known in his colorful television commercials as "Mattress Mack," was an excitable figure who was responsible for the event and made it possible. He was a self-made millionaire whose furniture business—"Gallery Furniture"—was the most successful of its kind in the United States. He was the live embodiment of the big-mouthed Texan—the familiar stereotype from a wide variety of jokes.

McIngvale was a self-professed patriot who preferred to wear shirts displaying the American flag and an unabashed fan of both Andy Roddick and especially of Andre Agassi. Both Roddick and Agassi were winners the U.S. Men's Clay Court Championships—another ATP event organized and run by the McIngvales at the Westside Tennis Club each year. Agassi praised McIngvale as a "phenomenal promoter" and "one of the greatest things to happen to tennis." The McIngvales professed that they invested more than $25 million in organizing the Tennis Masters Cup. They even went as far to advertise the tournament during the Super Bowl, shelling out around $1 million each for three television advertisements.

Federer's criticism of the facility and the tournament reached the ear of McIngvale, who took it as a personal insult. McIngvale confronted and scolded Federer in a manner that the Wimbledon champion was not accustomed to. Federer was confused, hurt, disappointed and angry. For a moment, he even considered withdrawing from the tournament and leaving. Fortunately, he reconsidered.

The *Houston Chronicle* speculated that Federer was not aware of who McIngvale was—and the newspaper explained to Federer that he was "the best thing for tennis since the introduction of the tie-break." The newspaper also stated that McIngvale recruited crazy fans to pump up the atmosphere at the event and unleashed the fans to cheer against Federer in his opening match with Agassi.

Not surprisingly, Federer seemed a bit uncomfortable against Agassi, who won the Australian Open at the start of the year. In the first-set tie-break, Federer quickly lost the first six points, only to lose 7-3. Rather than folding in the difficult conditions, Federer rallied and won the second set—only the second set he ever won from the American legend. When Federer took a 5-3 lead in the final set, a great triumph appeared imminent. But, like his Davis Cup experience against Hewitt two months earlier, Federer's nerves got the best of him when a major victory was in sight. A double fault allowed Agassi back in the match, tying the score at 5-5 in the third set. Many of McIngvale's fans jumped and screamed in approval. McIngvale himself was not shy in rooting openly for Agassi. Federer's disappointment was unmistakable. In the final-set tie-break, another double fault placed him in a 1-3 deficit. The end seemed near.

But the minutes that followed turned out to be the most important moments for Federer in the tournament—and possibly in his career. Perhaps benefiting from the fact that Agassi had not played a tournament since the US Open concluded two months earlier due to the birth of his second child, Federer was given a reprieve. Agassi missed what he called "a sitter forehand that I haven't missed since 1989" followed by a double fault to allow Federer back in the match. Agassi, however, reached match point at 6-5, only to miss a return of serve. Two points later, Agassi again reached match point at 7-6, with Federer saving himself with a brilliant forehand. A point later, Federer himself had a match point at 8-7. Agassi's return of serve landed dangerously close to the line—some observers even saying the ball was out. But without an out call from linesman, Federer played on—without distress—and hit a spectacular cross court forehand passing shot to punctuate his first-ever victory over the American legend. Game, set and match Federer 6-7 (3), 6-3, 7-6 (7)

Wearing a baseball hat, Federer walked into the post-match press conference around midnight and tried to play cool. The victory was very important to him—his best ever in the United States—and Federer, nonetheless, had difficulties hiding his emotions and expressing them in words. The victory had a liberating effect on Federer, as displayed two days later, when for the first time, he ended his hex against Nalbandian, defeating the Argentine for the first time in his professional career 6-3, 6-0. With Nalbandian's earlier win over Ferrero and Agassi's defeat of Ferrero, Federer clinched a spot in the semifinals as the winner of his difficult round-robin flight. Federer's bad mood was now a distant memory.

The quest for the year-end No. 1 ranking was also decided in round-robin play in the favor of Roddick, who held the No. 1 ranking since November 3. However, in a foreshadowing of things to come, Federer dismissed Roddick 7-6 (2), 6-2 in the semifinals to reach the Tennis Masters Cup final. Waiting in the final was Agassi, who finished second to Federer in their round-robin flight but defeated German Rainer Schuettler in the other semifinal. This time, Federer showed him no quarter from the beginning. Even after a two-and-a-half-hour rain delay, Federer dominated Agassi, winning the championship match 6-3, 6-0, 6-4 in just 88 minutes. "That was one of the best performances of my career," said Federer who didn't face a break point against both Roddick and Agassi. "I don't know if I have potential to improve, but I'm satisfied if I can maintain this level." His reward was lavish. He received $1.52 million in prize money—as well as a Mercedes convertible and 750 points that allowed him to squeeze past Ferrero into the No. 2 ranking behind Roddick. "Ending the year in second place isn't bad either," Federer said before leaving Texas. While the ATP computer ranked him No. 2, he ranked first for the year in number of tournament victories (7), match victories (78) and prize money earned ($4,000,680). Bud Collins of the *Boston Globe* agreed. "Forget the world rankings." Collins wrote. "Roger Federer is now the best in the business."

Only Mr. McIngvale appeared to have a distorted view of events from the highest row in the grandstands, where he sat during the championship match. Anybody listening to his endless address at the award ceremony would have assumed that it was Agassi who was the Tennis Masters Cup champion and not Federer. In his post-match ceremony remarks, McIngvale openly praised the exploits, talents and achievements of Agassi, reserving only one short sentence of praise for that of Federer, the man who had, in fact, won the event.

CHAPTER 20
An Abrupt End

There was no indication in Houston of any expected changes in Roger Federer's camp. Peter Lundgren was the man at Roger's side and everything was status quo. During an interview at the Westside Tennis Club, Lundgren discussed how the new strategy for the 2004 season was shaping up and what the training regime would be for December. "Roger can improve quite a bit. He still has a lot to do," he said. "We have to keep working on volleys and returns, the serve could be better and he could be stronger and faster."

In the meantime, many Swiss nationals grew very fond of Lundgren. He was the surrogate father who took on the "Crown Jewels of Swiss Tennis"—and took Federer under his wing like his own son. Who couldn't help liking the constantly smiling, friendly and vivacious Swede? He combined professionalism, looseness, seriousness and humor in a unique way. In contrast to many of his colleagues, Lundgren stood in the background of his charge, wisking away publicity and attention, preferring the spotlight to be upon his pupil. In addition, his tennis game was excellent at the age of 38—with a feel for the ball that one wouldn't quite expect due to his hefty appearance.

Despite the many bitter setbacks that Federer encountered during his long road to the top of the professional tennis world, Lundgren never lost his faith or belief in Federer, not even in the bleakest months when his breakthrough was late in arriving. Lundgren seemed also profitic in his predictions of Federer's success in 2003. By now, he seemed to become a part of Federer.

All of this made it all the more stunning when their separation was announced in December. The news was leaked in an unexpected way. Federer and Lundgren arranged a media conference for December 15 to mutually announce the end of their player-coach relationship but a resourceful journalist already broke the news of the split six days prior in the *Neue Zürcher Zeitung*. Federer and his management were forced to alter their plans and improvise.

A press release was hastily released, announcing the dissolution of their working relationship. "With the success and the skills that Roger has worked on with Peter Lundgren, he is very well-equipped for the challenges yet to come. But this also meant the desire for reorientation in his athletic training environment. Further information concerning a successor are still in progress. No decisions have yet been made."

That same evening, a press conference was orchestrated in Basel in the office of Federer's attorney, Bernhard Christen. The Wimbledon champion was in the midst of ramping up for the new season. He appeared with his mother, who was now a central figure on his team following his mid-year separation from the International Management Group (IMG). His face was grim and distant. The communication snafu did not sit well with someone who likes to have everything perfectly under control.

Federer found it difficult to express in words the reasons for the separation. He spoke about being burned out, about the long process of making the decision that started at the beginning of the 2003 season. "Our working relationship became too much of an everyday grind, especially in the last months," he said. "I have the feeling that I need something new, a new impulse, somebody who will take my tennis farther." He explained that he already told Lundgren a few weeks ago that he didn't feel as those things were working out. "He told me that if I had the feeling that I needed something else that he wouldn't stand in my way," said Federer. He said he had wrestled his way to making the difficult decision while on vacation in Mauritius. "Peter was just as disappointed as I was. We're quitting at the absolute peak of things and that makes it all the more difficult. I'm sure we'll remain friends."

The decision, which on the surface had no plausible explanation, caused many people to speculate on what really happened, if there was something else to the decision that was not discussed publicly. Some even criticized Federer for making such a rash decision when he was at his career apex. Did the two have a falling out? Was it a matter of money? Was the Swede becoming too expensive for Federer, who was now earning more prize money than any other player? Were other people involved? Had a successor already been named? Had Federer been poorly counseled and was he carelessly jeopardizing everything that he had worked for? The *Neue Zürcher Zeitung* immediately speculated that Mirka Vavrinec, "the first lady at the Federer Court," played a significant part in the process of relieving Lundgren. This theory was universally denied and didn't serve to lift the spirits of Federer and his girlfriend during these dank days of Christmas.

Viewed superficially, there was actually no reason for Federer to part ways with Lundgren after what was by far his best year. The working relationship with the Swede should have become much easier now that the pressure of finally winning a Grand Slam title was behind them. The Wimbledon and Tennis Masters Cup champion stood at the threshold of an exciting phase of his career where it seemed likely he would soon become the No. 1 player in the world and that he would win even more Grand Slam titles.

Once again, Federer acted instinctively—and how can one explain instinctive actions? He felt he was at the end of a journey with Lundgren, that the Swede had completed his mission. He was the ideal man who took him through the top 50 to the world's best and to a Wimbledon victory. Lundgren, himself denied great tournament victories as a player, could not have expected more. Federer felt that the Swede could not impart any more wisdom than he already gave. Lundgren gave him everything he had to give. Federer now expanded into regions that were also new to the coach and where he did not have experience.

Federer probably also sensed that something important was happening to him at this stage in his career. Tournament victories not only satisfied his appetite, but also stimulated it as well. He sought to achieve further greatness and perfection. Federer realized that he was a new player, with new goals, who needed other impulses in order to achieve an even higher level of success. It was immediately clear to him that this was his direction. If necessary, he was prepared to take the first steps by himself.

Lundgren followed the 2004 Australian Open from his home in the Swedish coastal village of Hunnebostrand. "I've traveled around for 22 years and am fed up with the constant travel and the hectic life of living out of suitcases," he explained over the phone. "I felt I needed a break. Houston was great but some of the tournaments at the end of the year were brutal. My kids cried whenever I went away. It was tough for my girlfriend, who was working. I think it was a good time for me to take a bit of a break." Lundgren's son, Lukas, was five by then and his daughter, Julia, was eight. She was suffering from diabetes and the entire daily routine revolved around her.

"I warned Roger that he was going to have some trouble explaining the reasons for our split to the media," said Lundgren. "But he knows what he wants. He was searching for new ideas and I said to him, 'We shouldn't go on if you feel that way.' I have my pride, too. I was a pro myself and understood him. I was not shocked. But when one has such a relationship, it's strange to quit so abruptly just like that."

Their friendship in fact remained untainted by the separation, even after Lundgren took on coaching one of Federer's biggest rivals, Marat Safin, a few months later. Federer and Lundgren met just before Christmas in Switzerland. Said Lundgren, "We had one of the best conversations in a long time."

CHAPTER 21
The Glittering Crowning

At the end of 2003, Roger Federer moved out of the house that he shared with his parents for two years in Bottmingen near Basel and moved into the neighboring town of Oberwil with girlfriend Mirka Vavrinec, their first apartment together. Meanwhile, he was honored in the Swiss capital of Bern as the nation's "Athlete of the Year" on December 13. The next day, after only three hours of sleep, he flew to London for a return visit to the All England Club to be the guest of honor as the Wimbledon champion in a British sports television program organized by the BBC.

Tim Phillips, the Wimbledon Chairman, received Federer, now an honorary member of the club, like an old friend. He accompanied Federer, his guests from Switzerland as well as two print reporters and the BBC television crew, for tea in the club room in the Centre Court building, where the Wimbledon trophies are displayed. Federer stared in wonder as he looked at the picture of him as Wimbledon champion located at the left above the entrance to Centre Court. The photo hung next to the famous quote by the famed British Nobel Prize laureate Rudyard Kipling: "If you can meet with triumph and disaster and treat those two imposters just the same."

Federer already met with disaster and now it was apparent that he could deal with triumph as well. The manner in which he composed himself on this day in London was impressive—also considering the hectic nature of his schedule and with such little sleep. He was modest but self-confident, friendly but determined. Boris Becker once called Centre Court at Wimbledon "my living room," and afterwards it became part of the Pete Sampras household in the 1990s. It now seemed that Federer was willing and able to transform it into his own personal parlor.

His return to his place of triumph visibly filled him with pride. He explained in minutiae what happened before and after his final-round match with Philippoussis just six months earlier. He took the three members of the media through the club house and around the tournament facilities and the empty courts upon which a wane December sun shined. "This entrance was full of elderly people but they immediately made way when I came," he said like a tour guide. "This is where I played together with Hewitt in doubles," or "this is where they took the victory photo but for some reason it looks completely different now." He gazed at Court No. 2 for a long time where he lay on the ground with excruciating back pain and thought he would have to quit.

Federer also visited the museum where the racquets, clothing and shoes that he used to win the tournament were on display. Not to be missed during this return journey to the All England Club was, of course, a visit to Centre Court. The court was surrounded by an electric fence to protect the grass against foxes and other animals. "Please don't stand on the grass," said the stern voice over the Centre Court loudspeaker. Federer burst out into laughter. As he gazed over the grass that he had conquered, he repeated the story about the moving award ceremony. "The moment when I could lift the trophy into the air for the first time was just magic. It was unreal," he said. "It's so beautiful, made from gold, not too heavy, not too light, just right. Everything here, the greenness, the grass, was always special for me. All of my favorite players played so well here. Wimbledon is my favorite Grand Slam tournament. So many people dream of winning here. And I thought, why me?"

On January 5, 2004, Federer was accorded an honor that he never expected. The Swiss television public elected him "Swiss of the Year," over such well-known and successful countrymen from industry, entertainment, sports and politics. Federer was greatly surprised—there was not a more prestigious award in his homeland. His name was engraved in stone in a mountain in the Canton of Obwalden, the supposed geographic middle of Switzerland.

When Federer arrived in Australia in January of 2004 in preparation for the Australian Open, criticism about his separation from Peter Lundgren already preceded him. The international media wanted to know the reasons.

Pat Cash, the Australian Wimbledon champion, hastily stated in London's *Sunday Times* that Federer made a mistake and was risking a career setback by ending his coaching relationship with Lundgren. Cash could neither understand the timing nor the motives for the separation and went as far to say that Federer was not yet ready for the new season and that he was allowing himself to be unduly influenced by his girlfriend. "Errors of judgment have already been made and the first thing Federer must do is ensure that his girlfriend returns to being just that," wrote Cash. "It's a simple matter of common sense."

Cash's aggressive—and below the belt—punch at Federer was unfounded. Federer not only would dispel all doubts cast on his professionalism, but also fundamentally call into question all theories about the importance of even having a coach. Federer was not lacking in offers from coaches around the world. After all, Federer was the only top 10 player without a coach. However, he didn't want to be overhasty. "Out on the court, I alone have to decide what I am doing," he said. "And nobody can help me with that anymore."

As the Australian Open began, questions about Federer's form and preparation mounted. He lost to Juan Carlos Ferrero at an exhibition tournament in Hong Kong, then at the Kooyong Classic in Melbourne, Andre Agassi polished him off in less than an hour with an ominous 6-2, 6-4 decision. Agassi, the four-time Australian Open, was firmly entrenched as the favorite at Melbourne Park having won his last 21 Australian Open matches.

Federer effortlessly reached the round of 16 and, thanks to his new found self-confidence, was able to avenge his Davis Cup loss to Hewitt, defeating the Aussie standout 4-6, 6-0, 6-3, 6-4 on the very same court where he tasted bitter defeat four months earlier in the Davis Cup semifinals. To make matters worse for Australian fans and Hewitt, Federer's victory occurred on all days but Australia Day, the Australian national holiday, with nearby fireworks going off in nearby downtown Melbourne.

Federer's fireworks continued in the quarterfinals against his nemesis David Nalbandian. In the decisive moments of the first set against the Argentine, Federer confirmed the sound state of his morale. Serving at 15-40 at 5-5 in the first set, Federer fired off four straight aces to win the game and carry him to win the first set and the eventual 7-5, 6-4, 5-7, 6-3 victory. His previous uncertainties with Nalbandian were now part of the past.

With world No. 1 Andy Roddick losing unexpectedly to Marat Safin in five sets in the quarterfinals, the door was open for Federer to take the No. 1 ranking. By reaching the semifinals, Federer was guaranteed to leap over Roddick in the rankings, but the No. 1 spot was still up in the air. If Ferrero, Federer's semifinal opponent, were to win the tournament, he would return to No. 1. Should Ferrero not win the tournament, Federer would ascend to the top for the first time. For the second time in his career, Federer was one match win from attaining his goal as world No. 1 when he took the court with Ferrero. After some initial tension in the opening set, the match was never in doubt. At 9:18 pm local time on January 30, after finishing his 6-4, 6-1, 6-4 domination of the Spanaird, Federer sank to his knees and raised his arms to the heavens. It was now certain. Federer would officially become the No. 1 ranked player when the next rankings were released on February 2.

"I wanted to enjoy this moment," he said. "You only get to be No. 1 once." But he remained adamant that his big goal was the title. "It would be a gigantic disappointment if I were to lose in the final."

Safin was Federer's unexpected opponent in the final. The Russian stunned Agassi in a five-set semifinal to reach the Australian Open final for the second time in three years. Although unseeded and ranked No. 86 in the world due to an extended layoff due to wrist surgery in 2003, the former world No. 1 was a powerhouse capable of winning matches and titles regardless of whom he played.

Federer, however, would not let anything stand in his way of victory. After he won the first set in a tie-break, Safin seemed increasingly tired and frustrated and resigned to defeat. Federer's 7-6 (3), 6-4, 6-2 final-round victory earned him his second Grand Slam tournament title and served as a stylish ascent to the world No. 1 ranking

"Becoming No. 1 was a goal but winning the title was bigger," he said.

He didn't forget Peter Lundgren either. At nearly every interview during his championship run, Federer mentioned the importance of his dismissed coach and even sent him a text message to Sweden, thanking him once again for his previous efforts.

There would be no discussion among experts in the tennis industry of the validity of the No. 1 ranked player. Having won Wimbledon, the Tennis Masters Cup and the Australian Open, Federer won three of the five most important titles in tennis in the last seven months. His success equaled the best run of success in men's tennis since Hewitt captured titles at Wimbledon, the US Open and the Tennis Masters Cup over a stretch of 10 months in 2001 and 2002.

The transitional phase in men's tennis that produced eight different Grand Slam tournament champions over a two-year-stretch was over. The ATP promoted this period in its "New Balls Please" campaign since nobody really knew who the next dominant figure would be in men's tennis. The discussion ceased. The age of Federer had dawned.

Three-year-old Roger attempts a forehand at the Ciba Tennis Club

Roger plays table tennis in 1984

Roger wins the Swiss national 12-and-under
championships in 1993

Roger and Peter Carter in 1998

Roger and his parents Robert and Lynette Federer in Klosers, Switzerland in 1998

The "blond" champion—Roger wins the Orange Bowl in 1998

© Siggi Bucher

Mirka Vavrinec—former WTA Tour professional and Roger's girlfriend

A debutant at the Tennis Masters Cup in Shanghai in 2002

Roger with Peter Lundgren at Wimbledon in 2003

With his fitness guru Pierre Paganini in Biel in 2003

Roger in tears at the trophy presentation at Wimbledon in 2003

Roger's most unusual trophy—his cow Juliette in Gstaad in 2003

Federer poses with the author, Stauffer, in a special return visit to the All England Club in December of 2003

CHAPTER 22
No. 1

In his autobiography *You Cannot Be Serious*, three-time Wimbledon champion John McEnroe compared reaching the No. 1 world ranking to climbing Mount Everest. "The very top, like the summit of Everest, is weird territory, impossible to understand unless you've actually been there," he said.

The New Yorker, who put an end to the Björn Borg era, concurred with the late Arthur Ashe, in the statement that there was "just as much difference between No. 10 in the world and No. 5 as there was between No. 100 and No. 10. Going from No. 5 to No. 4, he (Ashe) said, is like going from No. 10 to No. 5. And from there on up is inconceivable."

Roger Federer agreed with the assessment. "It's a long way to No. 1. You have to overcome many obstacles to get there," he said in spring of 2004. "I did it and now I have a lot of confidence." He said that it was only because of winning at Wimbledon, which released the enormous pressure of finally winning a Grand Slam event, that he was able to play so freely and without pressure in Houston and Melbourne. He no longer saw any reason to keep him from winning further major titles.

At 22 years and five months old, Federer was not the youngest world No. 1. Lleyton Hewitt, Jimmy Connors, Björn Borg, John McEnroe, Jim Courier, Pete Sampras, Marat Safin and Andy Roddick were all younger when they first made their appearances at the top spot. But Federer reached No. 1 before Boris Becker, Stefan Edberg, Ivan Lendl and Andre Agassi. As one of only three German speaking world-ranked No. 1 players (after Boris Becker and Thomas Muster), Federer could appreciate his status that was denied him in 2003. A childhood dream that just barely eluded him in the past months now was a reality.

It was by no means a matter of course that he would flourish as the top-ranked player. The No. 1 ranking was a burden for many of his predecessors.

The hunter became the hunted, the pursuer the pursued, the challenger the challenged. The No. 1 ranking also involved additional duties as the most important representative of the sport. It is expected that the world No. 1 shaped opinions on the sport. His word pulled weight and extra demands and attention made the world No. 1 constantly in demand. He stands at the center of the sport and is chased and surrounded by the media, fans and tournament directors, while also having the burden of continuing his training and maintaining his results to hold the No. 1 ranking.

Nonetheless the No. 1 ranking for most is the ultimate career goal—the fulfillment of a long-nurtured dream. Everybody who reaches it for the first time finds themselves at the end of a road and are forced to re-orient themselves. Not everybody copes well with the "No. 1" drug. It's not a bad life being ranked No. 2, No. 3 or No. 5—and it is much more relaxed.

Since the ATP rankings were introduced in 1973, many of the 22 players who achieved the No. 1 ranking disappeared shortly after attaining the top spot. Australian Patrick Rafter, Spaniards Carlos Moya and Juan Carlos Ferrero, the Chilean Marcelo Rios, the Austrian Thomas Muster and the Russian Yevgeny Kafelnikov were all only able to maintain the No. 1 ranking for less than a period of 10 weeks.

Federer, however, did not see himself at the end of a road but at the beginning of a new one. For him, it was immediately clear that he wanted to remain at the top as long as possible. This was his new mission that he had to sacrifice for and for which he had to set priorities. Unfortunately, the goal of maintaining the No. 1 ranking came, eventually, at the expense of Davis Cup. "Being No. 1 is fantastic. I recommend it to anybody," he said once. "I feel much better than when I was No. 5 or No. 6. I now play with much more confidence not only because I win a lot of matches and tournaments, but because I know no one can say that they are better than me. Perhaps on a certain day—but that's not enough to take the No. 1 position away from me." Federer confessed that he had no trouble with the expectations and increased hoopla of being the top man in men's tennis. When asked at the German Open in Hamburg if he liked being popular, he frankly confessed, "I like being the star. I love being the magnet to the public's attention."

Following his triumph in Australia and his ascension to the No. 1 ranking, Federer traveled home to Basel, where he was received by fans and sponsors with cowbells and flags bearing the words "No. 1." From there, he continued directly via private jet, provided by a wealthy dual Swiss-Romanian citizen, to Romania for the first round of the 2004 Davis Cup. Upon his early morning arrival at the Swiss team's hotel in Bucharest, he stepped out of his car into the lights of a bevy of Romanian TV camera crews. Just five days after winning the Australian Open, Federer was back in action on the other side of the world in a completely different place—the "Sala Polivalenta" in the middle of a run-down park in the Romanian capital. He only had two days to become accustomed to the time change, to adjust from the Australian summer to the European winter and switch from the hard courts of Melbourne to a clay court in Bucharest. Despite the massive transition, Federer led Switzerland to victory, winning both singles matches and pairing in doubles with good friend and Davis Cup debutant Yves Allegro to defeat Andrei Pavel and Gabriel Trifu 10-8 in the fifth set in the four-hour doubles match. It marked the fourth time in Federer's Davis Cup career where he accounted for three match victories in a tie.

The 2004 season was turning into a triumphal march for Federer. He was celebrated wherever he appeared. His results continued to be worthy of a world No. 1. His first defeat of the year—and in manner of three months—came in mid-February, when he lost to Tim Henman in the quarterfinals of Rotterdam. He quickly regained form and successfully defended his title in Dubai, defeating the Spainard Feliciano Lopez in the final. At the Tennis Masters Series event in Indian Wells, Federer avenged his loss to Henman in the championship match and realized his first "countable" victory against another of his early nemeses. The win over Henman was only his second in eight matches, with Federer's only previous win over the Brit in Key Biscayne in 2002 being decided when Henman was forced to quit after one set due to a stiff neck. His victory, therefore, was especially satisfying. "Now I believe that no opponent has a psychological advantage over me," he said.

An opponent that would bring Federer to his knees, however, appeared shortly after Indian Wells—illness. Immediately after the final, Federer began to run a fever and suffer from nausea and muscle pains. Despite his illness, he did not cancel his pre-arranged trip to Portland, Ore., the home of his clothing sponsor "Nike," for a promotional visit, but en route to Miami for the next tournament, Federer was forced to stop and check into an airport hotel in Los Angeles to rest and try to recover. As he and Mirka finally arrived in Florida, he considered withdrawing from the tournament, but when rain gave him an extra day of rest, he decided to give it a go.

After he was able to muster up enough strength to negotiate a three-set win in his first match against No. 54-ranked Nikolay Davydenko of Russia, Federer next drew the highly-regarded Spaniard Rafael Nadal. The 17-year-old left-hander from Mallorca played what he described at the time as the best match of his life and dominated the listless Federer 6-3, 6-3. The loss was the most decisive defeat Federer experienced in a year. Nadal also became the youngest player to defeat the Wimbledon champion. Federer was not surprised that he lost since he was not yet recovered from his illness. Nonetheless, he suspected that Nadal would be a dangerous rival coming of age. "He will become the most powerful left-hander in tennis in the coming years," Federer prophesized.

Following his loss in Key Biscayne, Federer recovered his health and played his first matches in Switzerland as the new world No. 1 during the Davis Cup quarterfinal match against France in Lausanne. Fans greeted him with cowbells, whistles and ear-splitting noise in the sold-out Malley hockey arena. Federer said later that he was almost frightened by the noise but enjoyed the experience "It's like a dream to be able to play in such an atmosphere," he said. Although he decisively defeated Nicolas Escude and Arnaud Clement each in straight sets, Federer and Yves Allegro were unable to win the doubles point, which proved pivotal in France's 3-2 win that avenged their loss to the Swiss in Toulouse from a year earlier.

In the clay court season, Federer won the German Open in Hamburg for a second time and registered his overall best clay court season. At the French Open, however, he was stopped in the third round, falling to three-time Roland Garros champion Gustavo Kuerten. "I can accept this defeat," Federer said, acknowledging the superb ability of his Brazilian opponent. Nobody suspected that this loss would be his only defeat for a very long time.

Federer's hype reached new heights at the coming of Wimbledon. As the No. 1 seed and the defending champion, he was more in demand than ever. He chose to stay in a three-bedroom house on Clifton Road in Wimbledon Village—the same house where Pete Sampras lived during his Wimbledon sorjourns. This year, Federer's physiotherapist Pavel Kovac did not have to sleep on the couch and could enjoy his own bedroom.

Reto Staubli, a friend and former Swiss interclub team colleague of Federer, joined the team for The Championships. A former touring professional who had taken a job as a banker, Staubli viewed traveling and helping Federer as an adventure and took care of details and errands normally left to coaches. As a former Swiss national champion player, he even occasionally practiced with Federer. The defending champion, however, isolated himself to the house and the courts. Questions about his coaching situation, meanwhile, all but disappeared. Why should he change a winning formula?

Federer was firmly placed as a favorite to defend his title at the All England Club. His rankings lead over No. 2-ranked Andy Roddick stood at approximately 1,000 points—the equivalent of a Grand Slam title. With another win at the pre-Wimbledon event in Halle, Federer extended his grass court winning streak to 17 straight matches. Federer felt at home on grass courts and even the predictably wet English weather failed to fluster him.

With four relatively routine victories, Federer confidently reached the quarterfinals where he met Lleyton Hewitt, who tested the defending champion in a dramatic stop and go match that was three times interrupted by rain. After losing the first set, Hewitt was able to muster a second-set tie-break, ending Federer's 26-set Wimbledon winning streak. After Federer streaked to win the third set 6-0, Hewitt was finally able to break Federer's serve—snapping a streak of 105 straight service holds—and take a 4-3 lead in the fourth set. A five-set thriller seemed apparent, but Federer rose the occasion to win the final three games and escape with a 6-1, 6-7 (1), 6-0, 6-4 victory.

The fleet-footed Frenchman Sebastien Grosjean faced Federer in the semifinals, but again, wet weather made the match a soggy mess. Rain forced the match to be postponed from Friday—with Federer leading 6-2, 6-3, 4-2—to Saturday morning, where Federer needed only 30 minutes to win the third set in a tie-break, almost a full 24 hours after the match began.

On a rainy, bitterly cold Fourth of July, Federer played Roddick, who not only was in his first Wimbledon final on his country's Independence Day, but on the birthday of his older brother John. Roddick clearly emerged as a solid No. 2 in the rankings behind Federer and took the identity of Federer's primary challenger, especially on grass. The head-to-head between the two stood at 5-1 in the favor of Federer, who unlike the year before in his semifinal match with Roddick, was now considered the heavy favorite.

But Roddick and his coach Brad Gilbert both did their homework. Roddick played with an intensity that was palpable all the way to the top rows of Centre Court. Roddick's power game dominated the early stages of the match as his brutal groundstrokes and lighting serve gave him the first set 6-4. The second set turned into a inexplicable rollercoaster ride—Federer took a 4-0 lead and had a point for 5-0, but lost two service games in a row and allowed Roddick to square the set at 4-4. But the tennis gods were in Federer's favor. At 6-5, a let court winner gave him a set point. A gorgeously played running cross court forehand winner on the next point gave Federer the set.

The defending champion, however, was still unable to seize complete control of the match. In the third set, he trailed 2-4 when the heavens intervened as rain forced a temporary suspension in the action. The delay lasted 40 minutes and—as strange as it may sound—proved to be a pivotal moment in the match.

The rain stoppage also provided the Australian Pat Cash enough time on the BBC TV coverage of the match to make another false prediction—he wouldn't bet any money on Federer winning the match. But Federer returned to the court as a man transformed and with a new tactic. As Cash used to do with much success, Federer rushed the net with greater frequency and began to win more and more points in that position. He won the third set in a tiebreak and was able to fend off six break points in the fourth set, before he broke Roddick's serve at 4-3 without losing a point. In just a matter of minutes, Federer was again the Wimbledon champion.

It was 5:55 pm local time in Great Britain when Federer sank to his knees and rolled onto his back having once again won the greatest title in tennis. The sun, meanwhile, came out from the clouds, and like the year before, showered the award ceremony in sunshine. As with the ceremony in 2003, the tears flowed. "At least this time I managed to hold them back a bit

during the award ceremony," he remarked. "I'm even happier than last year."
He admitted how surprised he was at Roddick's aggressive and solid play.
Federer said he himself made the decision during the rain delay in the third
set to change tactics and to play more serve and volley. Of this, he said,
he was proud. "Coach Federer is satisfied with Federer the tennis player,"
he quipped.

CHAPTER 23
Samson's Return

Roger Federer's second straight Wimbledon title firmly established him in the No. 1 ranking and allowed him to avoid the first potentially delicate situation in protecting his position in the top spot in men's tennis. If he had lost to Andy Roddick in the Wimbledon final, Federer would have only been 65 points ahead of the American and would have had to at least reach the semifinals at the Swiss Open, the following week in Gstaad, to maintain his position as the world No. 1. With his victory at the All England Club, he held a 665-point advantage over Roddick in the No. 2 position and allowed him to compete without the pressure of maintaining a fragile hold on the top ranking.

Once again, the tournament organizers in Gstaad had an original present in store for the Wimbledon champion—a full-scale sized alpenhorn. Federer struggled in Gstaad, surrendering a set in four of his five matches, but punctuated his week with a four-set win over Igor Andreev of Russia in the championship match. After 13 attempts—and three losses in tournament finals—Federer finally won an ATP tournament on his home soil. It didn't particularly matter at that point that his first Swiss title was in Gstaad and not at "his" tournament in Basel. Federer was the first Swiss champion at Gstaad since Heinz Günthardt in 1980 and attendance at the Swiss Open during his performance was record-breaking. His relief was as great as his weariness, "Finally," he said. "I can get some sleep."

After vacationing in the Arab Emirate city of Dubai, Federer returned to Basel and began his preparation for the summer hard court season that, in 2004, included a very special event—the Olympic Games in Athens. Federer declared the Olympic Games to be one of his three major goals of the year, in addition to defending his Wimbledon title and reaching the No. 1 ranking.

But first, Federer focused on the Tennis Masters Series tournaments in Toronto and Cincinnati, where he hoped to expand his lead in the world rankings.

On August 1, Switzerland's national holiday and on the second anniversary of the death of Peter Carter, Federer defeated Roddick 7-5, 6-3 in the final of Toronto. He dedicated what was already his eighth tournament victory of the year to Carter—and to "him alone." Federer's win also established a new superlative in tennis—he was the first player since Björn Borg in 1979 to win three consecutive tournaments on three different surfaces—grass (Wimbledon), clay (Gstaad) and on hard courts (Toronto). "I hope to be able to have coffee with Borg sometime and have a talk about these series," Federer said. He proudly pointed out that there were players who reached the No. 1 ranking but lacked titles on certain surfaces, including Boris Becker, who failed to win a title on clay during his career.

Winning the championship was not the only momentous experience for Federer in Toronto—he had his hair cut short. In April, Federer's flowing mane was reduced by several centimeters, visually giving him a strong resemblance to Peter Lundgren. His hair, now, was considerably shorter, with a layered look. He actually just wanted a trim, Mirka explained, but the hair dresser convinced him to try something new for a change.

Federer's new look, however, didn't sit well the "gods of tennis." His strength seemed to emanate from his hair, like Samson in the Bible. Samson possessed super-human powers but after the Philistines trimmed his flowing locks, his powers diminished. If Federer had known what was going to happen to him during the next few tournaments, he would have been wise to skip his visit to the hair dresser in Toronto.

In Cincinnati, Federer lost in surprising fashion in the first round to Dominik Hrbaty of Slovakia, ending his 23-match winning streak. The winning streak was the longest in professional tennis in five years and the loss was Federer's first in the opening round of a tournament since the French Open in 2003—a stretch of 15 months.

Federer, however, was quick to see the positive side of his early defeat —it gave him more time to prepare for the Olympic Games. The two-time Wimbledon champion was the star of the Swiss Olympic delegation and was considered certain to bring home a medal. He was highly motivated and he talked for months of the importance the trip to Greece was for him. Said Federer, "I've been looking forward to this tournament for four years." He said he dreamed of winning the gold medal and toasting to his victory—and to his partnership with Mirka, which, like the Olympic flame, was ignited under the Olympic flag four years earlier at the Sydney Games. After his disappointing loss to Arnaud DiPasquale of France in the bronze medal match in Sydney, Federer was especially motivated to step on the medal podium.

He lived modestly in the Olympic Village—in contrast to many other tennis professionals who preferred hotels. He received the honor of leading the entire Swiss Olympic delegation as the Swiss flag-bearer at the Opening Ceremonies. Yet, like most of the tennis players at the Opening Ceremonies, he stood out in the enormous mass of athletes from all around the world, who sacrificed much through the years for this one chance at glory. While many athletes soaked in the atmosphere of the Opening Ceremonies from the infield of the Olympic stadium, Federer found himself forced to entertain a constant stream of photograph and autograph requests from his fellow Olympic athletes.

The International Tennis Federation was charmed that Federer held the Olympic tournament in such high esteem. Many Olympic followers and representatives from different Olympic sports held the opinion that the highly-paid professional tennis players had no business at the Olympics (tennis had once again became an Olympic sport in 1988) and that they did not take the event as seriously as it deserved to be treated.

In an Olympic tennis competition that featured many surprises, Federer's second-round loss to the unknown 19-year-old Czech Thomas Berdych was perhaps the most unexpected result. To make matters worse, hours after his devastating 4-6, 7-5, 7-5 loss to the No. 79-ranked Berdych, he was also eliminated from the doubles competition with partner Yves Allegro, losing to India's Leander Paes and Mahesh Bhupathi.

Federer's losses were major disappointments not only to himself, but to the Swiss Olympic delegation, which received another medal blow on the same day when its medal-contending judo athlete Sergei Aschwanden, also was eliminated from medal contention. Federer appeared well-composed in the media center—but he was at a loss for an explanation. He said he felt somewhat pressured and was tired after the long season, it was difficult playing against a young player like Berdych whom he didn't know. A few months later and viewing his Olympic experience with some perspective, he quipped, "At least I carried the flag well in Athens."

In contrast to other Olympic athletes from other sports, Federer didn't have to wait for months or even years for the next opportunity to achieve a shining victory. Just a week after the conclusion of the Olympic tennis competition marked the start of the US Open. Federer quickly set his eyes on the future. "If I could have had the choice, I would have taken Olympic gold, but now that this dream has been shattered, I want to win the US Open," he said. He then departed for New York for the fourth and last Grand Slam tournament of the year.

The US Open is known as one of the most chaotic of the Grand Slam tournaments and a tournament that many find too difficult to win, including Björn Borg. "The US Open is the Grand Slam tournament that is the most difficult to win," said Andre Agassi. Many others agree with him. "Somebody could stand up in the grandstands and play saxophone and it wouldn't bother anybody," Boris Becker noted in his younger years.

Federer shed his once chronic lack of success in the United States by winning two of America's four biggest titles at the Tennis Masters Cup in Houston and the Pacific Life Open in Indian Wells. Like at Wimbledon, he arrived early in New York in order to calmly prepare for the tournament. Besides his practice sessions and workouts, he spent his time going to such Broadway musicals as *Beauty and the Beast* and *The Boy from Oz*. He also conducted pre-event media interviews and kept up with his sponsor obligations. He even supported his fellow Swiss Davis Cup team members, watching them compete in the US Open qualifying tournament—a very unusual thing for the world's No. 1 player to do.

The weaknesses that he showed in Cincinnati and at the Olympics were not evident at the US Open. Was it perhaps due to the fact that his hair began to grow back? In any case, he had little trouble advancing into the quarterfinals, where he faced Agassi, now age 34. After a European summer highlighted by physical problems and unexpected defeats, Agassi found his groove on the

American hard courts, defeating both Roddick and Hewitt to win the title in Cincinnati—his first title in over a year. Agassi's confidence was high.

In one of the US Open's celebrated night matches, Federer and Agassi battled on Wednesday evening, September 8, and Federer immediately found his rhythm. He was leading 6-3, 2-6, 7-5 when it began raining and play was postponed. The match resumed the following afternoon and the players were greeted with gale force winds—as part of the weather front that swept through New York as a leftover from Hurricane Frances that battered Florida earlier in the week. Federer described the wind swirls as being the worst conditions that he ever played under. "Just five years ago I would have gone nuts playing in such a wind," he said.

The wind forced Federer to change tactics. He no longer tried to go for winners and display his usual aggressive style, but concentrated on getting the ball and his serves over the net and simply into play—which in the windy conditions was itself a challenge. "I played just like at practice and that was the right recipe," he said. A 6-3, 2-6, 7-5, 3-6, 6-3 win over Agassi put him into the semifinals of the US Open for the first time, where he would face an old acquaintance, Tim Henman. The 30-year-old Brit won six of his eight career matches with his Swiss rival, but Federer was a different player than many of the previous matches, with more self-confidence and stamina. As in March in Indian Wells, Federer encountered little resistance with Henman, winning 6-3, 6-3, 6-4 to advance into the championship match at the US Open for the first time.

Awaiting him in the final was another of his past nemeses, Lleyton Hewitt, the 2001 US Open champion. The Australian skipped the Olympic Games, but won the two ATP tournaments played concurrently to the Olympics in Washington, D.C. and in Long Island. Entering his match with Federer, he won his last 16 matches and did not surrender a set in his six-match run to the final.

It only took 17 minutes for Federer to hand Hewitt his first lost set of the tournament, losing only five points in a near perfect execution of tennis. When Hewitt won his first game of the match after Federer led 6-0, 2-0, the crowd at Arthur Ashe Stadium gave him a standing ovation. Federer contin-ued to be the much stronger player, until a lapse of concentration and a run of errors and missed serves allowed Hewitt to win four straight games after trailing 2-5 in the second set.

"If he had managed to win the second set, it would have turned out to be an entirely different match," Federer said. "I forced myself to keep positive. I said to myself that I only got this break because I was playing against the wind and I was serving with old balls. When I changed sides, everything actually did go easier."

Federer held serve at 5-6 to force the tiebreak and won that 7-3. The two-set lead broke Hewitt's resistance and Federer plowed through the final set 6-0 to win his first US Open championship.

"First I was surprised that Lleyton was no longer getting to the ball," Federer said of his moment of victory. "Then I was suddenly lying on my back, looking into the sky at the lights of the stadium. I thought, 'That's unbelievable.' Once again I was close to tears."

CHAPTER 24

New York, New York

Roger Federer's victory at the 2004 US Open provided new content for the record books of tennis. Statisticians and historians of the game quickly discovered that he was only the second man in the "Open Era" of professional tennis (since 1968) to win a Grand Slam final with two 6-0 sets. The other was the Argentinean Guillermo Vilas, who dominated American Brian Gottfried 6-0, 6-3, 6-0 at Roland Garros in 1977. The last time a player won a final at the U.S. Championships with two 6-0 sets came back in 1884 in only the fourth edition of the U.S. national championship and in the days of tennis infancy.

In the United States, 6-0 sets are referred to as "bagels" with a "double bagel" being considered the bitterest variety when a match is lost 6-0, 6-0. In German-speaking countries, these whitewashes are called a "bicycle." Although, Lleyton Hewitt was able to force a second-set tie-break against Federer in the US Open final, he was not spared the shame of the "double bagel" or "the bicycle." The Australian Associated Press (AAP) exaggerated that Hewitt's loss was "the greatest humiliation in the history of Grand Slam finals." One reporter in the post-match press conference even had the audacity to ask Hewitt if it was difficult to swallow a "double bagel."

More importantly in historical significance was that Federer, with his victories at the Australian Open, Wimbledon and the US Open, became only the fourth man in the Open Era of tennis to win at least three of the four Grand Slam titles in a calendar year. Mats Wilander from Sweden was the last man to manage such a feat in 1988, as did Rod Laver, who won all four Grand Slams in 1969, and Jimmy Connors, who won the Australian, Wimbledon and the US Open in 1974. Don Budge was the first player to win all four major titles in the same year—the Grand Slam—in 1938. The term "Grand Slam" was first coined when American tennis writer Allison Danzig suggested in 1938 that Budge scored a Grand Slam of victories—like a winning bridge player—at the four most prestigious championships of the year.

Laver, a left-hander given the nickname the "Rockhampton Rocket," even managed to win the Grand Slam twice—once in 1962 as an amateur and again in 1969 as a professional. In Laver's time, however, this accomplishment had a different value and was less significant than today as three of the four Grand Slam events were played on grass courts, unlike the four different surfaces of today's game.

In women's tennis, three players have won the Grand Slam—the American Maureen Connolly (1953), the Australian Margaret Smith Court (1970), as well as Steffi Graf (1988). The German, who married Andre Agassi after her tennis career, also won at the Olympic Games in Seoul in 1988 giving her the distinction of winning what is called the "Golden Slam." Martina Hingis, like Federer, won the Australian Open, Wimbledon and the US Open in 1997, narrowly missing the Grand Slam, with her surprising loss to Iva Majoli in the French final preventing her from joining this elite club.

In New York, Federer once again proved his ability to amplify his performance in the final stages of the tournament. He became the first professional player to win all of his first four Grand Slam tournament finals. It was almost equally amazing that in this feat, he lost only one set in his eight matches in the semifinals and finals. In the meantime, Federer's US Open final marked the 11th straight victory in a tournament final. For Federer, a tournament final proved to be his greatest motivation. His attitude was simple—what's the use of all the effort and match victories if you ultimately lose in the final? Winners stay, losers go.

The coup at Flushing Meadows transformed him into a sports star on Broadway. The American media celebrated him lavishly and some journalists even asked the question at such a pre-mature stage if he would be the man who would break Pete Sampras' record of 14 Grand Slam titles.

Federer remained grounded and modest in the hour of his greatest achievement in the United States. "I honestly never expected to win the

US Open," he said. "Until a year ago, I always had problems in the United States. The Americans always play with more confidence in their home tournaments than anywhere else. Conditions are difficult with the high heat and humidity."

But he admitted something else; "I had a strange feeling before the final because everybody was talking about how long it had been since anybody had won his first four Grand Slam finals. I knew that I only had this one chance to do this." Some were already talking that Federer was in a position to achieve the Grand Slam, but he didn't allow these musings of grandeur to mislead him. "I would be really happy if I were to win one of the four Grand Slams next year," he said the day after his US Open triumph during an extended interview session with a select group of journalists. "I know that I have to work hard for each match and for each title. It's crazy what's happening to me now. It's out of this world."

Federer's US Open title generously extended his points lead on the No. 1 ranking. His margin between him at No. 1 and Roddick, his next challenger at No. 2, was extended from 1390 points to 2990 points—the equivalent of three Grand Slam titles. It would be impossible for any player to overtake him before the end of the year, even if Federer lost every match for the rest of the year. In the last four years, the year-end Tennis Masters Cup was the final determining tournament to decide the year-end No. 1 player. However, 2004 was not a normal year and thanks to the US Open, the year-end No. 1 was already in the books.

The Monday after the US Open brought Federer to the realization that the clocks tick differently in the American media world. He was chauffeured in a stretch limousine from one television station to another—7:45 am at ESPN's show "Cold Pizza," then at 8:30 am to the "CBS Early Show" and then at 9:30 am at "Live with Regis and Kelly," followed by a photo shoot in Times Square, and a meeting with a select group of print journalists at the Hard Rock Café. At 2:30 pm, he was a guest on John McEnroe's television talk show, and finally he appeared on the "Charlie Rose Show." He had to prove his dexterity at ping-pong at two of his television appearances. Many things are possible in the United States, but setting up a tennis court in a television studio is not one of them.

CHAPTER 25
Setting Records Around the World

Following his triumph at the US Open, Roger Federer and his girlfriend Mirka Vavrinec experienced four very exciting and diverse weeks. Arthur Cohn, an Academy Award-winning producer and, like Federer, a native of Basel, invited his friend to celebrate his US Open victory with him in Los Angeles. Roger and Mirka got their first introduction to Hollywood's glamorous world. They took up residence in a luxury suite in Beverly Hills, went shopping on Rodeo Drive, visited attractions such as the Walk of Fame and met film greats such as Kirk Douglas and Danny de Vito. In between it all, Federer treated his body to hours of relaxation in the spa. Another highlight of this trip was an excursion in a private jet to Las Vegas to take in magician David Copperfield's show at the Hotel Bellagio. Following the show, Federer met with Copperfield—a meeting of two magicians, one could say.

The jet-set life continued smoothly. Federer then jetted across the Pacific Ocean and the International Date Line and made a stop-over in Hong Kong, where he conducted a media day for the Asian press. The next stop was Bangkok and the Thailand Open. Traveling in a minivan from the tournament facilities to his hotel through the humid, rain-soaked metropolis, Federer explained that he enjoyed moving about in the world of the beautiful, the rich and the famous. "I wouldn't be doing this if I didn't want to," he said. "I find getting to know show business exciting. I used to have trouble with the world of red carpets and formal dinners but now I'm having fun. It's also not difficult for me to talk to other people. There's always something to say."

He particularly enjoyed Asia's hospitality and the enthusiasm of the people—he was also enamored with Asian cuisine. In contrast to the other players at the event, Federer stayed at the Oriental Hotel on the Chao Phraya River, a traditional, colonial-styled structure and the best hotel in the city. Federer, in the meantime, made the conscious decision to avoid the official tournament hotels. He noticed that he could settle down quicker and relax better when he stayed away from the tournament crowd. Hotel rooms were havens where he could recuperate and escape—and he was willing to pay extra dollar for this extra luxury, but as the king of the tennis world, he was still often offered special rates to stay in the best suites in the best hotels. In Paris, it may have been the noble Hotel du Crillon, or the seven star Burj al Arab in Dubai, or the Peninsula in New York.

Federer's trip to Bangkok ended in success—he won the Thailand Open with a 6-4, 6-0 win over Andy Roddick in a sold-out final in front of 10,000-plus spectators. It was his 12th consecutive victory in a tournament final, tying the all-time record set by Björn Borg and John McEnroe. He received the "Trophy of the King" at the award ceremony from Princess Ubolratana Rajakanya and expressed his gratitude in the country's customary way, making a slight bow with hands folded over his chest. "I was surprised at how attractive the Princess was. She looked 35," he said later after a long walk through many hallways accompanied by five bodyguards while retiring to his plain and windowless single dressing room. "She's supposed to be 55!"

His "jet-set" world tour was now in its sixth week but he did not return directly home after Bangkok. For the third time during the 2004 calendar year, Federer went to Dubai. What nobody knew was that the Australian coach Tony Roche was also in Dubai, on assignment to spend a few days of training with Federer in the initial stages of what later became their fascinating player-coach relationship.

By early October, Federer already won ten titles in the 2004 season. His match record stood at 69-6 and there were still four tournaments remaining on his schedule. Two more important ATP records were within reach—most victories in a season (86) and most tournament titles in a season (12), both set in 1995 by the left-handed Austrian clay courter Thomas Muster. But then, the unexpected happened. Federer withdrew from the event in Madrid because he didn't feel sufficiently rested after his world tour. He preferred to concentrate his energies on winning the event that was as high on his wish-list as the French Open—the Swiss Indoors. At the tournament's Monday opening presentation in Basel's town hall, Federer was in a fine mood, upbeat and told all the assembled media how well prepared he was for the week. However, just a few hours later, he was overtaken during a practice session by what must have been the curse of Basel—he suddenly felt an unusual pain in his left thigh. The pain persisted during his practice session on Tuesday. He hastily underwent a magnetic resonance imaging examination, which revealed a muscle fiber rupture—an injury common for tennis players.

Instead of his long-desired triumph in his hometown, the Swiss Indoors brought him some of the bitterest hours of his career. He showed up at the St. Jakobshalle Tuesday evening—when he was scheduled to make his tournament start—wearing street clothes. He withdrew from the tournament and explained to the media and the public what happened. "I never imagined that it would turn out like this," he said. "I had made perfect preparations and had a good chance at winning the tournament."

Federer recovered just in time to travel to Houston in his attempt to defend his title at the Tennis Masters Cup. However, the second year at the Westside Tennis Club was completely different than the previous year. Jim McIngvale—"Mattress Mack"—took last year's criticisms by Federer and his fellow players to heart and significantly improved the conditions of the tournament. Each of the eight participants now had their own dressing room. The differences between Federer and McIngvale were resolved and the tournament promoter and his wife warmly welcomed the world's No. 1 player and congratulated him graciously for his impressive 2004 season. Federer finally felt welcome and appreciated in Texas. McIngvale even facilitated for Federer a lunch with former American President George Bush Sr., a self-confessed tennis fan, and his wife Barbara, both residents of Houston. However, there was something that McIngvale could not facilitate with his influence and his deep pocketbook—good weather. Most of the week featured rainy and windy weather, spreading gloom among fans, players and officials and causing long and persistent match delays.

At least Federer was fully recovered from his thigh injury. Six weeks went by since his last tournament competition in Bangkok, but surprisingly, he had little trouble immediately finding his rhythm. Federer negotiated round-robin wins over Gaston Gaudio, Lleyton Hewiit and Carlos Moya to reach the semifinals, where he faced Marat Safin, who was now tutored by Federer's old coach Peter Lundgren.

The Federer-Safin semifinal was highlighted by the second-set tie-break that lasted 27 minutes and ended 20-18 in Federer's favor. The 38 points matched the record for the longest tie-break in tennis history—equaling the amount of points Björn Borg and Premjit Lall played at Wimbledon in 1973 and that Goran Ivanisevic and Daniel Nestor played at the 1993 US Open. "Too bad we didn't break the record," Federer joked. "We should have made an arrangement to do this." Federer was in a good mood because even though he blew seven match points, he also fought off six set points and won the match 6-3, 7-6 (18). Interestingly enough, television replays showed that Federer actually won the match on his third match point when leading 10-9, when the TV replay showed Federer was the victim of a bad line call. "I even saw the mark Safin's shot made and it was out," he stated. Almost any other player would have frantically protested such an injustice, especially at such a critical point in the match. Federer, however, reacted as if nothing had happened, even though he would have won the match on Safin's mistake. He remained entrenched in the dog fight and said he intentionally convinced himself that Safin's stroke probably landed in. "I would have gone nuts otherwise," he said.

In the other semifinal, Roddick's game buckled against Hewitt as the American lost the last 20 points of the match, losing 6-3, 6-2. Some cynics actually offered that Roddick may have welcomed defeat to avoid a fourth final-round loss to Federer for the year. Instead, it was now Federer against Hewitt for the sixth time on the season, and for the sixth time, Federer emerged the winner. The 6-3, 6-2 win gave Federer his 13th consecutive victory in a tournament final, breaking the record he previously shared with McEnroe and Borg for most consecutive victories in tournament finals.

As Federer toasted with Champagne in the player's lounge after his post-match interview with the press, he seemed like anybody who had just ended a normal work week. But on this day, a dream year came to a close. Federer won 11 titles, three Grand Slam tournaments as well as the Tennis Masters Cup. His won-loss record for the year stood at 74-6, marking the best winning percentage since John McEnroe went 82-3 in 1984. His reward was lavish. Just in this week—like the year before in Houston—he set a personal record in prize money winning $1.52 million and raised his season earnings to $6,357,547.

Since his devastating loss to Berdych at the Olympic Games, Federer went undefeated for the remainder of the year. He was now the champion of four Grand Slam tournaments and finished the year as the No. 1 player in the world. Federer still had one more wish before he and Mirka jetted off to the Maldive Islands for some rest and relaxation—"I would like to make time stand still and just enjoy this moment." But nobody, of course, could fulfill this wish.

CHAPTER 26
The Other Australian

Because of his success in the 2004 season, Roger Federer found himself in an interesting dilemma with regard to his coaching situation. He was without a coach for the entire year, making him the exception on the professional tour, yet he completed one of the greatest individual years in the history of the sport. Despite his success, he still sought new impulses. He still felt he had an even greater untapped potential and he wanted to continue to improve—especially his serve, his backhand and his net game. He knew that if he rested on his laurels and stayed stagnant, his game would regress.

However, he also knew the dangers that taking on a new coach would have not only for him, but for the coach as well. "If a player loses a few times, then they'll say that it was the coach's fault," Federer said in Bangkok. "As long as I don't have a coach, I don't think too much, and as long as I play well, I also don't have to change anything. That is the case right now, but I am also aware that there are going to be times when things won't run as smoothly. Then it would be better to have a coach."

Since the beginning of the 2004 season, rumors swirled that Federer was pursuing Darren Cahill as his coach. Cahill, who was actually a childhood school friend of Roger's deceased coach Peter Carter, was a standout Australian player who reached the semifinals at the 1988 US Open and was the former coach of Lleyton Hewitt. At the time, he was working with Andre Agassi and Federer was quick to deny the rumor at every opportunity. Truth be told, Federer had his eye cast on another prominent Australian of an older generation—Tony Roche. The unflappable man with the sun and wind-burned complexion was born in 1945 in Wagga Wagga—a city located between Melbourne and Sydney whose meaning is "the city of the many crows." He was one of the greats in tennis history, but won only one Grand Slam tournament title in singles, mainly due to the fact that the competition of his era consisted of legends such as Rod Laver, Roy Emerson, Ken Rosewall and John Newcombe.

In his prime, the left-hander was an imposing figure with a treacherous serve and brilliant net game that helped him secure 13 Grand Slam men's doubles titles and guided him to four Davis Cup titles representing Australia. In singles, he reached six Grand Slam tournament finals, including the Wimbledon final in 1968 and the US Open final in 1969 and 1970. His only Grand Slam triumph in singles came in 1966 on the slow clay courts at Roland Garros, where aggressive players like Roche are usually at a disadvantage. Roche is a gentleman and when asked about his victory in Paris, he immediately emphasized that he was only able to win the tournament thanks to the fairness of his final-round opponent, a Hungarian named Istvan Gulyas. "I injured my ankle and, without a doubt, would not have been able to play in the final if he had not allowed me to have an extra day off to rest," Roche said. "It was an incredible gesture of sportsmanship."

Roche is considered to be one of the world's premier tennis tacticians. He is a polite, quiet, extremely modest and very discreet. Even Australian journalists who meticulously cover the sport admit that there's a certain mystery to Roche. "He prefers to stay in the background when working with players," said Australian radio reporter Craig Gabriel. Even during his glamour years as a player, Roche preferred ceding the limelight to Newcombe, his long-time doubles partner. Roche won 12 of his 13 Grand Slam doubles titles with "Newk"—five at Wimbledon, four in Melbourne, two in Paris, and one in New York. Newk and "Rochey"—as he is referred to in Australian circles—led the Australian Davis Cup team as captain and coach respectively from 1994 to 2000.

But Roche didn't always manage to keep out of the headlines. At 29, following a series of unsuccessful treatments for serious shoulder and elbow problems, he consulted a miracle healer in the Philippines, who used acupuncture to treat his ailments and allow him the opportunity to achieve further accolades on the tennis court. Three years later in 1977, Roche starred in the

Davis Cup Final when he upset Adriano Panatta of Italy to help Australia win the Davis Cup title. The win over Panatta, next to his French Open triumph 11 years earlier, was his most celebrated victory in singles in his career.

As a mentor, "Coach Roche" led New Zealander Chris Lewis to his unexpected run to the Wimbledon final in 1983. In 1985, he teamed with Ivan Lendl and steered the Czech to seven of his eight Grand Slam singles titles, but unfortunately, not the elusive Wimbledon title that Lendl so desperately desired. After Lendl's retirement, Roche worked with fellow Australian Patrick Rafter, who won the US Open twice and became the No. 1 player in the world briefly in 1999. After the death of his coach Tim Gullikson in 1996, Pete Sampras even offered Roche a job as his personal coach, but Roche preferred to stay with Rafter. After Rafter's retirement, he worked primarily in Australia, working in women's tennis with the Australian Fed Cup team and also promoting up-and-coming Australian junior talents.

Both Lendl and Rafter still rave when asked about Roche and his influence on their tennis careers and their lives. When once asked who the most important person was in his career, Rafter answered without hesitation, "Rochey is my hero above all as a human being and not just as a tennis coach."

In October of 2004, Roche first trained with Federer in Dubai on a trial basis, but the Aussie legend didn't think the timing was right for him to start working with the No. 1 player in the world. He was approaching his 60th birthday and no longer wanted the excessive global travel that a full-time career in tennis demanded. Nonetheless, he offered to help Federer prepare for the new season. Just before Christmas in 2004, Federer traveled to Australia to train with Roche where he lived in Turramurra, a suburb of Sydney. He assumed this was going to be their last training session together and was saddened at the prospect of not having the full opportunity to work with the man he felt was best suited to help him. "Roche would have been a person who could have improved my game," he said at the time.

However, the personal chemistry between Federer and Roche clicked during the 10-day training camp. Despite the 36-year age difference, Federer and Roche got along fabulously. Federer made one last attempt—he told Roche he would be happy no matter how much or how little time Roche could dedicate to him as coach, he would take advantage of every opportunity. The Australian was impressed by Federer's persistence and was flattered that Federer traveled so far to Australia—and sacrificed celebrating the Christmas holidays at home—just to train with him. Roche relented. They shook hands on the deal without any sort of formal contract. The intention was that they would work together for about 10 weeks during the 2005 season.

After Christmas, Federer flew from Sydney to Doha, Qatar in the Middle East where he made his 2005 tournament debut at the Qatar Open. Federer chose the tournament as the stage for publicly announcing his agreement with Roche. "I'm glad that Tony changed his mind," he said. "I now have somebody who I can fall back on if necessary. Roche was a great serve, volley and return player in his day. He won't change my basic game but he will try to help me in certain areas. We also mutually respect and appreciate one another too which is great."

"If I were ten years younger, I would have jumped at the opportunity," Roche explained later on the eve of the Australian Open. "The fact that Roger made the sacrifice to come to me in Australia before Christmas demonstrated the great respect he has for me. That convinced me." For Roche, respect and trust were the most important elements for a partnership. As with Federer, Roche's previous deals with Lendl and Rafter were also sealed with simply a handshake.

Roche had a vision of how Federer could get stronger and become more efficient—improving his volleys and playing more at the net. By coming to the net more often, Federer could end points quicker and save energy. "He's a good athlete who can volley well and he has good reflexes," Roche said. "He could be even better. He should take more advantage of this. He already dominates from the baseline. I don't see any reason why he shouldn't be as dominant at the net."

The fact that Federer approached Roche demonstrated the great respect he has for tennis history. Federer knew that there was very little from a tactical and technical standpoint that was a mystery to Roche and that the Aussie had over 40 years of global experience in the sport. Like John McEnroe, Federer was fascinated by the rich history of his sport and held former champions in high regard. Who would be a better person to tell him about the strengths of Laver, Emerson, Borg, Lendl or Rafter than Roche, who had intimate knowledge of the minds and talents of the all-time greats.

Roche constantly pointed out the similarities between Federer and Laver as a person and as a player. Federer, like Laver, is an easy-going, relaxed person who likes to laugh and doesn't seem to be easily rattled. This attitude, he said, is an important base for success. The two agreed to travel together during the eight-week stretch between Hamburg in May and Wimbledon, but as the year developed, there would be down times where the two would hardly communicate with each other for several weeks. It was a strange player-coach relationship, but mutually agreeable.

As the 2005 season commenced, the relationship began auspiciously. Federer opened the 2005 season in Doha, losing just 23 games in five matches to win his fourth tournament in a row. To add to Federer's domination of the field was the fact that for the first time in his career, he won a title without having his serve broken. "I thought a lot about this stat and concentrated on not losing a service game," he said after dominating Croatian Ivan Ljubicic 6-3, 6-1 in the final.

Federer immediately flew back to Australia, where he also won the Kooyong Classic, an exhibition tournament featuring some of the bigger names in tennis held at the Kooyong Lawn Tennis Club, a previous site of the Australian Open. There was no question that the Australian Open favorite was Federer, who entered the event with a 21-match winning streak stretched over a five-month period. An Australian sports bookie reduced the odds of Federer winning to 1-8. Even Pete Sampras had not reached such odds for a Grand Slam tournament during his greatest days on the circuit. Approximately two thirds of the gambling public placed bets on the man from Switzerland to win the 2005 Australian Open.

En route to the semifinals, Federer did not lose a set, including a dominating 6-3, 6-4, 6-4 win over four-time Australian Open Andre Agassi in the quarterfinals. Marat Safin—and his coach Peter Lundgren—awaited Federer in the semifinals. Just like their second-set tie-break in Houston, their semifinal match became an epic and turned into the match of the year. Federer led two sets to one and by 5-2 in the fourth-set tie-break and had Safin in a virtual stranglehold. Federer held a match point at 6-5 and rushed the net, only to see Safin counter with a superb lob over his head. In his confident manner, Federer attempted an aggressive and risky between-the-legs retrieval of the lob, only to have his trick shot land in the net. Two points later, Safin won the fourth-set tie-break to even the match at two sets apiece. Before the start of the fifth set, Federer's foot was worked on by the medical staff, but the conclusion of the match was still a long way from being determined. Unlike the US Open, where a tie-break is played in the fifth set, the Australian Open, as well as the other two Grand Slam tournaments, play out a deciding set until one player wins by two games. Federer and Safin duked it out in a fifth set for another 80 minutes—almost as long as a full soccer game—before the winner was determined. After four hours and 28 minutes, the result was a bitter pill for Federer as Safin finally broke through on his seventh match point to register the shocking and unexpected 5-7, 6-4, 5-7, 7-6 (6), 9-7 upset victory.

In the wee hours of the morning, after Australian fans sang "Happy Birthday" to Safin who was minutes into his 25th birthday, Federer faced the fact that many of his winning streaks ended. His 26-match winning streak—his personal best—ended as well as his 24-match win streak against top 10 players. For the first time since Madrid in 2003, he lost a tournament after reaching the semifinals. His attempt to become the first player since Pete Sampras in 1993/1994 to win three consecutive Grand Slam tournaments also came up short.

Nonetheless, Federer seemed composed when he showed up at 1:30 in the morning for his post-match press conference. "I can only blame myself," he said. "I gave it my best. It was a good fight between two good men and in the end, the best man won." He did not mention that he entered the match with a painful left foot that became worse as the match progressed. In trying to favor the foot, he put extra stress on his back. In the fourth set, when he could have closed out the match, a pinched nerve radiated pain to his pointer finger, which adversely affected his forehand.

The loss dented Federer's armor. His point total in the world rankings sank by 550 and his advantage over the No. 2-ranked Lleyton Hewitt dropped as much as 1,000 points. His lead was still equivalent to two Grand Slam titles—but the year was still young and many things could happen. Although

Federer achieved his second-best result ever at the Australian Open and narrowly missed reaching the final, fundamental questions were being asked. Was Tony Roche the wrong man for the job as coach? Could Marat Safin, who won the title, threaten Roger and take his spot as world No. 1? Had Roger lost the aura of invincibility?

CHAPTER 27

A True Champion

Defending his position as the world's No. 1 player was one of Roger Federer's top priorities for 2005. In an effort to rest his body as a means to that end, Federer very reluctantly withdrew from Switzerland's Davis Cup first round match against The Netherlands in February. Not all of his fans sympathized with his decision. It was, after all, a home match for the Swiss and Federer was considered an avowed supporter of Davis Cup. Federer often said that bringing what some referred to as "the ugliest salad bowl in the world" to Switzerland for the first time was among his highest career goals. Additionally, a No. 2 Swiss player was coming of age in Stanislas Wawrinka, a young talent born in 1985, lending the Swiss team a fresh perspective. Wawrinka, who won the French Open junior championships in 2003, would rise from No. 162 to No. 55 in the rankings during the 2005 season and was considered one of the best up-and-coming players in Europe. Although Wawrinka and Federer's childhood friend, Marco Chiudinelli, gave it their best efforts, the Federer-less Swiss team lost to the Dutch by a 3-2 margin.

Federer responded to his crushing defeat in Melbourne like a true champion. He began another string of victories in his next tournament in Rotterdam, followed by wins in Dubai, Indian Wells and Key Biscayne for his 24th, 25th, 26th and 27th career titles in seven weeks. Even more impressive was the fact that the first two of these titles—in Holland and the United Arab Emirates—took place in consecutive weeks in completely different conditions. The title in Rotterdam was won in an indoor arena in the middle of the European winter, while the Dubai title was won outdoors in the hot conditions of the Persian Gulf.

While in Dubai, Federer had the distinction of facing off with Andre Agassi on two occasions in two very different scenarios. In a publicity stunt to promote Dubai and the tournament, the two tennis legends agreed to a special performance—hitting balls against each other on a special laid tennis court on the helicopter pad located 211 meters above the sea at the world famous seven-star hotel—Burj al-Arab. The temporary tennis court didn't possess the standard dimensions of a real tennis court, but it did offer breath-taking views of the land and sea surrounding the desert paradise. The spectacular video and still photos of Federer and Agassi were shown around the world. Said Federer, "That will always be a highlight in my career."

Agassi and Federer met again later in the week on a more traditional tennis court in the semifinals of the tournament. Federer had since found Agassi's number and defeated the American for the sixth consecutive time, giving up only four games in the process. Agassi didn't lose his sense of humor in the loss. "Maybe we should play our next match on top of the Burj al-Arab," he remarked.

By defeating Ivan Ljubicic in the final, Federer won his third successive title in Dubai—the first time he won the same tournament three times in a row. Dubai, with its extravagance, sports-friendly weather and its accessibility for globe-trotters, became sort of a second home for Federer. He admitted to journalists that he was considering acquiring a vacation residence in the Emirate. "I feel very welcome here," he said.

After defeating world No. 2 Lleyton Hewitt in the final of Indian Wells, Federer won the title in Key Biscayne, Fla., for the first time, defeating the young 18-year-old Spaniard Rafael Nadal, who defeated Federer decisively at the same event the previous year.

Entering Key Biscayne, Nadal moved to No. 6 in the year-to-date ATP Champions Race with victories in tournaments in Brazil's Costa do Sauipe and in Acapulco in Mexico. His match winning streak hit 15 as he entered the Key Biscayne final with Federer. The burly left-hander played fearlessly in his first appearance on the big stage of professional tennis and to everyone's amazement, he led Federer 6-2, 7-6, 4-1 after two hours of play. "I looked up at the scoreboard and only hoped that 6-1 would not appear there ten minutes later," Federer explained. "I blew one opportunity after another and I thought, 'This can't be happening.'" In an earlier time in such a situation, Federer would have thrown in the towel but these days were well in his past.

Somehow, he crawled back into the match and, came back from a two-sets-to-love deficit to win 2-6, 6-7 (4), 7-6 (5), 6-3, 6-1.

The Indian Wells/Key Biscayne "double" that went favorably for such players as Jim Courier, Michael Chang, Pete Sampras, Marcelo Rios and Andre Agassi before him, now garnered Federer 1,000 points in the world rankings, the equivalent of a Grand Slam title. He was now 2,245 points ahead of Hewitt in the No. 2 spot. The conversations that Federer may be in a "crisis" quickly faded. "This is a great moment in my career," Federer said after his win over Nadal. "Making a two-set comeback against a player of his caliber and then winning it isn't normal—even for me."

Following his win over Nadal, Federer made his first appearance in three years at the Monte Carlo Open in Monaco. His visit, however, ended in an unexpected defeat by the hands of another 18-year-old, Richard Gasquet of France. Like his first defeat of the season to Safin at the Australian Open, Federer was one point away from victory—he had three match points on Gasquet—but his 25-match win streak ended in a narrow 6-7 (1), 6-2, 7-6 (10) defeat. Nadal went on to win the tournament to move to No. 2 in the ATP Champions Race and further proved that he was now a top contender.

Following Monte Carlo, Federer took the next three weeks off in order to be treated for the tendonitis in both his feet that troubled him since the Australian Open. According to his fitness trainer Pierre Paganini, it was a purely precautionary measure. "Roger is so professional that he does not wait until the problem becomes so serious that he is forced to take an extended leave," Paganini said.

During Federer's hiatus, Nadal won tournaments in Barcelona and Rome that included an incredible victory over Guillermo Coria of Argentina in the Italian final that lasted five hours and 14 minutes, the longest-ever final on the ATP Tour. Suddenly Nadal was only a mere 10 points behind Federer in the ATP Champions Race. Federer finally had a challenger who was his equivalent. At the beginning of the year, most experts speculated that Hewitt, Safin and Roddick were the biggest threats to Federer's No. 1 ranking. Professional sports, however, are fast-moving businesses. What was true yesterday is outdated today. Suddenly all the talk and hype was about Nadal, who dominated the clay-court season like no player had in the last 10 years.

Federer returned to tournament tennis in Hamburg, where Nadal withdrew due to a blister on his hand suffered during his five-hour-plus marathon with Coria. Tony Roche was with Federer in Hamburg as part of his lead up to the French Open. Once again, Federer treated Hamburg's Rothenbaum Stadium as his own personal extravaganza, winning the title for the third time in four years. Federer did not lose a set en route to the title and was able to settle two old scores. In the second round, he took revenge against the Czech Tomas Berdych for his loss at the 2004 Olympics with 6-2, 6-1 victory. In the final, Federer avenged his Monte Carlo loss to Gasquet, defeating the Frenchman 6-3, 7-5, 7-6 (4) for his 19th straight victory in a tournament final. The title in Hamburg gave Federer the distinction of winning six of the ten last Masters Series tournaments. No one had ever accomplished this before.

From Hamburg, he flew directly to Estoril, a Portuguese spa and vacation resort near Lisbon and the site of the Laureus Awards ceremonies. The Laureus Foundation—derived from the Latin word laurus (laurels)—was established in 1999 in order to honor the best athletes and to achieve social improvements through sports. The foundation supports about three dozen children's relief projects world-wide. Despite its short existence, the Laureus Awards had the reputation as the "Oscars" of the sports world.

The award's great reputation and credibility are derived from its jury—a 40-member committee chaired by former Olympic track star Edwin Moses and reads like a "Who's Who" of sports—Seve Ballesteros, Franz Beckenbauer, Sebastian Coe, Emerson Fittipaldi, Michael Johnson, Michael Jordan, Jack Nicklaus, Pele, etc. Tennis is also well-represented by Boris Becker as its vice-president as well as by John McEnroe, Ilie Nastase and Martina Navratilova.

The Laureus Awards' "World Sportsman of the Year" honor is considered to be the ultimate crowning achievement for an athlete. Entering the awards show in Portugal, just three men held the distinction of earning the small Laureus statue designed by Cartier as the "Sportsman of Year"—Formula 1 racer and seven-time world champion Michael Schumacher, the golfer Tiger Woods, as well as Tour de France cycling champion Lance Armstrong. This year, Schumacher and Armstrong, as well as motorcycle world champion Valentino Rossi, six-time Olympic champion from the Athens Games Michael Phelps, two-time Olympic champion and middle-distance runner Hicham El

Guerrouj, and Federer were the athletes nominated by a nominating committee of hundreds of journalists around the world.

Federer was the only one of the six nominees present in Portugal but it was not clear whether or not he was the winner. When he showed up in the casino in his tuxedo, the scene was genuinely reminiscent of the real Oscars. Countless limousines drove up and the invited guests paraded on the immense red carpet toward the entrance, past a media grandstand with hundreds of photographers. The red carpet featured an endless stream of VIPs from all over the world, including superstars like David Beckham and his pop singer wife Victoria Adams, as well as film stars such as Jackie Chan and even King Juan Carlos of Spain. Roger Federer was in the middle of all the glitz and glamour as the guest of honor. He still claimed not to know the results of the voting. "You could show a pre-taped video if somebody else wins the award," he said in the barrage of flashing lights on the red carpet.

Perhaps to no one's surprise, the evening concluded with Federer winning the "World Sportsman of the Year" award. Cuba Gooding, Jr., the American actor, and Martina Navratilova presented Federer with his Cartier trophy. "I'm very honored," Federer said in his speech before the glamour-filled auditorium and approximately 500 million television viewers around the world. "I've already received many awards but this—this is the one." Federer received special applause when he said that, like the Laureus Foundation, he will continue to give back what sports gave to him.

"Winning Wimbledon, the title or the money, is nice, but such awards are something different," he said amidst the media tumult in the Congress Center. "And this is the one that I've always had in the back of my mind. It allows me to look back and realize that I really did have an extraordinary year."

CHAPTER 28
Fresh Tracks on Clay

Roger Federer lost out on his first opportunity to win a Grand Slam tournament in 2005 after losing to Marat Safin in the semifinals of the Australian Open. The French Open, however, offered him another opportunity for a career milestone—a milestone that only a very select few have achieved—the "Career Grand Slam." The term stands for winning all four major titles over a tennis career—a feat only achieved by five men in the history of the sport. Rod Laver and Don Budge are the only men who have won a "real" or calendar-year Grand Slam—winning all four major titles in the same year. Budge won the first Grand Slam in 1938, while Laver won a Grand Slam in 1962 as an amateur and then again in 1969 as a professional. Fred Perry of Great Britain clinched his career Grand Slam at the 1935 French Championships, while Roy Emerson of Australia completed his career quartette at Wimbledon in 1964 at age 27. Andre Agassi joined Laver as the only professional players to win a career Grand Slam when he won the French Open in 1999.

For Agassi, as well as for many other great players in the history of the game, the French Open or "Roland Garros" proved to be the toughest nut to crack. It took him 11 attempts and three trips to the championship match until he finally won in Paris. Even in his lucky third appearance in the singles final in 1999, he decisively lost the first two sets to the unseeded Ukrainian Andrei Medvedev before rallying for the five-set victory at age 29—seven years after winning his first Grand Slam tournament title.

Clay court tennis is in some regards a different form of tennis as it requires different footwork—a "sliding-into-the-ball" approach. The clay surface slows the velocity of the ball enough to give players on the defensive just a little more time to save a passed shot that on a faster surface would otherwise be a winner. Changes in temperature as well as variations in humidity levels provide for constantly changing playing conditions. Warm weather dries out clay courts and makes them play faster and favors the more aggressive players than when it is cold and moist, when the courts play much slower and favor the more defensive-minded players.

These extraordinary—and unpredictable—conditions explain why the French Open seems to always have the most unlikely champions of all four of the Grand Slam tournaments. The clay courts and the conditions create an environment where a larger pool of players become potential champions of the event as opposed to Wimbledon or the US Open. Some of the greatest serve-and-volley and aggressive-style players have routinely left Paris defeated. Yannick Noah's ability to play an aggressive style of play and defeat the defensive clay court style of Mats Wilander in the 1983 French final still seems like a minor miracle.

More than half of the 23 players who were ranked No. 1 in the world rankings entering 2007 do not have a French Open title on their resume. This includes Boris Becker, who reached the semifinals three times, Pete Sampras, who only reached the semifinals on one occasion in 13 attempts, John McEnroe, who lost a painful final to Ivan Lendl in 1984 after a two-sets-to-love lead, and Stefan Edberg, who led Michael Chang two sets to one in the 1989 final before losing. Jimmy Connors, who was either denied entry or did not enter the tournament for many years, is also part of the group of all-time greats without a French title. Other notables on the list include John Newcombe, Arthur Ashe, Patrick Rafter, Marat Safin and Lleyton Hewitt.

Although Federer's professional career began with 11 straight defeats on clay courts, he never allowed himself to become discouraged. In France, where he experienced the least amount of success of the Grand Slam tournaments, Federer constantly made reference to the fact that he grew up on clay courts and that this was "his surface" too. He had after all won three titles on clay at the German Open in Hamburg and proved repeatedly in Davis Cup play that he could compete with anybody on clay courts. However, to date, he was unable to even advance as far as the semifinals at Roland Garros.

Federer may have arrived in Paris with a season's record of 41-2 but he expressed caution before his seventh French Open. "The first rounds here are always treachrous," he said in a modest tone that was sometimes missing from previous years. "I'm not thinking about winning this tournament." He arrived in Paris directly from Portugal and had the privilege of being able to practice every day on the Centre Court at Roland Garros—the Philippe Chatrier Court—where he suffered many of his most devastating losses as a professional. Federer's excellent pre-event preparation and the tutoring from the now 60-year-old Tony Roche paid off. He won the first five matches of the tournament without dropping a set to reach the semifinals for the first time in his career. "It's almost going a bit too quickly for me," he said of his relatively easy jaunt to the semifinals.

However, waiting for Federer in the semifinals was none other than Nadal—whom he faced for the first time on a clay court. The young Spaniard was full of self-confidence and entered the match with a 22-match win streak. Due to a rain delay, as well the five-set match between Argentinean Mariano Puerta and Russian Nikolay Davydenko in the other men's semifinal, Federer and Nadal did not take the court until 6:20 pm local time in Paris. Federer struggled from the start and was troubled—particularly off the forehand—by Nadal's extreme topspin. After losing four of the first five games, Federer surrendered the first set 6-3—his first lost set of the tournament—as he had his serve broken an incredible four times. He managed to win the second set 6-4, but remained unusually nervous and committed nearly twice as many mistakes as Nadal in the third set. Nadal led 4-2, before Federer broke back to square the set. After Nadal held in the ninth game of the third set, he clinched the third set—and a two-sets-to-one lead—with a cross-court running forehand winner. Darkness started to fall in Paris and Federer was irritated. He seemed to be in a rush and requested the match be suspended due to darkness. The chair umpire did not allow it. Federer was flustered and Nadal took control of the match as he broke Federer's serve in the eighth game to take a 5-3 lead and closed out the 6-3, 4-6, 6-4, 6-3 victory one game later. "I started the match off badly and ended it badly," Federer summarized. "I played well in between but all in all, that was not enough."

Like at the Australian Open when Federer was defeated by Safin in the wee hours of the morning of Safin's 25th birthday, Federer was again a birthday victim at a Grand Slam event. This Friday—June 3rd—was the 19th birthday of Nadal—and like Safin—he would go on to win the tournament. In an exciting final between two left-handed players, Nadal defeated Puerta, who, as it turned out months later, tested positive for performance-enhancing drugs and was suspended from professional tennis.

The more time Federer pondered the loss to Nadal, the more positives he drew from it. He proved to himself and others that he had what it takes to win the French Open, despite what he thought was his worst performance in the later stages of a Grand Slam tournament. He was convinced that this loss to Nadal would be a learning experience. He now believed he could win the French Open and achieve the rare career Grand Slam. Another positive to temper his mood was the fact that the French public took a liking to him and rallied behind him during his matches, most notably against Nadal. "It was fantastic how they supported me," he said. "It was almost like a victory for me because it's not easy to win the crowd in Paris."

Since Federer's semifinal showing was a vast improvement from his third-round loss the year before, his grip on the No. 1 ranking rose to a record 6,980 points—giving him almost twice as many points as the No. 2-ranked Hewitt. Federer nonetheless maneuvered himself into a startling situation. He only lost three matches during the year but he stood empty-handed in Grand Slam titles. If he were to fail at Wimbledon as well, the only opportunity for a title remaining would be the always unpredictable US Open. His statement from the previous fall that he would be satisfied in 2005 with just one Grand Slam title suddenly took on new importance.

CHAPTER 29
Three Men at the Champions Dinner

"Guess Who's Coming To Dinner" was the title above a portrait of Roger Federer on the cover of Wimbledon's 2005 official program. It was a cryptic way of avowing who the overwhelming favorite for the title was. Anything but a victory by Federer, and with it his invitation to dinner—the Champions Dinner—would be a surprise. After winning five tournaments and 29 consecutive matches on grass courts—including his pre-event tournament triumph again at Halle—Federer once again journeyed to England as the big favorite. As the two-time defending champion, there was a tremendous pressure for him to succeed, but this time, he was firmly determined to enjoy the tournament. When not on site, Federer sequestered himself at his apartment near Centre Court, where he huddled with his closest entourage. While Wimbledon was not on the original "Federer Schedule," Tony Roche traveled with his charge to England for the first time, accompanied with his wife. The two men continued to bond and Roche began to tutor Federer not only in tennis tactics, but the rules and protocols of Australia's national sport, cricket.

Federer, along with the defending women's champion Maria Sharapova, were issued special "golden shoes" for The Championships by Nike as a publicity/advertising stunt. The shoes complemented his style of play in his first two matches of the tournament, but in the third round, he ran into a lot of trouble against the German Nicolas Kiefer. Federer lost a second-set tie-break and trailed 3-5 in the fourth, but prevented a fifth set by winning the last four games of the match. After defeating Juan Carlos Ferrero and Fernando Gonzalez, he reached the semifinals, where he once again met up with Lleyton Hewitt. The Australian was just finding his form after being off the circuit for several months—first because of a foot operation and then because of broken ribs sustained when he fell down the stairs at home. Hewitt was still ranked

No. 2 in the world, but was controversially seeded No. 3 behind Roddick after the All England Club deemed that Roddick's grass court results were stronger than that of the 2002 Wimbledon champion. Hewitt stood little chance of victory against Federer and lost 6-3, 6-4, 7-6 (4). Federer was into the final for a third consecutive year, and for a second straight year, Roddick was his opponent in the final.

Roche had a long and somewhat disastrous history with anything that had to do with a Wimbledon final. In his six finals that he either played in or coached a player in, his record was 0-6. As a player, Roche lost the 1968 Wimbledon final to Rod Laver 6-3, 6-4, 6-2 in his lone Wimbledon singles final. In 1983, his pupil Chris Lewis went down meekly to John McEnroe. Ivan Lendl, who served and volleyed on Wimbledon's grass like a wooden puppet, hired Roche to help him achieve his Wimbledon dream. But the Czech was unable to win a set against Boris Becker in the 1986 final and against Pat Cash in the 1987 final. Roche then guided his countryman Patrick Rafter to a pair of Wimbledon finals, in 2000 when he lost a narrow four-set battle to Pete Sampras, and in 2001 when he lost an epic five-set final to Goran Ivanisevic. Roche hoped Federer would finally bring him good fortune during a Wimbledon final.

Federer unleashed a storm against Roddick at the start of the match—winning the first set in 22 minutes—a glaring difference to the previous year when the American dominated him from the start. In the second set, after the two players exchanged early breaks, Federer dominated the tie-break, taking it 7-2 to take a two-sets-to-love lead.

Although it was barely drizzling, Wimbledon officials ordered a suspension of play after the second set. Most of the spectators stayed in their seats, including Robert Federer, who watched his son play live in a Grand Slam final for the first time. While wife Lynette sat in the players' box alongside Roche and Mirka Vavrinec, Robert sat on the complete opposite side of Centre Court.

Robert Federer didn't have good memories of Wimbledon and it required courage for him to even venture to Centre Court to watch his son. His memories from his last visit to the All England Club in 2002 were still vivid—when he sat in the Players' Box and expected to see his son roll through an easy first-round win over Croatia's Mario Ancic. Instead, he witnessed "Rotschi" suffer one of the most bitter defeats of his career. Robert considered himself to be bad luck since then. His son finally convinced him to come. "Forget it! If I lose, then it certainly won't be because of you," Roger told him.

Robert Federer followed his son's first two Wimbledon victories at home in Switzerland. When British reporters caught up with him afterwards, he explained that somebody had to look after the family cat. In 2005, he decided to come to Wimbledon from the beginning as a test. Most British reporters sitting only a few meters away from him in the Centre Court stands did not recognize him behind his sun glasses. The *Sun* actually ran a story about him, but the man in the photo associated with the story was not even him, but Federer's physiotherapist Pavel Kovac.

Robert Federer was still nervous during the rain delay, even if his son's two-sets-to-love lead calmed his nerves. "Even the points that Roger loses he plays well," he said during the intermission. "I've always told him that he has to play aggressively and follow through with his strokes—anything else won't work."

Neither the short break—nor the supposed "jinx" presence of his father—could prevent Federer from winning his third Wimbledon title. After 101 minutes of play, an ace sealed his 6-2, 7-6 (2), 6-4 victory. He fell to the ground and, as before, the tears flowed. Federer became the eighth man in history—and only the third player since World War II—to win three-straight Wimbledon singles titles. The other two to turn the "hat trick" in the last 50 years were Björn Borg and Pete Sampras, but Federer resisted the comparisons. After all, the Swede won Wimbledon five straight years and Sampras won seven times in eight years. What Federer didn't say and perhaps wasn't even aware of was the fact that his achievement in winning his three Wimbledon titles was, in fact, more dominant than the first three titles won by both Borg and Sampras. Borg gave up nine sets in the process while Sampras surrendered 11 sets. Federer, by contrast, lost only four sets.

Federer was at a loss for words for his near perfect performance in the final. "I really played a fantastic match—one of my best in my life," he said. "I was playing flawless. Everything was working."

Of the 35 grass court tennis matches Andy Roddick played over the last three years, he only lost on three occasions. All three losses were to Roger

Federer. "His performance this year was clearly better than last year's," said Roddick after his third-straight Wimbledon loss to Federer. "If I had played as well as today last year I probably would have won."

For a third year in a row Federer was the indeed the answer to the question "Guess Who is Coming To Dinner?" His guests for the Wimbledon Champions Dinner were Tony Roche and Robert Federer. Both men beamed with pride. The Wimbledon victory was very important to them as well.

"To me, Wimbledon is the greatest tournament in the world," said Roche, happy that he stayed in Europe with Federer for the grass season. "Playing against such a great opponent as Roddick in a Wimbledon final and playing at the level that he did—it can't get any better than that. On a scale from one to 10, that was a 10."

The Wimbledon champion was glad that his father was able to be with him at this special moment.

"He still gets upset if I miss a backhand or a forehand," he said to journalists the morning after his victory. "But I've learned to deal with this in the meantime because I know that he doesn't know as much about tennis as I used to think."

CHAPTER 30
An Evening in Flushing Meadows

For the first time, Roger Federer returned directly to his hometown of Basel after winning a Grand Slam tournament. A reception and ceremony was organized by the city in Basel's market square to welcome the new three-time Wimbledon champion. Federer was overwhelmed by the mass of fans and countrymen waiting for him. Thousands of people filled the picturesque square—a scene usually reserved for celebrations for Basel's soccer team. Federer stood on a small balcony of the city hall overlooking the square and waved to the crowd. "This is for you!" he shouted, pointing to the third replica Wimbledon trophy he now possessed.

Before yet another vacation to Dubai, Federer visited the doctor to have his feet examined. Despite his brilliant performance at Wimbledon, his feet troubled him. A magnetic resonance image was taken. The doctor advised Federer to skip the Tennis Masters Series event in Canada—where he was the defending champion. Even though his trip to Dubai was mostly for pleasure, he was soon joined by his fitness trainer Pierre Paganini and Tony Roche.

After almost a month and a half, Federer returned to tournament tennis in Cincinnati. His lead in the world rankings decreased by over 1,000 points. His main contender was no longer Lleyton Hewitt but now Rafael Nadal. During Federer's hiatus, the Spaniard won clay court tournaments in Bastad, Sweden and Stuttgart, Germany as well his first tournament title on a hard court in Montreal, defeating Andre Agassi in the final. Nadal was now the match-win leader on the ATP Tour with 65 victories, next to Federer's 58.

The Tennis Masters Series event Cincinnati was a tournament where Federer did not have a history of success. In his previous four appearances, Federer won only one match. The 2005 tournament would be a different story. He reached the final, where he faced Roddick yet again. And yet again,

Federer defeated his American rival 7-5, 6-3 for the title. The win created another milestone—Federer became the first player to win four Masters Series tournaments in a calendar year—to go with his titles in Indian Wells, Key Biscayne and Hamburg. Federer resumed his winning ways as the US Open in New York approached.

In the early rounds of the US Open, major surprise upsets narrowed the list of Federer's rivals for the title. Gilles Muller, a relatively unheralded player from the tiny nation of Luxembourg, shockingly defeated Roddick in the first round. Two rounds later Federer's other major rival, Rafael Nadal, also went down to defeat by the hands of James Blake of the United States. Federer, meanwhile, cruised through the draw. His straight-sets quarterfinal thrashing of David Nalbandian not only avenged his loss to the Argentine at the 2003 US Open, but placed him into the semifinals of his fourth Grand Slam tournament of the year—a feat only achieved in the Open Era of professional tennis by Rod Laver, Ivan Lendl and, ironically, Roche.

In the semifinals, Federer faced Hewitt in a rematch of the final 12 months earlier, while Agassi met fellow American Robby Ginepri. Most insiders expected that the all-American battle would be the second scheduled semifinal match on "Super Saturday" to take advantage of the larger television audience in the United States later in the afternoon. However, the 35-year-old Agassi, perhaps looking ahead to the Sunday final and receiving precious extra hours of recovery time, requested and received the earlier start time. Agassi and Ginepri battled for five sets, before the elder American advanced into his sixth US Open singles final. Federer struggled with a feisty Hewitt before prevailing in four sets. Federer immediately fixed his eyes on an ultimate final-round confrontation with Agassi. "This will be a highlight of my career," he said.

There was definitely something in the air in the late afternoon of Sunday, September 11, 2005 at Flushing Meadows. Spectators enthusiastically streamed into the 58-meter high Arthur Ashe Stadium, the largest tennis arena in the world. With a seating capacity of 23,352—and every last seat filled for this epic men's singles final—it seemed more imposing than usual. Television cameras captured many famous faces in the crowd—Robin Williams, Dustin Hoffman, Lance Armstrong, Donald Trump—none of them wanted to miss the battle of the titans. American flags fluttered in the wind and a giant flag was drawn over the court. It was the fourth anniversary of the September 11 attacks on the Twin Towers in Manhattan, amplifying the patriotic fervor. It was a perfect setting for Agassi to steal an unlikely victory.

"It can't get better for me," said Agassi to the CBS-TV after saying good-bye to his children and striding, confident of victory, into the arena for the final. It was nearly five o'clock, the sun was already settling low, shadows fell over the court. Floodlights soon illuminated the scene.

Federer must have felt like a slave in the Roman Coliseum who was about to be fed to the lions. The man from Basel, however, did not accept this role. He took control of the match from the beginning, taking a 5-2 lead, dampening the frenzied atmosphere. After Agassi fought off seven set points, Federer was able to put the first set in the books at 6-3. However, Agassi's fight at the end of the set showed his vigor, fight and determination. The match suddenly turned as Agassi jumped to a 3-0 lead in the second set and held on to tie the match with a 6-2 second-set victory. It was the most decisive set Federer lost all summer. High above in the TV commentators box, John McEnroe said, "Agassi couldn't be playing better." Agassi then bolted to a 4-2, 30-0 lead in the third set and seemed to gather all the momentum he needed to take him to his first Grand Slam tournament title in almost three years. Agassi's victory seemed just over the horizon, but Federer stopped the Agassi surge by breaking back to 4-3. After Agassi fought off four break points in the 11th game of the set, the two legends entered a pivotal tie-break to determine which player would take the important two-sets-to-one lead. After the players split the first two points, the situation became grim for Agassi. Federer rolled through six straight points to take the tie-break 7-1. The preverbal gas was let out of Agassi's balloon and in a matter of minutes, the scoreboard illuminated the final score of 6-3, 2-6, 7-6 (1), 6-1 in favor of Federer.

Following the match, Agassi had the highest of praise for Federer, calling him best player he ever faced. "Pete (Sampras) was great, no question," Agassi said. "But there was a place to get to with Pete. It could be on your terms. There's no such place with Roger. I think he's the best I've played against." Said Federer of Agassi's comments, "It's fantastic to be compared to all the players he's played throughout his career. We're talking about the best—some are the best of all time. And I still have chances to improve."

Federer, fighting off the partisan crowd and a determined and inspired Agassi, said he felt the match was lost in the third set. "I'm amazed that I did it and that it's already over," he said just after the match. "Agassi was like the fish that had gotten away from me." Next to Martina Navratilova, Agassi was the only living-legend still active on the tour. "Playing against him while I am at the peak of my career and his is coming to a close, in New York of all places, and in the final of the US Open—that was probably the most important match in my life."

Federer was not resentful—or surprised—of the biased crowd that cheered so vociferously for Agassi. "I was prepared for the worst but it was harder than I expected," he said of the crowd. "I hoped that there would have been more applause when I made good shots, but I understand the crowd. The stars were in the right alignment for Agassi to potentially end his career like Sampras or Ivanisevic by winning a Grand Slam title."

Now with six Grand Slam titles, Federer equaled the major title tally of his childhood idols Boris Becker and Stefan Edberg. He was just the third player to win at Wimbledon and the U.S. Championships two years in a row following the Americans Bill Tilden from 1920 and 1921 and Don Budge from 1937 and 1938. He was also the first player in 72 years to win all six of his first appearances in Grand Slam finals—becoming only the fifth player of all-time to go 6-0 in Grand Slam finals. The American Richard Sears and the Briton William Renshaw achieved the feat in the late 1800s, but in an era when the defending champion of an event only played the championship match as the "holder" of the event. The celebrated New Zealander, Tony Wilding, was also part of this select group, but he only defeated a total of three opponents for his three Wimbledon victories between 1911 and 1913, while Australia's John Herbert "Jack" Crawford of Australia, who was one set from winning the Grand Slam in 1933, rounded out the elite group of five that now included the man from Switzerland.

Federer celebrated his win with a good meal with a glass of wine at the Peninsula Hotel in Manhattan. Over dinner, Federer reviewed his road to victory in Flushing and remained as excited and full of adrenaline as if he was still playing in the final with Agassi. As with most of his successes, Federer was unable to sleep the night after his victory. He read the newspapers at five in the morning and watched the morning's television highlights of his final-round victory. He was in no hurry to leave New York. As in 2004, Federer made the rounds with the American media the day after his victory. However, the morning shows were excluded from the tour so he could sleep in a bit. He no longer needed to accept all the invitations for the American TV stations. Even the famed David Letterman had to wait his turn.

CHAPTER 31
The Savior of Shanghai

With the Grand Slam season of 2005 behind him, Roger Federer now focused on achieving his goals for the remainder of the calendar year. He wanted to play Davis Cup for Switzerland and help his homeland stay in the elite 16-team Davis Cup World Group and also protect his No. 1 ranking. He also wanted to defend his title in Bangkok, finally win the title in his hometown of Basel and, for the third year in a row, end the year with a victory at the Tennis Masters Cup. While he was at it, why not win titles in Madrid or in Paris at the Bercy tournament for the first time?

Federer's plan got off to a good start, beginning with the Davis Cup. He rejoined the Swiss team for its Play-off Round match against Great Britain in Geneva. Federer easily defeated Alan Mackin in the opening singles match, and after he and Yves Allegro defeated Andy Murray and Greg Rusedski in four sets in the doubles, Switzerland clinched the victory that allowed the nation to remain in the Davis Cup World Group for a 12th straight year. Federer encountered Murray, the talented Scottish teenager, one week later in the singles final in Bangkok, when he won his 24th straight match in a singles final. The win in Bangkok clinched the year-end No. 1 for Federer, giving him the distinction of being ranked No. 1 in the world for every week of the 2005 season—a feat only achieved by four other players (Jimmy Connors, Ivan Lendl, Pete Sampras and Lleyton Hewitt.) As a reward, he and girlfriend Mirka Vavrinec treated themselves to a few days of vacation in Bangkok where they toured temples and Buddha statues and enjoyed the Thai cuisine.

If not for Federer, Rafael Nadal was the clear cut No. 1 player for the 2005 season. The Spanish teenager won an astounding 11 tournaments, including the French Open and the Tennis Masters Series events in Monte Carlo, Rome,

Montreal and Madrid. Nadal's point total for the season ranked higher than four of the last five year-end No. 1 ranked players—Gustavo Kuerten (2000), Lleyton Hewitt (2001, 2002) and Andy Roddick (2003). In the era of Federer, this was only good enough for second place.

In October 11, Federer was in Allschwil, Switzerland training with countryman Michael Lammer, when he was once again struck by the "Curse of Basel." At the same facility where he suffered a muscle tear the previous year, Federer injured his right ankle. He felt a searing pain and fell to the court and could not get back up. "At first I thought I had broken something," he explained. The diagnosis was not that bad, but it was bad enough. Federer tore ligaments in his ankle and while surgery was not required, it forced him to withdraw from the events in Madrid, Basel and Paris. It was debatable if there was enough time for him to recover to play in the year-end Tennis Masters Cup in Shanghai in a month's time.

Federer's foot was in a cast and he was on crutches for two weeks. He did everything he could to accelerate the therapy to enable him to play in Shanghai. He underwent ultrasound, lymph drainage, massages, elevated the legs, special exercises—everything. To his benefit, he was not the only top player who was injured as the top 10 rankings at the time read more like a list of casualties. Three former Grand Slam tournament champions withdrew from Shanghai—Marat Safin was out with a bad left knee and Andy Roddick withdrew with a bad back. Lleyton Hewitt chose not to compete in Shanghai so he could spend time with his new wife, Bec Cartwright, who was expecting the couple's first child.

A fourth former Grand Slam tournament winner, Andre Agassi, arrived in China still gimpy after injuring ligaments in his left ankle around the same time as Federer's injury. After losing in his first round-robin match to Nikolay Davydenko 6-4, 6-2, Agassi also withdrew from the event. Since he won the tournament in Madrid in October, Nadal was troubled with a left-foot injury that caused him to withdraw from the events in Basel and Paris. Although he was in China with the expectation of competing, he also withdrew from the tournament just before his first scheduled match. Within a matter of hours, the tournament lost two of its most popular draws—Agassi and Nadal—and

Federer's start was still doubtful as well. The two-time defending champion arrived in Shanghai early to prepare, but he still didn't know until two days before the event began whether he would compete at all.

The typhoon-proof stadium in Shanghai was nearly sold out—but for the ambitious Chinese organizers—the situation was far worse than a typhoon. After a highly successful staging of the 2002 Tennis Masters Cup in Shanghai, Chinese officials were able to lure the event back to their country for three years starting in 2005. During the two-year stint of the tournament in Houston, the Chinese built the magnificent Qi Zhong Stadium that seats 15,000 spectators in the Minhang district in southwestern Shanghai. The facility features a retractable roof that is shaped like a blooming magnolia—the city's emblem. It is an eight-ton structure with eight retractable pieces that open and close. Since eight is Federer's favorite number—because his birthday is on the eighth day of the eighth month—it made for a special connection between him and the tournament. Shanghai was also special for Federer since it was the site of his Tennis Masters Cup debut in 2002—and the memories were still fond. He even made an extra trip to take part of the official opening in the stadium in early October.

Federer's injury was definitely the most serious of his career to date. While he was healthy enough to play in the tournament, his expectations were low. He did not properly prepare for the event and did not rule out the possibility of losing all three of his round-robin matches.

In his opening match, Federer surprised himself when he was able to defeat David Nalbandian 6-3, 2-6, 6-4. He described the victory as one of the finest wins of his career, which gave some indication how ill-prepared for the tournament he actually felt.

Federer's next match with Ivan Ljubicic became a high-point of the tournament. Ljubicic was regarded as a threat to win the title after posting the best indoor record of any player during the year. After Federer gave fans—and organizers—a scare when he called for a trainer to treat him on court before the third set, he saved three match points before prevailing in a 7-4 final-set tie-break. The win clinched Federer's spot in the semifinals as the winner of his group.

In the semifinals, Federer registered an incredible 6-0, 6-0 thrashing of Gaston Gaudio of Argentina that not only moved him into the Tennis Masters Cup final for a third straight year, but gave him an 81-3 record for the year. He was within one match victory of tying John McEnroe's record for the best won-loss record in the history of men's tennis. In 1984, McEnroe won both the US Open and Wimbledon and achieved a record of 82-3. Nalbandian, whom Federer defeated in his opening round-robin match, was the only barrier that stood in his way of tying this important record. However, unlike round-robin play, the final was a best-of-five set affair, making the achievement that much more difficult for the out-of-match-practice Federer. Tie-breaks decided the first two sets, with Federer winning a first-set tie-break 7-4 and a second-set tie-break 13-11. With two hours of arduous tennis needed to take the two-sets-to-love lead, Federer began to look weary in the early stages of the third set. Nalbandian took advantage and crawled back into the match. During a stretch in the fourth and fifth sets, Federer lost 10 straight games to trail 0-4 in the fifth set. At 0-30 in the fifth game of the final set, Federer, perhaps motivated by chants of "Roger! Roger!" as well as by his own will and pride, began to rally back into the match. Forty-five minutes later, he was just two points from victory serving for the match at 6-5, 30-0. Nalbandian, however, turned the tide again. Federer would later say, "I wasn't playing to win any longer but just to make it as hard as possible for him."

After breaking Federer back to force the final-set tie-break, Nalbandian rallied to win the match 6-7 (4), 6-7(11), 6-2, 6-1, 7-6 (3). Federer watched Nalbandian sink to the ground after the greatest victory of his career and as the first Argentinean Masters champion in 31 years. "I came closer to winning the tournament than I had thought," said Federer. "Under these circumstances, this was one of the best performances of my career. This tournament was probably the most emotional one for me this year."

Whether satisfied with his effort or not, the loss, nonetheless, meant the end of several of Federer's streaks. It was his first defeat since the semifinals of the French Open in early June—a streak of 35 matches and the fifth-longest match winning streak in ATP history. (Nalbandian's countryman Guillermo Vilas is the record-holder with 46 straight victories). The loss also marked his first defeat in a tournament final since July of 2003—a streak of 24 straight final-round matches. Although he only lost four matches, he ranked his 2005 season worse than 2004, since two of his four defeats happened at Grand Slam tournaments. "But this season was unbelievable as well," he said. "At some stages, I felt invincible."

Thanks to the star power of Federer, the Tennis Masters Cup was not a complete disaster for the Chinese promoters. The fledgling tennis movement in Asia continued. A few months later, the ATP renewed its contract for Shanghai to assume organization for the Masters through 2008. "If the tournament had been damaged by the many forfeits, then it was compensated for by one of the most exciting matches of the year," the *Shanghai Daily* wrote the day after the epic Federer-Nalbandian final. John McEnroe was also satisfied. "It was nice to see how hard Federer fought to break my record," McEnroe said. "Perhaps people will now realize that it's not so easy to achieve a record of 82-3."

CHAPTER 32
Chasing Ghosts

Rod Laver is such a modest person that people tend to overlook him. Even the organizers of the Australian Open didn't come up with and implement the idea of re-naming their Centre Court the Rod Laver Arena until 2000—twelve years after the opening of the facility.

Laver is still the only man to win the Grand Slam twice—in 1962 as an amateur and again in 1969 in the Open Era open to amateurs and professionals. The short, red-haired left-hander is considered by fellow tennis players to be a epitome of a tennis legend. However, when asked how Roger Federer compares to him, in typical modest fashion, Laver said, "I would be honored just to be compared with Roger. Roger could become the greatest tennis player of all time."

The "Rockhampton Rocket" went even further in an interview before the Australian Open in 2006 when he stated, "I firmly believe that Roger is capable of winning the Grand Slam this season. He is such a wonderful player and has such unbelievable talent...Of all the players who I have seen since winning the Grand Slam, he is probably the only one that has the talent to do it."

To Laver and most followers of the sport, winning the Grand Slam in the modern day game carries much more value than it did in Laver's time. "The demands are much greater now than back when I was playing," Laver said. "The opponents are stronger and quicker and the racquets allow balls to be hit with incredible power. We just had wood racquets. There are also so many more young talented players on the tour now that have no fear of the top players." While Laver's comments where well-intended, they did, however, have a boomerang effect of Federer. They increased the already heavy pressure weighing upon him as the 2006 season began.

As was the case at the Tennis Masters Cup in China, injuries affected the first Grand Slam tournament of the year in Melbourne. Defending champion Marat Safin was not in the field. Rafael Nadal and Andre Agassi also were not fully recovered from their injuries to make the trip "Down Under." Federer, by contrast, recovered from his torn ligaments even if the right foot was still somewhat stiff and he wore a support bandage as a precaution. With Safin, Nadal and Agassi out of the field, Federer was more clearly favored than any player if the bookies' odds were any indication. Whoever bet on Federer to win the event would only receive 1-5 odds.

Federer rolled through his first three matches with the form of the over-whelming favorite—surrendering only 22 games in three straight-set victories. But he ran into difficulties in the round of 16 against a difficult opponent—Tommy Haas—who beat him previously in the same round at the Australian Open in 2002 and who beat him in the semifinals of the Olympics—also in Australia. After winning the first two sets decisively, Federer lost the third set and soon found himself in a five-set struggle. Federer, however, came through in the clutch to win 6-4, 6-0, 3-6, 4-6, 6-2—his first five-set win at the Australian Open. In the quarterfinals, Federer again encountered more difficulties than usual against Russia's Nikolay Davydenko. He fought off five set points in the third set—that would have had him trail two-sets-to-one—before registering the 6-4, 3-6, 7-6 (7), 7-6 (5) victory. Nicolas Kiefer offered some initial stiff resistance in the semifinals, but after two sets of drama, Federer advanced into the Australian Open final for a second time with a 5-7, 7-5, 6-0, 6-2 win.

In his six matches en route to the final, Federer lost four sets—more than previously surrendered while reaching a Grand Slam final. The man from Basel, however, was still the overwhelming favorite to win the title when he faced unseeded upstart Marcos Baghdatis—a 200-1 outsider to win the title. The 20-year-old bearded maverick from the island of Cyprus was the major story of the tournament—defeating Andy Roddick, Ivan Ljubicic and David Nalbandian in succession to become an unlikely Grand Slam finalist. Cyprus, a small island nation off the Greek and Turkish coast in the Mediterranean with no tennis history whatsoever, was suddenly stricken with tennis fever as businesses closed and children skipped school to watch his matches. Baghdatis was unseeded, ranked No. 54 in the world and had never won an ATP tournament in his career at the time. To boot, he held an 0-3 record against Federer and Federer had never lost a Grand Slam final—let alone to an unseeded player.

The *Melbourne Age* newspaper carried the headline "The Wizard And The Apprentice" before the final, but as the match began, the question was which was which. Baghdatis, supported throughout the fortnight by the many Greeks in Melbourne who created a soccer-stadium atmosphere with chants, cheers and flag-waving, continued to play boldly, aggressively and on the offensive—as he had the entire tournament—while Federer struggled, particularly off the forehand side. Federer lost the first set 7-5 and saved two break points to prevent a double-service-break 0-3 deficit in the second set. After he held serve, Federer then broke the Cypriot's serve in the next game to square the set at 2-2. After the two players exchanged service holds, a stroke of good luck benefited Federer late in the set as an overruled call on set point gave Federer the second set 7-5. The momentum immediately turned in Federer's favor and the challenge to his supremacy ended. Federer's 5-7, 7-5, 6-0, 6-2 victory secured him his seventh Grand Slam title—tying him with such legends as Richard Sears and William Renshaw—heroes of the 1880s—as well as John McEnroe, John Newcombe, Mats Wilander and two of four French Musketeers, Rene Lacoste and Henri Cochet.

Federer showed no exuberance as the award ceremony began, but when Rod Laver bestowed the Norman Brookes Trophy upon him, he was overcome with emotions. "I don't know what to say," he said at the start of his victory speech, before he fell silent. He barely managed to congratulate Baghdatis and thank his entourage and sponsors. When he mentioned Laver and that the title meant a great deal to him, his voice cracked, just like at his first Wimbledon victory, and he could no longer hold back his tears.

"I was terribly nervous," Federer told Swiss television commentator Heinz Günthardt after he left the court. "It was an immense burden to be so clearly favored against a newcomer." With seven Grand Slam titles, Federer began to compete not only against his contemporaries on the other side of the net, but against the ghosts of tennis history, including Pete Sampras and Rod Laver, who was standing next to him on this day.

CHAPTER 33
A Rivalry Is Born

Following his victory in Melbourne in January of 2006, it was clear to Roger Federer that he had to do everything in his power so that he could be in top form for Paris. A victory at Roland Garros would give him the distinction of being the first player to hold all four Grand Slam titles since Rod Laver in 1969. It would be a "Roger Slam"—a phrase borrowed from the "Serena Slam" coined when Serena Williams held all four Grand Slam tournament titles during an impressive run in 2002 and 2003. "That would be as valuable to me as the real Grand Slam," said Tony Roche, an aficionado of tennis history. "I don't want to denigrate Rod Laver's and Don Budge's accomplishments who were the only men to manage the Grand Slam, but you can't forget that three of these tournaments were played on grass back then." Only one player won the four great titles of tennis when played on four different court surfaces—Andre Agassi.

Federer took a break in February and, like the year before, didn't participate in the Davis Cup first round so he could concentrate solely on condition training and carefully plan his competitions and his rest and recovery periods. The tournament titles continued to pile up. After losing to No. 2-ranked Rafael Nadal on a hard court in Dubai, Federer won the Tennis Masters Series events in Indian Wells for a third year in a row and again in Key Biscayne for the second consecutive year. The clay court season also began with promise as he reached the final of the Monte Carlo Open for the first time in his career, only to lose to Nadal in a tight four-set struggle 6-2, 6-7 (2), 6-3, 7-6 (5). A few weeks later, the two met again in the final of Rome, where the No. 1 and No. 2 players played in one of the best matches of the 2006 season. Federer led 4-1 in the fifth set and botched two match points at 6-5 in the fifth set before losing in a five-hour-and-six-minute struggle 6-7(0), 7-6 (5), 6-4,

2-6, 7-6 (5). The match not only proved that Federer was catching up to the clay court prowess of Nadal, but also firmly cemented the rivalry between Federer-Nadal as one of the best in global sports.

During the dramatic Rome final, journalists sitting in the media grandstand overheard Federer shout some unusual words to the players' box. "Everything all right, Tony?" Had his almost 61-year-old coach Tony Roche taken ill during the match? No. Federer later explained that he was not speaking to Tony Roche but Nadal's uncle and coach Toni. He said he was angry that "Uncle Toni" was allegedly giving illegal coaching to his nephew—an incident that Federer said he noticed against Nadal in the Dubai and Monte Carlo finals earlier in the year. Federer also shared his displeasure over the alleged illegal coaching with ATP officials. Federer said ATP officials should not just sit there and enjoy the tennis, but they should make sure that rules are followed. "You can otherwise just throw the rule book away," he said.

Federer's intervention during the match did not escape Nadal. They shook hands coldly after the match. Their relationship became strained for the first time. Back on Mallorca following the final, Nadal accused Federer of being a sore loser during an interview with Spanish press. "He has to learn to be a gentleman even when he loses," Nadal stated. Although both athletes skipped the tournament in Hamburg following the marathon match in Rome, their paths crossed once again a few days later. At the Laureus Awards ceremony in Barcelona, Federer was chosen again as the "Sportsman of the Year" and Nadal was honored as "Newcomer of the Year."

"We sat at the same table with the Princess of Spain between us and we noticed that it wasn't such a big deal," Federer said. "Everything had blown over by the time we were in Paris."

At Roland Garros, Federer effortlessly reached the semifinals—losing only one set in the process to Nicolas Massu of Chile in the third round. David Nalbandian, Federer's former nemesis, waited in the semifinals and after only 39 minutes of play, the Argentine surprisingly lead 6-4, 3-0. Nalbandian, however, was troubled by a stomach injury and as the match progressed, it became too much to bear. With the score knotted at one set a piece and Federer leading 5-2 in the third set, Nalbandian was forced to retire from the match.

It seemed as though 2006 was Federer's year. He was one match away from the "Roger Slam" but once again, Nadal waited in the final. The Spaniard entered the final having won his last 59 matches on clay courts—his first-round win over Sweden's Robin Soderling broke the all-time clay court streak of 53 matches set by Guillermo Vilas in 1977.

Federer, however, was convinced he could beat him. He and Tony Roche analyzed the left-hander's game and pondered his tactics. In contrast to right-handed players, Nadal had a completely different range distribution. He covered his left half of the court much better than most players and he was able to more consistently work on Federer's weaker backhand side with his forehand.

The final was one of the most highly-anticipated matches in memory. Black market prices for the final reached four digit figures in euros. The media outdid itself with previews and headlines—"Prince against the Pirate" ran the headlines of the British *Independent on Sunday*. Former French heavyweight boxing champion Jean-Claude Bouttier said the final reminded him of one of the greatest fights in boxing history. "A stylist is meeting a puncher at this match," he said. "Nadal is Marvin Hagler. Federer is Sugar Ray Leonard."

The match began fantastically for Federer. Carried by a wave of sympathy from the spectators accorded the No. 1-seeded "underdog," he won the first set 6-1 on the hot afternoon with temperatures hovering near 90 degrees Fahrenheit. The turning point in the match, however, came quickly and brutally. At 0-1 in the second set and after leading 40-0 on his serve, Federer missed an easy volley at the net to lose his serve and go down an early break in the second set. His tremendous momentum was lost. Months later, Federer said that this moment "broke his neck." While Federer fell apart, Nadal got his second wind and rallied for the 1-6, 6-1, 6-4, 7-6 (4) victory. It was Federer's first loss in a Grand Slam final.

Even months later, Federer could not say exactly what happened during the three-hour final. "I wasn't nervous," he said. "To the contrary, I was even astonished at how cool I was. The fact that I wasn't able to pull it off had to do with Nadal. He was impressive coming back after the first set." Was there something he would do differently if he could play this final again? "Yes. I would have changed my game after the first set even though I was winning," he said. "I should have stood farther up, played more aggressively and I needed to try to put more pressure on him."

Although he reached the final of every tournament he played to date in 2006, there was now an unmistakable blemish on this record. His four losses in 2006 were all to Nadal and all in finals. His first loss was on the hard courts of Dubai, with the next three coming on clay in the finals of Monte Carlo, Rome and Paris. In the meantime, his career record against Nadal was 1-6, with his lone victory being achieved after coming back from a two-sets-to-love deficit in the Key Biscayne final in 2005. Nadal, however, was cautious to not lay claim to the No. 1 ranking. "I can't say that I'm better than Roger because that wouldn't be true," he said in Paris.

The comforts of the grass courts of Wimbledon—still considered Federer's realm—followed the disappointment of Paris. Federer thought of something special for this year at the All England Club and showed up for his opening round match against Richard Gasquet on Centre Court with a bit of flair. He sported a classy custom tailored white jacket with an emblem embroidered on the left breast pocket displaying a stylized "F" for Federer, three racquets symbolizing his three Wimbledon titles, a Swiss Cross representing his country of origin, a lion for his zodiac sign, a bushel of grass for the grass season, and his name.

Federer's 6-3, 6-2, 6-2 victory over the talented Frenchman was surprising in its ease and lack of drama, but not in the final result. The victory was Federer's 42nd consecutive win on grass and breaking the all-time grass court record held by Björn Borg, who won 41 straight matches from 1976 to 1981. In humble fashion, Federer gave more credit to Borg's streak since all of his matches were won at Wimbledon. "The five Wimbledons and the sixth final is something beyond all possibilities for any player," said Federer, who nearly had his grass court streak end two weeks earlier in Halle, fighting off four match points against Olivier Rochus of Belgium.

Federer had no trouble reaching his fourth straight Wimbledon final and his fifth straight Grand Slam tournament final. For the first time in his career, he reached a Grand Slam final without losing a set. And for the first time in 54 years, the Wimbledon men's final was a rematch of the French Open final of the same year as Nadal also bullied his way into the final. The Spaniard only managed to win three matches in his three previous Wimbledon appearances, but played with more vigor, fight and confidence than previous years. In the second round, he rallied from a two-sets-to-love deficit to beat American qualifier Robert Kendrick 6-7 (4), 3-6, 7-6 (2), 7-5, 6-4 and then ended the Wimbledon career of Andre Agassi in the third round. A straight-sets win in the semifinals over the upstart Cypriot Marcos Baghdatis gave Nadal the distinction of being the second Spanish man to reach the Wimbledon final—joining 1966 Wimbledon Champion Manolo Santana.

But any and all statistics were of secondary importance on July 9, 2006. Although Federer couldn't be overtaken in the world rankings, another defeat at the hands of Nadal would deprive him of feeling that he could still claim to be No. 1 in the world. He just fought for the "Roger Slam" in Paris and now he was just one defeat away from losing his mystique as the world's best player.

The fifth meeting between Federer and Nadal for the 2006 season began just like the one in Paris. Federer dominated the first set—blanking Nadal with a 6-0 set, but he then lost his first service game of the second set. Wimbledon, however, was not Paris and the Swiss fought his way back in the set, breaking back for 5-5 before the two settled into a second-set tie-break. After trailing 1-3 in the tie-break, Federer took a comfortable two-sets-to-love lead winning the second-set tie-break 7-5. Nadal did not go away and persisted and won the third-set tie-break. He could smell his opportunity.

After a rain delay, Federer returned to Centre Court and gave a stunning performance, streaking to a 5-1 lead in the fourth set before holding on to close out the fourth set—and the match—6-3. Clinching his fourth straight Wimbledon title, Federer did not sink to the ground and seemed more composed than the previous three years. His satisfaction and relief, however, were immense. "This was overall my best Grand Slam tournament," he said. His third-set loss to Nadal in the final was the only set he lost during the fortnight. He lost only four service games in his seven matches. Nobody since Björn Borg, who won Wimbledon in 1976 without losing a set, prevailed so supremely at The Championships.

Federer once again proved his mental toughness in addition to his competitive mettle. "I was aware of the importance of the match," he stated. "If

Nadal won, he would have been the first player since Borg to have won both Paris and Wimbledon in the same year. I was very relaxed during the match because I was playing so well. I said to myself: 'He's beaten me a few times already but that was on his surface; that shouldn't affect our matches on grass or hard-courts. One shouldn't be discouraged by defeats.'"

Federer accepted the Wimbledon trophy with his white jacket and proudly displayed it, along with his favorite gold cup, during his victory lap around Centre Court. The jacket served its purpose and was then retired to the Wimbledon Museum. The man from Basel was just the third player since World War I to win Wimbledon for a fourth consecutive time—joining Borg and Pete Sampras.

Two weeks vacation in Dubai followed his virtuoso performance at the All England Club, but preparations for the summer hard court season began soon at the tail end of his trip to the Persian Gulf. His return to the ATP Tour didn't go quite so smoothly as his efforts at Wimbledon, but he still managed to win the Tennis Masters Series event in Toronto, but lost four sets en route to his ninth consecutive title in a North American event.

The following week in Cincinnati, much to the delight of British journalists, Federer suffered only his fifth defeat of the season when he was upset in the second round by the upstart British player Andy Murray. The British writers—desperate for their nation to have a Grand Slam-worthy champion—followed every move of the young Scot and were convinced that his win over Federer was a major career development in their man's potential destiny of becoming the first British man to win a Grand Slam title since Fred Perry in the 1930s.

The loss to Murray ended two significant streaks. It was Federer's first defeat in North America after 55 triumphs in two years and for the first time in 14 months and 17 tournaments, Federer failed to reach a singles final. The early-round upset loss, however, did not shake his confidence as the 2006 US Open approached.

CHAPTER 34

Two New Friends: Woods and Sampras

When Tiger Woods achieved the "Tiger Slam" in 2000 and 2001—winning all four of golf's major championships in a row—Roger Federer was not yet 20 years old. The way that Woods dominated golf and reignited interest in the sport certainly caught the attention of the young Federer. However, he never thought that he would ever be compared to someone as dominant as Woods. "His story is completely different from mine," he said in the spring of 2006. "Even as a kid his goal was to break the record for winning the most majors. I was just dreaming of just once meeting Boris Becker or being able to play at Wimbledon some time."

Despite their different developments and the differences between their sports, the commonalities between Woods and Federer became unmistakable through the years. Like the four-time Masters champion, Federer is in full pursuit of sports history. While Woods is pursuing Jack Nicklaus and his 18 major championships, Federer is chasing Pete Sampras and his 14 Grand Slam singles titles. Both Woods and Federer are amazing because of their mental resilience, which is evident from the fact that they manage to make the most terrific shots under the greatest of difficulties.

Unlike his parents, Roger Federer is not a passionate golfer, but he follows Woods' career with great interest. "It would be interesting to meet him and to see what he's like in person," Federer said in Key Biscayne in 2006.

Both Federer and Woods are clients of the International Management Group (IMG) and Federer's agent, Tony Godsick, is friends with Mark Steinberg, the agent of Woods. In the summer of 2006, Federer asked Godsick if he could arrange a meeting with Woods. "The next thing I heard was that Woods would be delighted to come to the US Open final," Federer recollected. "At that time the tournament hadn't even started. I would have preferred meeting him in a more relaxed atmosphere than on the day of the US Open final—and I still had to get there first."

The public had no idea that a spectacular meeting was in the making behind the scenes at the US Open. After Federer defeated the Russian Nikolay Davydenko in the semifinals, he was informed that Woods was going to make good on his promise. He flew to New York from Florida on his private jet with his wife, Elin, to watch the US Open final in person. To everyone's surprise, Woods took a seat in Federer's guest box—which was quite noteworthy given the fact that Federer faced an American, Andy Roddick, in the final. "The fact that Tiger was sitting there put me under extra pressure," Federer later admitted. "It was just like when I was younger when my parents or Marc Rosset watched me play in person. You want to play especially well."

Woods' timing was perfect. He watched and cheered as Federer won his third straight US Open title, defeating the resurgent Roddick 6-2, 4-6, 7-5, 6-1. For the third year in a row, Federer won both Wimbledon and the US Open—a record that he didn't have to share with anyone.

While Federer briefly met Woods before the final, the two spent well over an hour together in the locker room following the match, drinking Champagne and gazing at the US Open trophy that Federer just won. Woods even talked on the phone to Federer's parents who were at home in bed as it was nearly three in the morning in Switzerland.

"I was impressed by how much we had in common," Federer explained when Woods was on his way back to Florida. "He knew exactly what I was going through and I see what he has to go through. I've never spoken with anybody who was so familiar with the feeling of being invincible."

"It was terrific for me to see him go into my player's box, shake his fist, and enjoy himself," he recollected a few weeks later. "He was the loudest one in my box. I was surprised how loose he was about it. He was happy as a kid to be able to watch the final. I think we'll do things together more often."

The appearance of Woods at the 2006 US Open final sparked more comparisons—and debates—between the two "athletes of the century" as to who was greater and more dominant. With all due respect to Woods, James Blake came out in favor of Federer. "In tennis, it's a tournament where you have one bad day and you're out," said Blake. "That's what we do every single week. Roger is winning every Grand Slam except for the French, winning every Masters Series tournament. That means he can't have one bad day—that's incredible. Not to mention he has to be out here for four hours running as opposed to walking while carrying one club—again not taking anything away from golf. Tiger's proven himself every Sunday every time he has a lead. But look at Roger's record in Grand Slam finals, too. In Grand Slam finals, he's 8-1. That's unheard of."

The Woods camp and golf fans pointed out that the American, in contrast to Federer, already won all four major tournaments in his sport and instead of only having to defeat seven opponents at the biggest tournaments, Woods had to fight off around 150 contenders. Tennis aficionados emphasized that Grand Slam tournaments lasted two weeks and not just four days and that in tennis, having an off day is enough to get knocked out whereas in golf, players could always save the day in such a situation.

Still others highlighted the commonalities between the two. "Despite their total dominance, Tiger Woods and Roger Federer show a modest self-discipline that would have impressed the most chivalrous medieval knight," *The Daily Telegraph* of Britain wrote. The *Calgary Sun* stated unequivocally which of the two super athletes it favored—"(Federer) is infinitely more human than Tiger Woods, more precise, more likable, more honest, less robotic, seemingly enjoying his place as a tennis player for the ages." The *Daily News* of Los Angeles, by contrast, questioned all of these comparisons. "You say the Swiss dude is definitely the greatest tennis player of all time? Good, then we can switch back to the Bengals-Chiefs. Equating Roger Federer to Tiger Woods isn't a backhanded compliment, it's a forehanded insult. An athlete of Federer's all-around refinement deserves better than to be defined in terms of another athlete."

After his US Open victory, Federer returned home to Switzerland when he received a surprise phone call. Pete Sampras, whose legacy and records were now one of Federer's biggest rivals, called to offer congratulations. "He had already text messaged me three days ago and now he was calling me to congratulate me personally," said Federer shortly after the US Open. "He asked if I had gotten the message. I said I was just about to reply. It was almost embarrassing. Perhaps I should have replied quicker." Sampras told Federer how much he liked to watch him play and emphasized that he now was more clearly dominant than he was during his prime. "To hear something like this from him was incredible," Federer said. "It's never happened to me before that my earlier idol called me to compliment me."

Sampras and Federer continued their text message relationship, with Sampras offering more good wishes over the following few months. Before the tournament in Indian Wells in March of 2007, Federer then took the initiative and called Sampras, who meanwhile announced he was returning to competitive tennis on the Champions circuit run by his contemporary Jim Courier. Federer asked Sampras if he would like to hit some balls and train together. "I wanted to see how well he could still play because, after all, he was one of my favorite players growing up," Federer explained. With a wink in his eye and devilish grin, he then said, "beating him in his backyard in Wimbledon was so special to me, so I wanted to try and beat him in his house."

Federer and Sampras only played once during their careers—the memorable round of 16 match at Wimbledon in 2001. Late in Pete's career, the two had one brief practice session together in Hamburg. "It started to rain," Federer recollected. "I was so disappointed, but he was happy to get off."

After their training session together in Los Angeles in the spring of 2007, Federer expressed his surprise at how well Sampras could still keep up during their practice session. "We played some great sets and tie-breaks. I'm glad to see that he's actually still enjoying tennis." The scores of these practice matches? "They're secret," Federer said. "Surprisingly, he was very good, but not good enough to beat me!"

Federer found that he and Sampras shared many commonalities and could talk in great detail of their respective lives and pressures on the tour, as well as common experiences, experiences at particular tournaments and even about players who they both played against. With Woods, this was not the case. "Pete and I played the same tournaments and even played against the same opponents," Federer said. "I have much more in common with Pete than I have with Tiger off court."

"When I was new on the tour, I hardly ever spoke to Pete," he continued. "First of all, he was never around at the courts, and when he would come into the locker room, everything was quiet because he was respected so

Roger clinches the No. 1 ranking against Juan Carlos Ferrero in Australia in 2004

Roger and Tony Roche at
Wimbledon in 2005

New rival Rafael Nadal after their 2005 semifinal match at Roland Garros

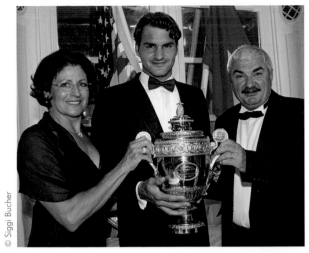

With his parents at the
Wimbledon Champions
Dinner in 2005

The celebrated champion after his third Wimbledon title in 2005

"This trophy is for you" Roger tells the crowd at the Basel Marketplace in 2005

He always has time for his fans—signing autographs at the 2005 US Open

An off-court photo
shoot in the California
desert before Indian Wells
in 2004

The jet-set lifestyle—
Roger and Mirka at the
Wimbledon Champions
Dinner in 2005

© Siggi Bucher

Roger and Tim Henman share a laugh at the tsunami fundraiser at Indian Wells in 2005

© RF Management

Roger at the New Briton Township in South Africa in 2005

Federer and Andre Agassi enjoy a friendly—and scenic—hit at the world's most unique tennis court on the the helipad of the Burj Al Arab, the world's most luxurious hotel, in Dubai in 2005.

Federer poses with Rod Laver and Marcos Baghdatis after the 2006 Australian Open men's final

Who is the more dominant athlete Roger Federer or Tiger Woods? Both champions pose with the US Open tennis trophy after Federer won the title in 2006.

Stauffer, in Geneva, during one of his many exclusive interviews with Federer

much by all the other players." Several years later, Federer finally got a chance to find out what made Sampras so unique and what brought him so close to perfection.

Before the end of 2006, Federer received another opportunity for an in-person visit with Woods. Just two months after the US Open, Federer, Tony Roche and Mirka Vavrinec followed Woods for six holes in the first round of the HSBC Golf Championship at the Sheshan Golf Club in Shanghai before the Tennis Masters Cup. Woods shot a mediocre round of 72 on the day—"Unfortunately, I was hitting wild shots everywhere," he said.

Woods finished second in Shanghai that week but Federer one-upped him and put forth plenty of fireworks en route to winning his third Tennis Masters Cup title. Unlike the previous three years, Federer arrived at the Tennis Masters Cup after an extremely successful fall season and without any major injuries.

After the US Open, he returned to Davis Cup play, guiding Switzerland to victory over Serbia—and back into the Davis Cup World Group—defeating both Janko Tipsarevic and Novak Djokovic in singles. He then traveled to Japan for the first time in his life and defeated Tim Henman to win the title in Tokyo. Two weeks later, he won his first title on Spanish soil, defeating Fernando Gonzalez of Chile to win the Masters Series event in Madrid. A week later, Federer achieved one of his most important career goals when he finally won his hometown event—the Swiss Indoors in Basel. Federer again met Gonzalez in the final, and after his 6-3, 6-2, 7-6 (3) victory, he celebrated by buying and eating pizza with the ball kids at the St. Jakobshalle. He did not forget that years before, he too was a ball kid at the event.

In Shanghai, Federer's lone challenger ended up being Roddick, who held three match points against him in their round-robin match before faltering. After an impressive semifinal win over his chief rival Rafael Nadal, Federer trounced Blake, the surprise finalist, 6-0, 6-3, 6-4 to win the championship. "I've never seen any one play better tennis," Roche said exuberantly. The title was Federer's first in China and his win over Blake extended his winning streak to 29 matches.

After Federer's dream year, the tennis history books were again revised. Although he only competed in 17 tournaments during the 2006 season, he earned $8,343,885 in prize money, besting Pete Sampras' record by nearly two million dollars. "The Masters title in Shanghai is the perfect end to an incredible season," said Federer, who reached the final of 16 of the 17 events he played, while winning a career-best 12 titles. With a 92-5 won-loss record, he became the first player since 1982 to win over 90 matches in a single season. Federer was also the first professional player to win at least 10 tournaments three years in a row.

In retrospect, he was only two sets shy of becoming the third man to win the Grand Slam. Had he not lost the four-set final to Nadal at the French Open, a Grand Slam would have been achieved, although the pressure he would have faced at Wimbledon and the US Open would have been, of course, much more intense.

CHAPTER 35
The Perfect 10

After his victory in Shanghai that capped his most successful season to date, Roger Federer treated himself to an extended vacation. He and Mirka Vavrinec traveled to the Maldives where he relaxed on the beach and watched DVDs, leaving the tennis world far behind.

After two weeks of training in December in Dubai with Tony Roche and Pierre Paganini, Federer, in his new role as UNICEF Ambassador, traveled to India just before Christmas, where he visited schools, orphanages and HIV-education programs in Tamil Nadu the Indian state most devastated by the 2004 tsunami.

"The 2006 season was my best by far," he said. "I don't think I could be playing any better. Now, it's a matter of maintaining this level." In order to achieve this, he wanted to allocate his energy even more efficiently. "I've learned that it is more important to take a break between competitions and to be well-prepared for the next event than it is to play in all of the tournaments," he admitted. This philosophy, unfortunately, came at the expense of Davis Cup once again. For the third consecutive year, he skipped his Davis Cup obligations, even though Switzerland hosted an attractive home tie against Spain. Despite Roche's initial opposition, Federer also decided to skip the first tournament of the year in Doha, where he started his season with tournament victories the last two years. Federer's new motto was now "Less is more."

After a few more days off between Christmas and New Years, Federer arrived in Melbourne and the 2007 Australian Open without an official ATP event as a warm-up. He did get some match-play experience at the Kooyong Classic, the pre-event exhibition at Melbourne's Kooyong Tennis Club. Surprisingly,

Federer lost in the final of the tournament to Andy Roddick, but since it was not an officially-sanctioned match, he was not upset at all with the loss.

Spurred by new coach Jimmy Connors, Roddick's career was back on the up-swing. In addition to his runner-up showing at the US Open, Roddick won the Tennis Masters Series event in Cincinnati and after his strong performancees against Federer in the US Open final and Shanghai, as well as his exhibition victory over the Swiss at the Kooyong Classic, many speculated that Roddick was on Federer's heels. The hype increased when the two faced each other again in the Australian Open semifinals. Roddick lost 12 of the 13 encounters with Federer but the longer this losing streak continued, the greater the likelihood that Federer would eventually stumble and lose to Roddick.

In what many people predicted would be an upset victory for Roddick turned into one of the bitterest days of the American's tennis career. Federer pulled off a masterpiece—one of the best matches of his career. He trailed 3-4 in the first set and then rolled off 15 of the next 17 games and won the semifinal match 6-4, 6-0, 6-2 in 83 minutes. "It was almost surreal," Federer said. "I'm shocked myself at how well I played." The statistics were incredibly lopsided as Federer hit as many winners in the match as Roddick won points. Federer hit 45 winners to Roddick's 11, while he won 83 points to Roddick's 45. Federer also out-aced Roddick 10 to four, never lost his serve, and converted all seven break-point chances on Roddick's serve. At one point, Federer won 12 straight games to take a 3-0 lead in the third set. The signature shot in the match came on the opening point of the fourth game of the second set. Roddick unleashed a fierce forehand from short range that landed close to the baseline. Rather than getting out of the way of the rocket forehand, Federer leaned left into the ball and hit a reflex backhand half-volley that traveled cross-court for a winner.

"Darling, you are a maniac," Mirka told Federer after returning from his day's work to the locker room. Two-time Grand Slam winner Rod Laver, who witnessed the flawless display of tennis, also showed up in the locker room and congratulated the victor. "Roger played fantastic," said Laver. "He used all the strokes there were and Andy was a little frustrated. The only thing you could do is go to the net, shake hands and say, 'That was too good.'"

Roddick's post-match press conference was one of the most difficult of his career, but the American took the defeat like a man and was at least able to treat the humbling defeat with some humor. "It was frustrating. You know, it was miserable. It sucked. It was terrible. Besides that, it was fine," he said. Federer, he said, deserved all the praise that was being bestowed on him.

Federer reached his seventh straight Grand Slam tournament final—tying the 73-year-old record held by Australian Jack Crawford. By reaching the semifinals, Federer broke Ivan Lendl's record of 10 straight Grand Slam semifinal appearances. He was careful not to celebrate prematurely. A year ago in the Australian Open final, he nearly crashed and burned against the unseeded upstart Marcos Baghdatis. His final-round opponent was the red-hot Fernando Gonzalez and Federer did not want to let his nerves—or another slow start—prevent him from closing out another Grand Slam title. Gonzalez defeated Lleyton Hewitt, James Blake, Rafael Nadal and Tommy Haas en route to his first Grand Slam final. He was the third Chilean Grand Slam finalist after Luis Ayala, a finalist at the French in 1958 and 1960, and Marcelo Rios, who also was a finalist at the Australian Open in 1998. Gonzalez desperately wanted to become the first player from his country to win a Grand Slam singles title.

For the second time, Federer reached a Grand Slam final without surrendering a set. In 2006 at Wimbledon, he also won 18 straight sets en route to the final before Nadal managed to win a set in a tie-break to spoil a perfect run to a Grand Slam title. Gonzalez began his first Grand Slam final on a cool January evening undaunted by Federer's quest for a perfect run through a Grand Slam draw. The Chilean, in fact, had two chances to immediately stop Federer's run to perfection in the first set. Serving for the first set at 5-4, Gonzalez held two set points at 40-15, but Federer hit an elegant volley to save the first set point, and benefited from the hard-hitting Chilean netting a blistering forehand on the next set point. As it turned out, it would be the only chances Gonzalez had in the match.

Nothing could stop Federer after he confidently won the first-set tiebreak 7-2. He did not shy away from engaging the Chilean's whipping forehand, while converting winners off his backhand side and at the net.

At 10:08 pm local time in Melbourne, Federer fell to the court after converting on his first match point in his 7-6 (2), 6-4, 6-4 victory. He yelled out in joy and lay on the court in exultation. Federer's parents, Lynette and Robert, traveled to Australia for the first time and looked on from Federer's box along with his late coach Peter Carter's parents.

The match was a perfect 10. The victory was his 10th in 10 career matches with Gonzalez—the Chilean being the first player to lose 10 straight matches to Federer. It was Federer's 10th career Grand Slam title and the first time he won a Grand Slam without losing a set. Federer became the first player to win a Grand Slam tournament without losing a set since Björn Borg won the 1980 French Open. The only two other players to win a Grand Slam event without losing a set in the Open Era were Ilie Nastase at the 1973 French Open and Ken Rosewall at the 1971 Australian Open. In his quest to find perfection, Federer was nearer to his goal than ever before. The headline in the newspaper *Age* the next day read: "The Perfect 10."

With his 10th Grand Slam title, Federer moved into fifth place in the all-time rankings list—tied with American Bill Tilden who, in the 1920's and early 1930's, was the paragon of the tennis world. "Moving from nine to 10 is a big step," Federer said after his 36th consecutive match victory. He now only needed four more Grand Slam titles to catch up to Pete Sampras and his record 14 Grand Slam titles. Besides the American, only Australian Roy Emerson (12) as well as Rod Laver and Björn Borg (with 11 each) were ahead of him. Federer won nine of the last 13 and six of the last seven Grand Slam tournaments and he also was a finalist in Paris—marking an unprecedented run on Grand Slam trophies.

Federer was quite familiar with the ghosts of tennis history and of his new rivals—the record books of tennis. On February 26, 2007, his name appeared at the top of the ATP rankings for a 161st straight week—breaking the record of Jimmy Connors, who sat at the No. 1 ranking for 160 consecutive weeks in the 1970s. Federer next set his sights on achieving another ranking record—the 286 total weeks as world No. 1 set by Sampras. "My goal is to hold my top ranking as long as possible and to win as many tournaments as possible, preferably Grand Slam tournaments," he said. "But I'm not going to drive myself nuts like Tiger Woods who only wants to beat Jack Nicklaus' 18 major titles."

Because Federer is almost 10 years younger to the day than Sampras, his development is easily compared to the seven-time Wimbledon champion. The 25-year-old Federer won Grand Slam titles nine and 10 in a little less time than Sampras, who at the same age only won his ninth Grand Slam title at the 1997 Australian Open. Sampras won Wimbledon—his 10th Grand Slam title—later in his 26th year and then won four more Grand Slam titles before playing his last match at the 2002 US Open after his 31st birthday.

The 14 Grand Slam titles appeared to be a record that Sampras would hold for many years. In the meantime, however, most observers in the game stated it was only a matter of time before Federer breaks this record as well. "It's beginning to look interesting," Federer said in the fall of 2006 of the record 14 Grand Slam titles. "Earlier I had said that it wasn't worth mentioning if I hadn't yet reached the halfway mark. Now I'm way past the halfway point and I am playing with the thought that I could do it."

According to a poll conducted by the ATP at the beginning of February of 2007, 92 percent of over 40,000 participants were of the opinion that Federer would also break the Sampras record. Some 68 percent predicted Federer would win 17 or more Grand Slam tournaments, while 28 percent even expect he win as many as 20 Grand Slams. "He'll continue to improve," Sampras said of Federer at the start of the 2007 season. "I think he'll win 17, 18 or 19 Grand Slam titles. He's just gotten to the middle of his career."

After now having twice won three Grand Slam titles in a row—another first of the Open Era—Federer was now also convinced he could win the Grand Slam and join Don Budge and Rod Laver as the only men to achieve the improbable task. "This may not be my goal for the season but I'll do everything I can to give myself the best chances," he said at the beginning of 2007.

Despite his massive success, Federer did not lose his humility. "I view each of my big victories as if it were the last," he said. Federer learned from the history of the game that opportunities should be seized when presented and that even phases of invincible dominance can abruptly come to an end, such as the cases of Björn Borg or John McEnroe. Mats Wilander once wrote that it is impossible to tell which Grand Slam title is a player's last. After winning three of the four Grand Slam titles in 1988, Wilander failed to win another title and his Grand Slam count ended at seven. "The biggest problem is not age but motivation," Laver stated of how a Grand Slam count can end for a champion. "One becomes mentally exhausted and the will to win fades."

Roche said that Federer is only in the beginning stages of his peak years—with the 26, 27 and 28-year-old Federer being the peak age athletically and mentally. "I understand that the hunger can begin to disappear at some point," Federer admitted. "You invest so much and at some point, the body becomes tired. You have to go through a lot in a career. But as a boy I always dreamed of becoming No. 1 and it would be wrong if my drive were to fail me now at this point." He said that it's sometimes hard and that sometimes he's tired and just doesn't feel like playing or traveling. "That comes with age," he said. "But I don't think that I'll just quit one day and retire early because I'm tired. I really don't."

He has already set his sights on the year 2012. He will turn 31 and the Olympic Games will take place in London. The Olympic tennis event will be played at a special place for Federer—Wimbledon—the venue of his greatest victories. Said Federer, "That would be the ideal moment to consider making my exit."

PART II

THE PERSON
Nice but Firm

Roger Federer was still a teenager and just emerging as an up-and-coming player when I first heard him utter the sentence that would become his life's motto—"It's nice to be important—but it's more important to be nice." I once ran across these words of wisdom in a book by philanthropist Robert Dedman, an American, who started his career as a dishwasher and succeeded in becoming a successful millionaire building resorts and private clubs. Dedman made this one of his 10 golden rules. He wrote that "it's easy to be nice when life is good to you and everything is going fine. But it's a greater challenge when you're not doing well. Being nice then demands a greater personality when you're tempted to be just the opposite."

In the intervening time, Roger Federer has since proven that he can and will live by this motto. He is not just paying lip service with this saying; it has become his life's guiding principle. Even in difficult situations, he is pleasant and respectful—and there are many difficult situations for the No. 1 tennis player in the world who everybody wants a piece of. Has anybody ever found Roger Federer to be unpleasant, a braggart, an arrogant snob? Even if he's not feeling well, if he has to deal with bitter defeats, if he has to answer the same question for the twelfth time in one day, is tired, in pain or would just rather go back to his hotel—he is friendly. He also answers uncomfortable questions without getting irritated or suspicious.

In Shanghai, at the 2005 Tennis Masters Cup, at a round-table interview, where the players sit for an hour at a table and answer questions from the media, one of the many Chinese reporters asked him an innocent question. "Roger, so many fans chase you but still you're friendly. How can you be so friendly with everybody?" The reporter had to repeat the question twice in poor English as Federer could not understand her but listened patiently and answered spontaneously. It seemed to be the easiest question of the day for him. "Why should I be unpleasant when I can just as well be nice? That's how easy it is for me."

Said Andy Roddick of Federer after the 2005 Wimbledon final, "I'd really like to hate you but you're just too nice." Rafael Nadal received a congratulatory text message from Federer after winning the tournament in Madrid in 2005 and after duplicating Federer's record of winning four Tennis Masters Series titles in the same year. When Nadal arrived in Basel shortly afterwards for the Swiss Indoors, only to withdraw due to injury, Federer visited him in the hotel. The two best tennis players of the year, who dueled for much of the season for titles and the No. 1 ranking, chatted for twenty minutes, far away from all the cameras. "We've also telephoned each other a few times," said Nadal. "Federer is not only a good world's top-ranked player and a great person, he is also quiet, calm and most importantly, he's nice."

Finding positive character traits about Federer as a person is the simplest thing in the world for a biographer. He's patient, cooperative, helpful and attentive. He has a big heart for the poor and the disadvantaged as well as for his own charitable foundation. He is fair and credible and plays everything straight. If he says that the ball was out, everybody immediately believes him. He is worldly, cosmopolitan, multi-lingual, expresses himself well and thinks before he speaks. He is modest, unpretentious, loyal, well-balanced, dependable and sympathetic. There are no similarities to those athletes who are so self-centered, they just want to talk about themselves the entire evening in the company of others—and there are plenty of those!

No detail is too small to interest Federer. People are continuously amazed at the interest he expresses in their lives. He always tries to remember people's names and to address them accordingly.

Federer lives according to established principles and values, most of which he doubtlessly acquired from his parents over the years. Among them are integrity, honesty, genuineness, modesty and loyalty. People he trusts will find that they have a friend for life in him. Former classmates who have nothing to do with the world of tennis are still among his closest friends. "You could always rely on him, talk with him, and count on him," said fellow Swiss player Marco Chiudinelli. "He could keep things to himself."

One of these principles is that Federer either does something properly or not at all. Said Yves Allegro, "When he makes a decision, his heart is completely in it." Allegro, who keeps in regular contact with Federer, never ceases to be amazed at his uncompromising will and his professionalism when it comes to managing his career. "Tennis is his life and his career has top priority," he said. "He does everything to keep improving. He thoroughly enjoys this life and savors it. He loves tennis and everything about it, but it's not always easy for him. When I see everything that he has to do, I sometimes think to myself it's lucky I'm not No. 1."

Federer is aware that his tennis career is ephemeral—a phase in his life. He knows that he will have enough time left over to catch up with other things—snowboarding, playing golf, raising children, mowing the lawn, grilling sausages or drinking beer with friends.

Allegro experienced the extent to which Federer is helpful and dependable in 2003 when he asked Roger if he wanted to contribute anything to the Grône tennis club in Wallis for its 25th anniversary. Allegro's father founded the club, which at the time, was deeply in debt. Federer spontaneously agreed to help by playing an exhibition match free of charge. Despite the fact that he just recently won at Wimbledon and had reached the final of Gstaad, he showed up as promised at the club and played the exhibition match before 3,000 spectators, which saved the club from financial collapse.

When one-time roommate Michael Lammer competed in the qualifying rounds of the US Open in 2005, Federer was in the stands cheering him on. Over dinners in New York, he tutored and advised his slightly younger countryman. "He offered to help me on his own initiative," said Lammer, whose tutoring from Federer helped him through the qualifying rounds and into the second round at Flushing Meadows. "I think it was fun for him. He has his own entourage, but not hundreds of friends on the tour. He probably wouldn't mind if there were more strong Swiss players."

Federer's conviviality, together with a pinch of patriotism, is also the reason why the time he spends with the Davis Cup team means so much to him. These days and weeks are a welcome change of pace for him from the grind of tournament tennis since he goes from being a singles competitor to a team member, which is all the easier for him since he is friends with most of the people on the team. "The Davis Cup is less stressful for him than other tournaments," said Allegro. "Normal problems fade into the background. We play cards, have fun, everybody gets along with one another." It's clear to Allegro that the positive atmosphere is a reason why he plays some of his best tennis in Davis Cup. "He enjoys playing for his country and when he feels good, he's nearly invincible anyway."

If Federer wasn't a tennis professional, his life probably would have led him to a career in professional soccer. He has established good relationships with top Swiss soccer players like Benjamin Huggel or Murat Yakin and follows his favorite team—FC Basel—wherever he is in the world and gets upset if he misses any of the team's big victories. Gigi Oeri, Vice President of FC Basel, even attended Wimbledon as a guest of Federer.

"Sometimes I dream like a kid about becoming a soccer player and shooting a goal in a crowded stadium," Federer said as late as 2003. A year later, he was permitted to train with FC Basel's first team in the spring. FC Basel Coach Christian Gross noted afterwards that Federer's feel for the ball was certainly not limited to the tennis courts. "With a little persistence, he could have had a career for sure," he said. A Swiss radio commentator once said of the Swiss Wimbledon champion, "Federer is like the little dog next door. Give him a ball and he's happy."

Like a genuine fan, Federer is willing to make sacrifices to enjoy his passion for soccer. When Switzerland played against Turkey in the deciding game for qualification for the World Cup in 2005, he followed the match live on television in Shanghai—despite the game not concluding until 4 am local time and him having a big match the next day in the Tennis Masters Cup against Guillermo Coria.

Of course, Federer is enormously ambitious and hates losing—but where would he be now if he weren't so ambitious? But even in defeat, he's always fair. He can lose with objectivity—and doubtlessly losing becomes easier the less one has to experience it.

People who know Federer from his youth and haven't seen him for quite a while always discover with a mixture of amazement and pleasure that he's hardly changed at all. Federer is living proof that someone who becomes rich and famous can also be normal. He noticed long ago that things go best if he just stays himself—even in the most tumultuous situations.

Although he doesn't claim to be a star, Federer enjoys immense international popularity and has a wide fan following. By the beginning of 2007, the number of registered members of his official website at www.rogerfederer.com reached 100,000. He may not be the type of person who young girls cry, scream or faint over like David Beckham or Robbie Williams, but Federer has a following among women who are more interested in the person than in the tennis player. He's done his fair share of modeling—posing for photo shoots and feature story spreads for such big magazines as *Vogue* and *GQ*. He was even twice included in *People* magazine's "Sexiest Man Alive" issue, featured in the "international men of sexiness" section. The honor seemed to amuse him more than flatter him.

Federer may not be a trendsetter like Beckham or Brad Pitt but he is very fashion-conscious and is open to all fashion designs and styles. "I used to just have some shirts and two pairs of pants in my closet, but now it's jam-packed," he said in the summer of 2005. Behind every fashionable man is no doubt a fashionable woman, and Mirka Vavrinec, has served him well in the fashion department. Both often consult with stylists and fashion industry friends prior to important fashionable events or photo shoots. Anna Wintour, the editor-in-chief of the U.S. edition of *Vogue* and one of the most influential people in the fashion industry, is a close friend of the couple.

Like all individual athletes, Federer lives egocentrically and has his entourage and inner circle sacrifice much for his success. Mental toughness and keeping an edge and aura is important for success. No one, however, would accuse Federer of being "macho." His other side—the gentle, vulnerable, emotional side—is too easily recognizable. Has any one seen an athlete cry so often in public than Federer? The man from Basel does not construe this as a weakness but as a sign of his great sensitivity and respect for the sport.

He's also not the kind that creates scandal or is chased by the paparazzi, like Boris Becker or John McEnroe in their days. Aside from a few nice, pre-arranged photo spreads taken mostly on vacation and consisting of beautiful, posed shots, Federer hasn't had his photo featured in the gossip photo pages.

Even his relationship with Mirka hasn't produced many stories for the society press over the years. The couple is not one that dives head first into the nightlife during their leisure time. Their vacations are rather uneventful. "On vacation, I do the opposite of what I do at tournaments. Nothing," said Federer. "I lie on the beach, sleep, go out for a nice meal, maybe do a little shopping if I have the energy."

Roger and Mirka lead a quiet, harmonious life together and seem compatible with each other. "Mirka likes to cook and I like to eat. That's a perfect arrangement," he said. "I help from time to time, make the beds, vacuum or dry the dishes. We make sure that we divide the work *evenly*." He knows that his girlfriend sacrifices a great deal for him and he tries to do something in return whenever the opportunity presents itself. He goes with her to the movies, to the theater, to concerts. He said that "on vacation, I'm willing to change roles. Then she's the center of attention."

The fact that Mirka is three years older and is familiar with professional tennis from first-hand experience lends additional stability to the partnership. Since Boris Becker's career, tennis years have acquired the reputation of being counted in "dog years," one year multiplied by seven. "Sometimes Roger is like a twelve-year-old but then again, he can be like a 35-year-old," said Mirka. "It's not a problem for me that I'm three years older."

She is not the type who overburdens her boyfriend with unrealistic demands because she knows what it means to be at the top. Above all, she's terribly proud of him and is therefore willing to make compromises. "I'm not in a big hurry to get married," she said in 2004. "When I consider that my parents married at 18 and had me at 21—I can't imagine that." She added that she didn't want to wait until she was 40 to have children "but when I have a child, I want the father to be around to play soccer, hockey and tennis with him or her instead of being away for 40 weeks at tournaments."

Because Roger is so friendly with the media, the media is friendly with him. They respect the fact that he makes the rules and they follow them. Federer is therefore one of the few Swiss celebrities to date who has not allowed reporters in his home to do a story. Roger and Mirka in the bathtub? Unthinkable. When a reporter once asked him what his apartment looked like, he responded with disarming candor, "This is very private. It's something

I don't discuss at all. Only my closest friends and family are permitted to see the apartment." End of discussion. Next question.

Federer is a Leo and his favorite animal is the lion—which fits him well. He is proud, has natural authority and likes to have everything under control—not just on the tennis court. His successes and the professionalism that he conducts his career with make him a natural leader in personal as well as in business matters. He may have shunned making decisions in the past, always asking his parents or his trainer first, but these days are long gone. Federer no longer needs anyone to tell him what needs to be done. Even during marathon matches lasting for hours, he won't look up to his box or to his support group.

Like a lion, Federer can sometimes bare his teeth and show an uncompromising side that is incongruous with his normally gentle and nice nature. This happened, for example, when he pushed Jakob Hlasek from his position as Davis Cup captain when he was just 19 or when, to everybody's astonishment, he parted ways with his friend and coach, Peter Lundgren. After that incident, the *Neue Zürcher Zeitung* described Federer as the "Terminator," who, in regards to "mental execution has since been equipped with a stubborn head and courage." The newspaper continued to state that he is a "power person that disdains marionettes."

Federer is a person not daunted by consequences after making decisions that he thinks are right. It was a shock for him to inform Lundgren that their working partnership was over, he said. It was as if somebody else had made the decision, a kind of alter-ego. His unwillingness to compromise even in with the smallest of matters has contributed to his authority and has made him a figure of respect—even for people many years his senior. As an example, most people in his entourage don't agree to interviews without first securing the approval and blessings of the boss—Federer.

Who could blame Federer for wanting to maintain maximum control over his career? After all, he has spent virtually his entire life in the attempt to master a difficult sport in the most professional and successful way he can. In doing so, he has learned that the smallest details can be the difference between victory and defeat—and that his initial instincts are almost always correct.

THE PLAYER
Like a Chameleon

The physical requirements and demands on professional tennis players are among the most grueling of all sports. Anyone who wants to win major tournaments and become a top player must be as quick as a sprinter, have the endurance of a marathon runner, take punishment like a boxer and execute like a forward in soccer. He or she must have the overview and cleverness of a chess grandmaster, the nerves of a mountaineer, the strength of a decathlon competitor as well as the calm hand of a painter, the patience of a sailor during a lull in the winds and the courage and cold-bloodedness of a matador. To be properly marketed, it's also nice to be relatively attractive and, if possible, have a penchant for showmanship because, after all, people want to be entertained.

"I'm tired of tennis. It drained me," Pete Sampras said in an interview after he retired in 2002. "I never had a single peaceful night's sleep my entire career. Not until it was over was I able to sleep the entire night trouble free." The 14-time Grand Slam tournament champion, who reigned for six years as the world's No. 1 ranked player, didn't touch a racquet for months after his retirement.

The experts are unanimous in the opinion that Roger Federer has all the qualities that make up a tennis champion. His coach, Tony Roche, is also in agreement. "He is a cross between Ivan Lendl, the hard worker at the baseline, and Patrick Rafter, the explosive aggressive player," said the Australian, who hasn't missed much in tennis in the past 40 years and worked with both Lendl and Rafter for many years. Federer's shot variations also remind Roche of Rod Laver, the only player in history to win the Grand Slam twice. "Some of the things that he does are simply incredible—nobody else has mastered them," said Roche. "I sometimes wonder, 'How did he do that?'"

Federer not only has the talent to dictate play, hit a winning shot from anywhere on the court, but also can play defensive tennis with the best of them. His quick legs and anticipation allows him to retrieve shots that would be winners against a normal player. Not only can Federer reach balls, but with a flick of the wrist can sometimes improvise winning shots seldom seen on a tennis court. ESPN, the American sports broadcast network, often shows a highlight reel of Federer's brilliant shot-making in what they affectionately call the "Federer Fun House."

Watching Federer on a tennis court often leaves you with the impression that the clock is ticking differently for him than for others—slower. The time between his opponent's shot and his own seems to give him more options than other players—as if he experienced everything in slow-motion—while he himself is moving in real time. No one has the reactions of Federer or gives up fewer aces.

Federer—like no other player—can alter the height, spin and speed of the ball. He has the innate ability to "hold the shot" until the last moment allowing him to disguise his intentions with expert ability. He covers the court exceptionally well and has such tremendous balance that when he prepares, he is able to "freeze" his opponent in that fraction of a moment between the end of his backswing and the beginning of his forward launch at the ball. This moment of truth forces them to guess which way he will hit the ball. When they are wrong, they are made to look foolish. This ability, this talent, is demoralizing to his many opponents. This mastery, when it is in full flow, positively emboldens the Swiss superstar. His game is the perfect marriage between art (when, where, and why to hit the appropriate shot) and science (perfected technique on his strokes).

"He's never in a hurry," says Roche. "The hallmark of champions in every kind of sport is that they have more time than others."

Federer has a poker face reminiscent of Björn Borg. He is remarkable with his elegance, his virtuosity, his unpredictability, his joy in the game, his creativity and his fascinating wealth of shot variations. Former Swiss great Heinz Günthardt, himself once a precise technician on the court and now a sharp-eyed television analyst, says Federer plays tennis like nobody ever has. "He plays as he pleases," Günthardt wrote in a column in the Swiss newspaper

Sonntags Zeitung. "He'll rush the net, play from the baseline, defend, attack, play fast, play with emotion, with topspin, with slice. His shot variation is ingenious. Anybody observing his game will come to the conclusion at some point that he plays like all the greats from the past 20 years—and because of this, like nobody else."

Günthardt pointed out early on that Federer's diversity of shots also posed a potential dilemma in that Federer, more than any other player, could become bogged down with too many options. Federer has not mastered the "art of economy" or the strength of knowing that he only has a handful of shots in his repertoire. With many shots at his disposal, Federer sometimes is burdened with "thinking too much" on the court on which shot to hit in certain situations.

From his early professional days, Federer was a "show-off" who enjoyed trying to hit spectacular—but low percentage—shots and therefore constantly lost matches that he should have won due to his lack of a conservative game plan.

"Back then I wanted to show everybody what I was capable of, the difficult strokes I had mastered," he once admitted. "But at some point it became clear to me that I would get more attention if I were among the top players in the world and if I were to play on the big Centre Courts."

Federer learned to manage the theatrics and began to play more for the scoreboard and not as much the spectators. The willingness to take big risks and his uncompromising aggressiveness gave way to a more calculating tactic that also took the weaknesses of his opponents into consideration. Without this reorientation and change of tactics, Federer never would have become No. 1 in the world.

"I believe that talent alone brought me to No. 10 in the world rankings," he told *L'Equipe* at the end of 2005 after the newspaper declared him the "Champion of the Champions." "After this, I had to take a few extra steps because today, the matches are so physically and mentally demanding and talent alone is no longer sufficient."

Federer the tennis champion is a puzzle of many pieces. It took years for all the pieces to fit together. Everything fell into place with each moving part working in synchronicity—talent, athleticism, mental strength, self-confidence, ability to concentrate, determination, tactical perception, professionalism, ambition and pride. As Andy Roddick once asked with resignation after a defeat, "How can you beat a player who doesn't have any weaknesses?"

One important point in Federer's development was finding the right degree of on-court emotion and temperment. The inner unrest and aggression that characterized him as a junior gave way to an unflappable calm and confidence. The process that Federer underwent to reach this point, however, was long, difficult and took place on many levels.

The first improvement in this area came when Federer moved from junior tournaments to the professional tour. As he began to play matches of greater significance and in front of larger audiences, the more he forced himself to stay in control and not throw his racquet, yell and scream. The higher he climbed in the world rankings and the better he became, the less reason he had to become agitated. Of course, the speed at which he rose to the top was never fast enough for him. He relapsed in his temper tantrums from time to time, especially in the early rounds or on outside courts.

Between 1998 and the spring of 2000, Federer worked with sports psychologist Chris Marcolli, who in addition to working with Federer, also provided his services to ice hockey clubs and other sports organizations. This was a phase in Federer's career where he posted some strong tournament results but also suffered very many disappointments and unnecessary defeats. His mental work, at times, also had negative effects on him as on occasion he became too relaxed. At Key Biscayne in 1999, after losing to the lower-ranked Kenneth Carlsen of Denmark, Federer explained a surprising lack of motivation. "I was almost bored on the court," he said early in the 2003 season. "I no longer showed emotion and had to discover what was best for my game. Now I know how I have to behave in order to play well."

According to Federer, his biggest improvement came with his mental game. Parallel to this was the decisive improvement in the area of physical conditioning that Federer began in December of 2000 with fitness expert Pierre Paganini. It was Paganini who developed a three-year plan with the goal of maximizing Federer's physical performance so that he could have greater endurance. The work yielded rapid results. "I have less trouble in long matches," he said at the beginning of 2003. "That also means that I can play longer in a tournament or that I can play four tournaments in a row without cracking. I tell myself to keep calm and that being tired is normal. Suddenly at the end, there is the chance to win a tournament."

It sometimes seems incredible to Federer himself how much he has changed. "Before, when my coach told me that I should calm down, that seemed impossible to me," he said in 2004. "I simply had to get rid of this tension and these demons in my head. No one could help me. It had to come from me."

Without the physical conditioning, Federer would have long failed at trying to get his emotions under control. The extra work that he invested in his career under Paganini's guidance also fortified his self-confidence and his ambitions grew. He admitted at the US Open in 2005 that in his junior years and in his early years as a professional, he sometimes lost matches where he didn't give his best effort. He sometimes had the terrible feeling that his opponent deserved the victory more than himself. Why? "Because I had the impression that he trained harder than me," he said. "I had the fortune, after all, to come from Switzerland."

How does Roger Federer play exactly? In the summer of 2005, he described it as "retro-style" to the *New York Times*. He is really bringing tennis back to an era when it was a game characterized by wood racquets, artistry, tactics and athleticism.

"I'm very all-around, of course. Not the big weapon, let's say, but players who play me, they know what the weapon is," he said to the *Times*. "They know if they give me a short ball, it's gone, even if it doesn't look that dramatic. It's more of a fluid game, which has no scratches, you know, which is round and that makes it more dangerous. My ability is to be like a chameleon, maybe."

Anticipation, Federer believes, is one of the best attributes. "I have the impression that I sense how a ball is coming and my reactions are automatic."

Many things that make Federer strong are hardly perceptible to the average spectator, perhaps because they don't seem as spectacular or as sensational as a cracking forehand shot accompanied by a loud groan or an ace served at 140 miles per hour. Anybody can see that Federer's serves are not as fast as Andy Roddick or Ivan Ljubicic—but only opponents notice to what extent Federer is able to vary speed, placement and spin with his serve, and how his variations can catch players off guard or exploit weaknesses in a players return game.

His shot variety is one of most impressive attributes. He can always come up with a different shot. He can fake a high-bouncing kick serve and slow his hand at the last second to such an extent that his irritated opponent no longer knows what's happening to him. He can put so much topspin on a forehand that the line judge is ready to call it out when the ball in fact drops like rock in bounds. He can undercut a backhand in such a way that as to create a difficult-to-play dying ball that hardly bounces and spins out of bounds so that the opponent can at best only helplessly shovel the ball over the net and the winning point is just a technicality.

"He invents strokes and attempts things that you think can't be real," said Marc Rosset. "I don't know anybody who has such a good feel for the sport."

Federer wears opponents down with such ease that it makes tennis look like a cinch. "He's like an artist, a painter or a sculptor, who creates the impression that everything is easy," Yves Allegro, Federer's frequent doubles partner, remarked.

Philippe Bouin, the tennis writer from *L'Equipe* and one of the greatest international tennis experts, described Federer's game as a "permanent miracle." Bouin, however, also pointed out the downside of such an attribute. "His misfortune is that his talent allows him to make the most difficult shots look easy," he said. "People will be all the more disappointed on the day when the magician reaches into his hat and will be bitten by his own rabbit."

Federer's mental strength may also be largely natural. From an early age, he had the capacity to grow beyond himself when the going got tough. Even in his formative times as a tennis player, he was a decidedly competitive type who could summon his best performance at the crucial moment and whose performances in practice didn't really reflect his true playing strength.

To play your best in crucial moments, you need to be mentally strong. If you are not in tune mentally and don't believe in yourself, there is no way that you can utilize your full potential at the crucial moment.

In this sense, athletes competing in individual sports are at risk to unravel and become unnerved with disturbing and self-destructive thoughts—even more so than in team sports, where substitutions and teammates can prevent a mentally-weak athlete from single-handedly deciding the outcome of a game. "We tennis players have the tendency to be delicate. A single grain of sand in the works is enough to derail one's game," Federer said in 2004. "I've always attempted to keep calm and collected. I therefore tend to look up at my box less than other players."

Federer has done an exemplary job in shutting out distractions, as if they bead up and run off an invisible shell. He does not overestimate himself or underestimate his opponent—not matter how great the ranking separation. He is prepared for anything—which is why he is seldom surprised or thrown off track. Even during his long winning streaks, one will hear Federer say such repeated sentences as, "I'm far from becoming a legend." "I'm expecting the worst." "I'm always surprised when I win so easily." "I never underestimate an opponent."

The No. 1 ranking is a source for Federer where he draws strength and motivation, unlike other players who perceive the top ranking as burden. "I enjoy being the favorite, not just the favorite but the big favorite," he said in 2005. "After all, it's up to the challenger to do the work while the favorite looks around first and sees what the others are doing. Of course, I have to make sure that I win my matches, but I'm mentally so strong that I don't have a problem with this situation."

While other players may become unglued over a faulty call rendered by a line judge, Federer only shakes his head at such a moment and continues play as if nothing happened. When, for example, he was playing in the 2005 US Open final against Agassi—with over 23,000 fans cheering vociferously for his American opponent and some even provocatively heckling him—he managed to remain focused with blinders on and concentrated on the one essential thing—getting the ball over the net one time more than his opponent.

THE OPPONENT
Just to be in his Shoes

Shortly after his debut on the ATP Tour, Roger Federer was quickly considered the new Pete Sampras. Early on and at first glance, the playful newcomer strongly resembled Sampras in many ways—Wilson racquet, Nike clothes, the strong serve, the brilliant forehand and the one-handed topspin backhand.

Boris Becker was one of the experts who quickly and correctly assessed Federer's potential. At the start of the 2000 season, when Federer was still losing more than winning, the three-time Wimbledon champion already had high praise for the young Swiss stating, "Roger is one of the greatest talents that world tennis has ever produced." Due to his incomparable style and his infinite potential, Federer was showered with premature laurels that, in the meantime, did not make his development easy. It was reminiscent of the Bible passage: "From everyone who has been given much, much will be demanded."

While Federer grew up relatively pressure free in Switzerland, once he turned professional and the global tennis community first began to see his natural talent and abilities, the stress of his high expectations mercilessly took hold of him. He had trouble dealing with all of the effusive compliments since he felt that he hadn't proven anything yet. The fact that his breakthrough was years in the making did not silence the hymns of praise even though comments were increasingly mixed with impatience, regret and sometimes frustration or pity. Many people in Switzerland and around the tennis world increasingly hoped that Federer would finally transform his obvious potential into becoming a great champion.

At the start of the new century, professional tennis needed a new star at the top of the game—an attractive leading figure who would create fresh publicity for the sport. Tennis needed a spark to help sustain its status in the tough competitive, sports-saturated global marketplace. The sport needed to identify its next star to sustain and generate new spectators, sponsors and broader media coverage—similar to what golf found in Tiger Woods.

After Sampras played the final match of his career in the 2002 US Open final, tennis missed the standard-setting legendary figure who dominated the sport over the previous decade. A vacuum arose in men's tennis starting in 1999, when Sampras last finished the year ranked No. 1 in the world. The next five years proved to be an extensive transitional phase, where nine players earned the No. 1 ranking, causing confusion as to who was the central figure in the sport to take the mantle.

There is no doubt—the tennis world was ready for Federer to be a champion before he himself was ready to become a champion. There was a long learning curve before he won his first Grand Slam title in 2003. "He rose from being a world class player to rising to the caliber of a Grand Slam champion," said Becker after Federer's Wimbledon victory in 2003. "For the sport of tennis, he is a godsend, especially in Europe. Finally, there is another charismatic player from Europe—from Switzerland which is a neutral country—who will revitalize the sport across the continent. We have all gained something from Federer's victory at Wimbledon. Finally, tennis once again has a player with a classic technique, who can do everything, and not just deliver a 220 km/h serve."

John McEnroe was also an early cheerleader for Federer. The former "enfant terrible" and himself a talented artist on the court, described Federer as the "most perfect player who has ever lived." The serve-and-volley virtuoso said in France in the fall of 2003 that "I dreamed of playing like Federer. Watching him play is the greatest treat. If he continues like this over the next three or four years, he'll become the greatest champion I have ever seen in my life." Federer, said McEnroe, was the "Sampras of the twenty-first century," and any child beginning to play tennis should take him as a model.

Mats Wilander, who won three of the four Grand Slam titles in 1988, also was an early admirer of the man from Basel. "How I'd love to see Roger win in Paris," he wrote in a newspaper column before the French Open in 2004. "In reality, I'd love to see him win across the board. Federer levitates over all the others and he's not even reached his prime yet." Later in the year, Wilander refined his praise of Federer stating, "I'd like to be in his shoes for one day to know what it feels like to play that way."

Sampras, who officially announced his retirement from tennis at the 2003 US Open, had nothing but praise for his successor to the tennis throne. Although he only played Federer on one memorable occasion in the round of 16 of Wimbledon in 2001, Sampras was not oblivious to Federer's impressive development.

Without a trace of envy, he stated that "he's head and shoulders above everybody else. He's also the best athlete and moves the best of all of them." Also impressive, said Sampras, was Federer's ability to maintain the highest level of play without spending an inordinate amount of energy. "That's why he can give his best throughout the entire season," he said.

Sampras admitted to many similarities with Federer. "We have the same temperament and he has the same light way of playing that I have," he said. "He dominates like I was able to for a while." In a later interview, the American expressed himself more precisely. "Federer is better from the base-line than me," he said. "His backhand is also better and his forehand is just as good. The record books will be his greatest challenge over the next four or five years."

Praise for Federer was not limited to the men's tour. Top players on the WTA Tour were not shy in their euphoria over Federer's style in play. "Roger has this natural instinct to improve," said fellow Swiss Martina Hingis. "I always had someone to explain to me why something wasn't working, but he feels it by himself." Serena Williams, who, like Hingis, dominated women's tennis for a long time, gushed that "I wish I could play like him."

Other past tennis greats also chimed in with songs of praise for Federer. "Nothing bothers him out there. I sometimes ask myself if he even has a pulse," said Jimmy Connors at Wimbledon in 2005 when he was commentating for the BBC. That same year, Ivan Lendl, who confided in the same coach, Tony Roche, for many years, compared Federer with Tiger Woods on the eve of the US Open. "Roger and Tiger both have in common that they have enormous talent and invest a great deal of time in their careers," he said. "That's why they're so hard to beat." The native Czech and later Americanized citizen did not rule out the possibility of having already seen equally talented athletes like Federer. "There have been other extremely talented players but they have not managed to achieve the things that Federer is now achieving," said Lendl.

There have been a few players who encountered a fair degree of success against Federer, especially Tim Henman, David Nalbandian, Lleyton Hewitt and Rafael Nadal. Hewitt won seven of the first nine matches against him, while Henman and Nalbandian took six of the first ten. But at some point, Federer discovered the key to winning against his "feared rivals" and took control of these rivalries. After losing six of his first seven matches with Rafael Nadal, Federer is gaining on his Spanish rival, winning key matches in 2006 in the Wimbledon final and at the Tennis Masters Cup.

"If you take Roddick's serve, Agassi's return, my volley and Hewitt's quickness, you'd have a chance against Federer," said Henman after losing to Federer in the semifinals of the 2004 US Open. "But you'd need quite a few players for that." When Gaston Gaudio was asked what the difference was between his Argentinean colleague Nalbandian and the Wimbledon champion, he dryly commented, "Federer, like Nalbandian, is a complete player, but Federer is a genius."

How have the top players reacted to the misfortune that their playing days coincide with those of Federer? Hewitt, himself the No. 1 player in the world before Federer's reign began in 2004, lost all nine matches against Federer in 2004 and 2005 during which he lost five sets by a 6-0 margin. Five of these defeats took place in Grand Slam tournaments—one in the final of the US Open and one in the final of the Tennis Masters Cup. Hewitt consistently pointed out through the years that Federer brought tennis to a new level with his ascent to the dominant position as the world No. 1, but the Aussie admitted he has not given up in his pursuit to also reach Federer's level of excellence.

"Everybody needs a while to catch up with him," Hewitt said after losing to Federer in the semifinals of the 2005 US Open—his ninth straight defeat to the man from Basel. "That is the reason that somebody like Agassi at 35-years-old still wants to improve. Of course it was frustrating, but you have to see the big picture. I think I'm a better player now than I was when I was No. 1."

Roddick, Federer's immediate predecessor as world No. 1, has not fared much better. In a direct comparison, the American trailed 13-1 in his head-to-head series with Federer following his destruction in the semifinals of the 2007 Australian Open. Six of the last eight matches were in tournament finals—two of them at Wimbledon and one at the US Open. Roddick, who is a year younger than Federer, bravely promised not to allow himself to become discouraged. "I would like to play against him again and again until my record is 31-1," he said after the Wimbledon final in 2005.

After that match, Roddick called him "the most physically-gifted player I've played against. But with that, he's just become a mental force, too. You put those two together, and it's a tough combination." Asked if Federer could become the best player ever, Roddick added, "I think you're not stretching it far to make that argument, that's for sure. I think time will tell. If he keeps up this level, then I think so. I don't know many people in history who would beat him."

He explained that Federer even manages to win points which Roddick, in his opinion, could not play better. "It's really tough," he said. "I remember, it was in his service game, I think it might have been 30-all. I hit about as good of a return as I could up-the-line, hit it really hard. He kind of got there. I came in and just took a full swing at a forehand, laced it cross-court and he was there and just hit it past me. I don't know if I could have hit two better shots. You know, it deflates you and it puts more pressure on you because you feel like, 'Okay, if I'm playing points like that, maybe I have to try and do something better, but I don't know if I can."

Agassi somewhat dominated Federer in their first three matches, but after eight defeats in a row—their last match being the 2005 US Open final—their head-to-head will forever stand at 8-3 in favor of Federer. Agassi, who like Hewitt lost a US Open final and the Tennis Masters Cup final to Federer, is not reserved with extolling the virtues of Federer's abilities.

At the Tennis Masters Cup in Houston in 2003, where he lost to Federer twice in a span of six days, Agassi said of Federer, "He does everything great. He moves great, plays great from both sides, from the baseline and at the net. His serve is extremely effective and accurate and he knows the game really well. He's as good as anybody can be." In a statement during the post-match award ceremony in Houston that sounded more like a declaration of love, Agassi said to Federer, "Man, you're my inspiration."

A year later in the quarterfinals of the 2005 Australian Open, Agassi complemented Federer on improvements to his serve and leg work, but resisted comparing Federer with other all-time greats such as Sampras.

"It's not fair to compare the great players with each other," he said at the time. "Each one has certain strengths and weaknesses." However, after losing to Federer in the final of the US Open later in the year, Agassi delved into a monologue in the packed post-match interview room inside Arthur Ashe Stadium. Agassi spoke with deep conviction and awe—almost as if he just experienced a close encounter of the third kind.

"It's disappointing to lose, but the first thing you have to assess is why did you lose and I just lost to a guy who is better," said Agassi. "I mean, there's only so long you can deny it, but he's the best I've ever played against. There's nowhere to go. There's nothing to do except hit fairways, hit greens and make putts. I mean, every shot has that sort of urgency on it. If you do what you're supposed to do, you feel like it gives you a chance to win the point. That's just too good.

"I've played against a lot of people over the years and they all had safety zones that I could concentrate on, but he has a response for everything you try. At some point he presses the button and makes you change your plan again. He plays this game in a special way. I haven't seen it before."

"I'm just speaking of the standard and the options and the talent and the execution that he shows in all the biggest matches. It's crazy..."

"Pete was great, no question. But there was a place to get to with Pete. You knew what you had to do. If you do it, it could be on your terms. There's no such place with Roger. I think he's the best I've played against...."

"Roger is the only guy I've ever played against where you hold serve to go 1-0 and you're thinking, "All right, good" and I'm not just making fun of it, I'm literally telling you the way it is. He can hurt you at any point. You're serving 30-Love, he wins the point. It's 30-15, the pressure you feel at 30-15 is different than anybody else. So there's a sense of urgency on every point, on every shot. It's an incredible challenge..."

"He hits that short chip, moves you forward, moves you back. He uses your pace against you. If you take pace off, so that he can't use your pace, he can step around and hurt you with the forehand. Just the amount of options he has to get around any particular stage of the match where maybe something's out of sync is -- seems to be endless. His success out there is just a mere reflection of all the things that he can do..."

"To beat him, something has to not be working for him and you have to manage to play the craziest tennis you have ever played. But even when you have him with his back to the wall, he has better options at his disposal than most. But you can't just talk about his talent. You have to respect him for the hard work, the discipline, and the dedication and the attitude that he brings to the court, again and again...

"You do step on the court feeling like you have to play a perfect match to beat him. He has to execute and has to do what he does. But if he does, you have to play a perfect match to win."

THE ENTREPRENEUR
Sign of the Hippo

Lynette Federer was astonished to read one of her son's first interviews in a Swiss newspaper when he was still a youngster. The question to Federer was "What would you buy with your first prize money paycheck?" and the answer actually printed in the paper was "A Mercedes." Roger was still in school at the time and didn't even have a driver's license. His mother knew him well enough to know that the answer couldn't be correct. She called the editors of the paper and asked to hear the taped conversation. The mother's intuition was correct. He had really said, "More CD's."

Roger Federer never had extravagant tastes. Money was never the main incentive for him to improve. It was rather a pleasant by-product of his success. It is a fact that the most successful tennis players are gold-plated and are among the highest-paid individual athletes in the world. Normally, the top 100 players in the world rankings can make ends meet financially without any difficulties—but nationality plays a crucial role in this. The best player from Japan, a country that's crazy about tennis and is an economic power house, may be only ranked No. 300 but he could still be earning substantially more than the tenth-best Spanish player even if the Spaniard is ranked 200 positions ahead of the Japanese player. Profits from advertising, endorsement contracts as well as other opportunities that arise for a top player in a particular nation sometimes greatly exceed their prize money earnings.

Anybody who asks a professional tennis player how many dollars or euros they win in a tournament will seldom receive an exact answer. For most, the total prize winnings are an abstract number on a paper and when it has finally been transferred to a bank account, it doesn't look too good anyways after taxes. By contrast, every player knows exactly how many ATP or WTA points they accumulate and how many are still out there to be gathered and where. These points ultimately decide where a player is ranked, which in turn determines the tournaments a player can or cannot compete in.

While tennis, for the most part, is an individual sport, it's hardly an individual effort when it comes to the daily routine. Nobody can function without outside help to plan and coordinate practice sessions, to get racquets, strings, shoes and clothes ready, to make travel arrangements, to apply for visas, to work out a tournament schedules, to field questions and inquiries from the media, sponsors and fans, to maintain a website, to manage financial and legal matters, to ensure physical fitness and treat minor as well as major injuries, to maximize nutrition intake and—something that is becoming increasingly important—to make sure that any sort of illegal substance is not mistakenly ingested.

Tennis professionals are forced to build a team around themselves that are like small corporations. This already starts in junior tennis, although sometimes a nation's national association will help with many of a player's duties—as the Swiss Tennis Federation did with Federer.

Virtually all top players are represented by small or large sports agencies, where agents and their staff offer their services—not always altruistically—to players. The reputations of agents and sports agencies are not always positive as many put their own financial goals ahead of what is best for their client.

The International Management Group or IMG—the largest sports agency in the world—signed Martina Hingis when she was only 12 years old. Federer also drew the attention of the company's talent scouts at a very young age. IMG signed a contract with the Federer family when Roger was 15 years old. Régis Brunet, who also managed the career of fellow Swiss Marc Rosset, was assigned to work with the young Federer. Lynette and Robert Federer invested a great deal of time and money in their son's career but were also in a relatively privileged position because Roger was able to take advantage of the assistance of local and national structures early on. For years, Swiss Tennis picked up the bill for his travel and accommodations at many of his matches and also provided opportunities for training and sports support care.

From an early age, Federer began to earn more money in the sport than his contemporaries. By age 18, he already won $110,000 in prize money on the professional tour and by 19, he had earned over $500,000. As Federer became a top professional, his prize money earnings catapulted. At age 20, his earnings soared to $1.5 million. By the time he was 23, his official winnings surpassed $10 million and at 24, the $20 million mark was eclipsed. At the end of 2005, Federer was already in seventh place in the all-time prize money list for men's tennis and was almost half-way to earning the $43 million that Pete Sampras earned as the top-paid player of all-time before his retirement.

At the age of 17, Federer already signed endorsement contracts with sporting good giants Nike (clothes and shoes) as well as Wilson (racquets). Babolat supplied him with one hundred natural gut strings each year while Swisscom picked up the bill for his cell phone use—which the teenager found pretty cool considering his numerous calls.

Federer did not care much for the details of his early business dealings. "I don't even want to know if I am receiving money from Head and Wilson or just equipment, because if I care too much about things like that, it could change my attitude towards tennis," he said in an interview at that time. "The prize money is transferred to my bank account and will be used later when I begin to travel even more." He then added somewhat hastily that "I will never buy anything big. I live very frugally."

Federer was never a player who would do anything to earn or save extra money. He also didn't move to Monte Carlo—the traditional tax haven for tennis players—to save on his taxed earnings like many professional tennis players such as his Swiss countrymen Marc Rosset, Jakob Hlasek and Heinz Günthardt. In 2002, he told *Schweizer Illustrierte,* "What would I do there? I don't like Monaco. I'm staying in Switzerland!"

He was less tempted to chase after the quick buck for several reasons. First, he was already earning considerably more money than his peers at such an early age. Second, as a Swiss citizen, there were fewer corporate opportunities than players from other countries such as the United States and Germany. Third, his creed was always "Quality before Quantity" and he wanted to concentrate on the development of his game in the hope that his success would reap larger rewards later in his career.

Federer, however, was always very aware of his value. He slowly but steadily moved up the totem pole of pro tennis and he observed the type of opportunities that opened up for the top players. When I asked him in Bangkok in the fall of 2004 if he was tempted to earn as much money as quickly as possible, he said, "I'm in the best phase of my life and I don't want to sleep it away. I have a lot of inquiries but most importantly, any new partners have to conform to my plans. They can't take up too much of my time and their ad campaigns have to be right. I'm not the type of person who runs after money. I could play smaller tournaments, for example, where there are big monetary guarantees, but I don't let it drive me nuts. The most important thing for me now is that my performance is right and that I have my career under control."

The fact that Federer does not go for the quick, easy dollar shows in his tournament schedule. After he became a top player, he only played in a very few number of smaller tournaments on the ATP Tour where players can be lured to compete with large guaranteed pay days (this is not permitted at the Masters Series and the Grand Slam tournaments). At these events, the going rate for stars the caliber of a Federer or an Andre Agassi could reach six digits. Federer is considered to be a player who is worth the price since he attracts fans and local sponsors and is certain to deliver a top performance. He won all ten tournaments in the "International Series" that he competed in between March, 2004 and January, 2006—an incredibly consistent performance.

Federer's strategy of looking at the big picture has panned out. He has developed into the champion that he is today because he hasn't been sidetracked by distractions and has remained focused on the lone goal of maximizing his on-court performance. His successes and his reputation as a champion with high credibility have increased his marketability over the years.

The number of Federer's advertising contracts was always manageable—in contrast to Björn Borg, for example, who had to keep 40 contract partners satisfied when he was in his prime. At 20, Federer signed a contract with the luxury watch maker Rolex—the brand that is also associated with Wimbledon. In June of 2004, Federer's contract with Rolex was dissolved and he signed a five-year contract as the "ambassador" for the Swiss watch maker Maurice Lacroix.

This partnership was prematurely dissolved after two years. Since Rolex became aware of the value Federer had as a partner, they signed him to another contract in the summer of 2006, replacing Maurice Lacroix.

In addition to this, he signed contracts with Emmi, a milk company in Lucerne (which seemed appropriate for someone who owns his own cow), as well as with the financial management company Atag Asset Management in Bern (until July, 2004) and with Swiss International Air Lines. All of the contracts were heavily performance-related in general and have increased substantially in value with Federer's successes.

Federer is a very reliable partner for companies. He was associated with his sporting goods sponsors Wilson (racquets) and Nike (clothing and shoes) since the beginning of his career and probably will be forever. His agreement with Nike was renewed for another five years in March of 2003 after the contract expired in the fall of 2002. The new contract was at the time considered to be the most lucrative ever signed by a Swiss athlete. Like almost all of Nike contracts, it contains a clause forbidding additional advertising on his clothing—or "patch" advertising—which is something that Nike also compensates Federer for.

But the renegotiation of the Nike contract was a long and tiresome process, which was one of the reasons that Federer dissolved his working relationship with IMG in June of 2003. In the spring of that year, he said that "one thing and another happened at IMG. Those are things that I can't and am not allowed to go into." It was a matter of money, he said, but not just that. "There were too many things that I didn't like."

From that point forward, Federer only wanted to work with people who he trusted implicitly. He noticed that the best control doesn't work if there is no trust. He gave his environment a new structure that became known as "In-House Management," based on his conviction that family companies are the best kind of enterprises. John McEnroe's father—a lawyer—frequently managed business affairs on behalf of his son—and it all worked out well for him. Federer's parents became the mainstay of his management and established "The Hippo Company" with headquarters in Bottmingen, Switzerland to manage their son's affairs. "Hippo," of course, was chosen in association with South Africa, the homeland of Roger's mother. "My wife and I had often observed hippos during our vacations to South Africa and have come to love them," Robert Federer explained once.

After 33 years, Lynette Federer left the Ciba Corporation in the fall of 2003 and became her son's full-time help (she doesn't like to be called a manager). "We grew into this business," she said months later. "If we need expert opinion about a specific question, we're not afraid to ask professionals." The two main goals for their son were to "build Roger into an international brand name" and to "maximize profits over a lifetime." The native South African, who, in contrast to Mirka Vavrinec, only occasionally traveled to the tournaments, worked very much in the background, which is exactly what her son wanted. It's important, Federer said in 2005, that his parents go about their private lives in peace despite their business connections to him. "I don't want them to have to suffer because of my fame," he said. "I also pay close attention that they are not in the center of media attention very often and only rarely give interviews."

Robert Federer continued to work for Ciba until the summer of 2006 when he took his early retirement at the age of 60. Robert, however, was always part of the core of his son's management for years. "I view myself as working in an advisory capacity and try to disburden Roger wherever possible," he said in the summer of 2003. "But even if we have a great relationship that is based on trust and respect, we still sometimes have trouble."

In 2003, Federer's girlfriend officially assumed responsibility for coordinating his travels and his schedule, especially with the media and with sponsors. Mirka's new role and responsibility gave her a new purpose in life following the injury-related interruption of her own professional tennis career. While mixing a business relationship with a personal relationship can sometimes cause problems, both Roger and Mirka say balancing the two has been easier for the couple than they first anticipated. Mirka treats both roles independently as best as she can and soon decided "not to get stressed any more" when requests and requirements of her boyfriend/client pile up.

"I've made everyone realize that they have to put in their requests a long time in advance and it works great," she said in 2004. She makes sure to expeditiously bring the most pressing matters to Roger's attention while seeing to it that he is not unnecessarily disturbed by what she believes to be trivial matters.

Nicola Arzani, the European communications director of the ATP Tour, extols the working relationship he has with Mirka. "I work regularly with Mirka and it works great," he said. "We coordinate all inquiries and set Roger's schedule according to priorities—usually a long time in advance." Federer, like all players, is supported by the communications professionals on the ATP Tour or with the International Tennis Federation at the Grand Slam events.

Mirka took up additional activities in 2003 as the driving force behind a Roger Federer branded line of cosmetics and cosmetic care products that were introduced during the Swiss Indoors in Basel. RF Cosmetic Corporation was thus born and Federer actively helped create the scent for his perfume called "Feel the Touch." Even if this perfume was generally met with wide acceptance, experts in the business believe that launching this line of cosmetics was extremely risky and premature, considering Federer's youth.

Federer had hardly replaced IMG with his In-House Management when his breakthrough months in 2003 and 2004 followed and provided many opportunities and requests for him—and a lot of work for his entourage. Within seven months, Federer won at Wimbledon, the Tennis Masters Cup and the Australian Open and then became the No. 1 ranked player. All of his successes and its consequences subjected the structure of his management to a tough stress test. "We were all taken by surprise, no question," Federer said. He admitted that he wanted to be informed about all activities and perceived himself to be the head of the In-House Management.

On July 1, 2004, Thomas Werder joined the team as new "Director of Communications" responsible for trademark management, public and media relations, as well as fan communication. This working relationship, however, was soon terminated nearly a year later. The German consulting agency Hering Schuppener with headquarters in Düsseldorf was then introduced as a partner to manage international public relations. But it remained mostly in the background.

With the exception of Maurice Lacroix, new sponsorship agreements were not initially announced. In February, 2004, when his son became the No. 1 ranked player in the world, Robert Federer said that while they were engaged in negotiations with various businesses, space for other partners was nonetheless "not infinite." "We're taking our time," he said. "We don't want to force anything. Roger can't have 20 contracts because each contract takes up part of his time."

According to marketing experts, the fact that Roger Federer's attempts to take better advantage of his commercial opportunities did not initially lead to additional advertising contracts not only had to do with this restraint, but also with his team's lack of contacts in the corporate advertising world. In addition, Federer was not the first choice for many international companies as an advertising medium, which specifically had to do with his nationality, his image, and—as absurd as it may sound—with his athletic superiority.

Federer had a limited corporate market at home in Switzerland from which to draw and, like all non-Americans, he had difficulties reaching into the financial honey jars of the corporate advertising industry. Such an undertaking, without the help of a professional sports marketing agency that knows the American market and that has the necessary connections, is nearly impossible. Federer's reputation as a fair, dependable and excellent athlete may also have made him not flamboyant or charismatic enough for many companies. Federer doesn't smash racquets or get into shouting matches like John McEnroe or Ilie Nastase used to. He doesn't grab at his crotch like the street fighter Jimmy Connors and, at the time, he was not considered to be a legend like Björn Borg, who looks like a Swedish god. He doesn't dive over the court until his knees are bloody like Boris Becker and he also doesn't surround himself with beautiful film starlettes like some of this colleagues, for instance McEnroe, whose first wife was actress Tatum O'Neal and his second, the rock star Patty Smythe, as well as Andre Agassi, who married the actress Brooke Shields, before being settling down with fellow tennis superstar Steffi Graf.

Anybody who likes convertibles, safaris, playing cards with friends, good music and good food, sun, sand and sea, is too normal and unspectacular. Federer was still missing something. During his first two years as the world No. 1, Federer lacked a rival that was somewhat his equal. Tennis thrives from its classic confrontations between rival competitors. Borg had Connors and later McEnroe. McEnroe had both Connors and Borg and later Ivan Lendl. After McEnroe and Connors, Lendl had Boris Becker. Becker had Stefan Edberg and Andre Agassi had Pete Sampras. In the women's game, there was no greater rivalry than Martina Navratilova and Chris Evert. Roger Federer didn't have anybody between 2004 and 2005 who could hold a candle to him. During the 2004 and 2005 seasons, Federer lost only 10 times to nine different players, seven of whom were not in the top 10. A real rivalry only grew starting in 2006 with Rafael Nadal.

When in July of 2005 *Forbes* magazine came out with its list of the world's top-paid athletes, Federer did not make the list. His annual income (from prize money, start guarantees, advertising and sporting goods contracts) was estimated to be about $14 million. *Forbes* tallied only two tennis players on their list—Andre Agassi, who, at $28.2 million, came in seventh overall on the list, as well as Maria Sharapova, the attractive Russian Wimbledon champion of 2004 whose estimated annual income was at around $18.3 million due to various advertising contracts. The *Forbes* list was dominated by basketball and baseball players with golf star Tiger Woods ($80.3 million) and Formula 1 world champion Michael Schumacher ($80.0 million) holding the top positions.

Given the undeniable need to play catch up to his fellow elite athletes on the *Forbes* list and gain more of a foothold in the commercial advertising space, nobody was surprised when Federer once again augmented his management with a professional international agency in 2005. It was a surprise, however, when he chose to rehire IMG after a two-year hiatus, despite such offers made by Octagon, SFX and other top agencies. However, the world's largest sports marketing agency was only announced as an addition to the In-House Management with the goal of "concentrating intensively on his economic opportunities." This was an optimal situation, Federer said, explaining that "I'm continuing to work with my present team, taking advantage of its lean structure while at the same time having a world-wide network at my disposal."

American Tony Godsick became Federer's manager. A tennis insider who also managed the tennis career of former Wimbledon, US and Australian Open champion Lindsay Davenport, Godsick was also married to Mary Joe Fernandez, the former top tennis player who owned three pieces of hardware that Federer desperately envied—two gold medals and one bronze medal from the 1992 and 1996 Olympics.

Following the 2003 death of IMG's founder, Mark McCormack, the company was sold. The Cleveland, Ohio-based company then reduced its staff of 2,700 considerably, sold many of its properties and parts of its business, apparently to remedy its financial woes. IMG's stake in professional tennis was also reduced as the company dumped its stake in events in Scottsdale, Ariz., Los Angeles and Indian Wells. The incoming IMG owner was Ted Forstmann, an investor who buys and sells companies at will, and made personal efforts to Federer to have his new company do business with him. The American was said to have paid $750 million for IMG and some insiders immediately speculated that Federer was signed to help increase the market value of the company and that he would share in the accruing profits if IMG were to be re-sold or listed on the stock market. No official comments came from either camp regarding this speculation.

Asked during the 2006 Australian Open if his new working relationship with IMG changed things for him and if he was now more active in off-the-court endeavors, Federer was unequivocal in stating that he was now in a new and much stronger position vis a vis IMG than before: "I don't want much more to do because I'm booked pretty solid. I've made it clear to IMG that this is the reason that I'm coming back. It's the opposite: IMG have to do more than before."

IMG quickly became very active in order to optimize Federer's economic situation and better exploit his potential. The goal was to find ideal partners and contracts that accurately reflected his status as a "worldwide sports icon." In 2006, existing contracts were re-negotiated, cancelled (Maurice Lacroix) and new ones were signed (Rolex, Jura coffee machines). Federer also signed a lifetime contract with Wilson, despite attractive offers from rival racquet companies in Japan and Austria.

Early in 2007, Federer signed his first big endorsement contract with a company that was not related to tennis or to a Swiss company. In Dubai, he was unveiled as the newest brand ambassador of the new Gillette "Champions" program, together with Tiger Woods and French soccer star Thierry Henry. "These three ambassadors were selected not only for their sporting accomplishments, but also for their behaviour away from the game," the company explained. "They are as much champions in their personal lives as they are in their sports."

The highly-paid contract was a stepping-stone for Federer and reflected that he had become an international megastar. The multi-faceted marketing initiatives, including global print and broadcast advertising in over 150 markets, helped him increase his popularity outside the sports world.

When I asked Federer in the end of 2006, if his relation to money had changed over the years, he said, "Suddenly, money turned into a lot of money, and in the beginning, I had problems with this." He felt that some articles suggested the impression that top tennis players are a modern version of globetrotters who run after the money from town to town. He did not feel this was an accurate portrayal of his priorities. "It's not true," he said. "All I'm trying to do is fulfill my dreams as a tennis player."

The Everyday Media Routine

It was July 3, 2004—the evening before the Wimbledon final between Roger Federer and Andy Roddick. Our reports for the *Sonntags Zeitung* had already been sent off to Zurich and my colleague Simon Graf and I were gathering our stuff in the press room at the All England Club when my cell phone rang. The name "Vavrinec" was illuminated in the display but it was not Mirka on the line, but Roger himself. I was surprised because it was rather unusual for him to call personally, especially the night before a Wimbledon final. Our paper was printing a major story on his girlfriend for the following day and had sent an electronic courtesy copy of the article to her via email. The fact that Roger was calling me did not seem to be a good sign.

It was known that Federer was reluctant to see anybody in his camp become too closely examined in the media spotlight and he felt obligated to protect them. After many attempts to convince Mirka to sit down for an in-depth personal interview, she finally spoke candidly about her daily routine, her relationship to Roger, about children and about marriage. The thought occurred to me that Roger now wanted to pull the emergency brake and stop the publication of the interview—which was impossible to do at such a late hour. In any case, it must have been something important if he were on the line personally the evening before one of the biggest matches of his career.

He seemed to have anticipated my thoughts, but also seemed amused and quickly dispelled my misgivings. His only concern about the interview was that the answer to the question about his friend Reto Staubli's role in his camp needed to be more exactly defined. Staubli, a former professional tennis player from Switzerland, accompanied Federer to tournaments at the time after Federer's separation from Peter Lundgren. He sometimes trained with him and appeared to have assumed the role of coach. Federer's reason for calling was to have this part of the story more concretely portrayed in order to save any trouble for his friend, who still held a job as a banker back in Switzerland. "Reto doesn't want to risk losing his job at the bank and so far he has used all his vacation time to work with us," Federer explained over the phone. "Thanks to the generosity of his employers in complying with his wishes, he has now received unpaid vacation time."

This small incident illustrates three of Federer's character traits—his willingness to help friends, his effort to keep all the collateral consequences of his career under control, and his ability to just act naturally. He always had a relaxed relationship with the media and he was always a very social person. Even as a junior, he was not afraid to talk to journalists about an article that he didn't agree with. As the No. 1 player in the world, *Forbes* magazine counted 24,396 stories about Federer over a 12-month period making the task of keeping track of his press virtually impossible.

There is no escape from the media for successful tennis players. It grows up with them and creates an involuntary community of purpose. They have to give interviews to the media after every match—so press conferences have become as much part of the game as showers and massages. Conversations with the media, however, can be stressful with difficult questions being asked and more than niceties being exchanged. Sometimes skeletons are dragged out of closets, provocative questions posed and prejudices reaffirmed. Many players therefore view press conferences as an irksome duty—a frustrating waste of time. Players answer questions suspiciously and become reticent or evasive and attempt to create distance between themselves and the media. Those who say nothing can't say anything wrong. They can also retreat from their exposed positions more quickly where cameras and microphones mercilessly catch every movement and every word and broadcast them to the world.

These mandatory post-match interviews are normally conducted in English first and then, if necessary, in the player's native language. On some occasions, press interviews can last longer than the matches themselves. The growth and development in the media world have contributed to a greater demand by television, radio stations and internet websites to cover events in person and gain quotes and comments from the players.

It may be a blessing that Federer, in addition to Swiss German, also has a near perfect command of High German, English and French—but sometimes his multilingualism is a disadvantage in these interview sessions. His press conferences routinely last the longest of any player because, next to English and German, he also has to provide quotes in French, which in the meantime has become a second native language for him and is the second official language of Switzerland behind German. Federer is also often accompanied by a small group of French-speaking Swiss journalists at the bigger tournaments.

With the other players, such as the Argentineans, press conferences are almost a walk in the park. Guillermo Coria, for example, even after five years on the professional tour, only appeared at press conferences accompanied by a translator and then only spoke Spanish. David Nalbandian is such a master at the art of evasion and economy of words that his interview transcript rarely takes up more than one page.

Some players, on the other hand, use the press conference as a forum to settle personal scores, to take revenge for unwelcome articles. Time and again there are instances when certain interviewers are boycotted or ejected from the room. Even John McEnroe, for example, had no reservations about doing this. Boris Becker also used to humiliate journalists, though somewhat more gently. He would sometimes answer questions from people who he had known for years and on familiar terms with only to maliciously begin addressing them in formal terms.

Playing these kinds of wicked games is unimaginable for Federer. He is a person who greets journalists when he comes in and then says good-bye to them when he leaves—even after defeats. When he first started to play professional tennis, he constantly astounded reporters after interviews by thanking them for having come to his match and his press conference. He notices when there is a familiar face who he hasn't seen for a long time in the press room, approaches the media to ask which journalist is covering which tournament, and sometimes even poses questions back to the reporters during press conferences.

Federer is not the type of person who makes a spectacle of himself with a big mouth, whose statements can be made into headlines or scandalous stories. He seems to have internalized Benjamin Franklin's motto—"The heart of a fool is in his mouth but the mouth of a wise man is in his heart." His amicability and candor with the media undoubtedly contributes to his popularity and his good press image. He takes his interviewing partners seriously and is also taken seriously by them. Federer has developed a way of integrating the media into his career, which is an exception among top players. After big tournaments, such as the Tennis Masters Cup in Houston, he offered the Swiss media people Champagne, played ping-pong with them and showed them the Players' Lounge or the dressing room. In the spring of 2004, he visited the editorial department at the *L'Equipe* newspaper in Paris before the French Open. The reporters were astounded and sang his praises in their columns.

There is no doubt that Federer has mastered the game with the microphone and notebook just as he has mastered the game with the racquet and tennis ball. He benefits from having the same qualities required by both—perspective, patience, respect for the opponent and the desire to always give his best.

The way he works with the media also makes setting limits easier. If he does not want to say something about a specific topic, most of the media immediately respect his wishes. For example, questions about his required military service—Federer was declared unfit for military service and was assigned to alternative community service—are taboo as are overly personal questions, and the public usually finds out where he was on vacation only after the fact.

Federer, however, has also had his difficulties with the media, especially in 2001 and 2002 when he struggled to break through and win his first major title. "After press conferences, I sometimes had the feeling that I had been hanged upside down by the legs and shaken out," he admitted after his third Wimbledon victory. "I came out and thought: 'O.K., I have to re-think my entire tennis game.' I feel better today. I know what I can do and what I can't do, what I can say and what I can't say in order not to be influenced negatively."

It's almost impossible to provoke him. The closest it comes are those questions that show a lack of respect for his person or his accomplishments. For example, when a reporter asked him twice if he really believed that he could defeat Andre Agassi after he had already beat him on two previous occasions, his answer was rather short. Federer was also not very enthused about a story in 2004 right before the Olympic Games when an astrologist predicted a bad constellation of stars for Athens. "You have to come up with something better than that," he said but emphasized that he doesn't let himself be distracted by such side-shows anymore. "It doesn't matter what these experts say," he said. "I can't be bothered with it. I can't control what is written and I don't even want to. I don't have to prove anything to anybody but myself."

Federer views the media as fellow sojourners but the tranquil days when he could grant an impromptu one-on-one interview are long gone. "Back then I could spontaneously grant interviews, but now they have to sign up months in advance," he said after his first Wimbledon victory. "I've noticed that I like to plan things. That way I can get ready for dates with the press or sponsors early and enjoy it." Even when it comes to exclusive interviews, his motto is still—quality before quantity.

According to Nicola Arzani, one of the ATP's top communications officers, demand for Federer is growing after each big victory. "The more he wins and maintains his image as a serious ambassador, the more doors open up for him," Arzani said at the beginning of 2006. "You can take him to anybody in the media world and arrange any kind of events. He has become an international star and he has also conquered the American media market as well, which is not easy. The reports about him have been the best that I have ever seen. Federer was more of a Swiss hero before, but now he's an international star. That's why he has more inquiries and engagements abroad. But he's still quite accessible to the Swiss media."

Sometimes Federer upsets his entire schedule because he can't keep from cultivating contacts with the media. Who could still be surprised that the media awarded him the "Prix Orange" at the French Open as the most friendly and approachable player?

THE CELEBRATED MAN
The Media's View

Wherever Roger Federer makes an appearance, he is met with a wide array of appreciation and praise from the media, regardless of where he happens to be playing in the world. He appears to inspire journalists worldwide to make extraordinary comparisons and colorful statements regarding his style and manner of how he plays the sport.

"Federer puts in performances like nobody before him carrying a Swiss passport, or at least since Ursi Andress emerged from Doctor No's lagoon in her white bikini," the *Süddeutsche Zeitung* wrote after his first Wimbledon victory, evoking the image from a James Bond film. "Watching him play tennis is like watching Michelangelo at work on the Sistine Chapel," the German magazine *Stern* stated, adding "if men's tennis, which has a deficit of heroes, were to wish itself a savior at some point, it would look like Roger Federer."

During Wimbledon, Federer usually finds himself the subject of even more extraordinary accolades in the press. It seems journalists are themselves competing against each other to best describe the elegance and stature of the man from Basel. Even John Parsons, the rather reserved and sober journalist for the *Daily Telegraph* and one of tennis world's most respected writers until his passing in 2004, also became caught up in hyperboles about Federer. "Take the ice-cool Wimbledon temperament of Björn Borg, add the elegant volleying skills of Stefan Edberg, stir with the serving authority of Pete Sampras and the returning qualities of Andre Agassi and there you would have a taste of the new Wimbledon champion," he wrote. "He could become a giant among champions."

Among the most ardent admirers of the man from Basel is the *Times* of London, whose extraordinary columnist, Simon Barnes, elevated Federer to the aristocracy early in his career and described him as the "Harry Potter of tennis." "There are actually people who believe that art no longer exists in tennis. That was modern art," Barnes wrote right after Federer's semifinal against Andy Roddick in 2003. When Federer managed to pull off the Wimbledon coup with his first victory at the All England Club, the editors of the *Times* appeared to be beside themselves with joy. "Sound the alpenhorns and let all the cuckoo clocks sing out," the paper stated. "Yodel the good news from peak to peak and break open the Toblerone. Roger Federer's victory at Wimbledon has confirmed the Swiss as a nation of sporting heroes, a land where giants emerge from their mountain meadows to sail the seas, balloon around the globe and swashbuckle their way to grassy tennis fame."

Barnes even drew a rather unusual comparison between Federer and the world's best soccer players: "It's just like watching Brazil! But Brazil weren't trying to be beautiful when they won the World Cup any more than Federer was when he took the title. Beauty was the art with which he destroyed his opponent." John Roberts, the humorous correspondent for the *Independent*, found his comparison in automobiles. "He showed the public at Centre Court and millions of spectators that it was worth having waited so long for a virtuoso like him. He is the Rolls-Royce of the tennis courts." Neil Harman, the tennis expert for the *Times*, once again celebrated Federer in December of 2003. "Federer cast a magic spell on the championship in a style that conjures memories of the golden age when the sport was still a cheerful meeting between player, racquet and ball," Harman wrote.

The *Times'* fascination with Federer remained consistent even when he won Wimbledon for the third time in 2005. "You thought that was boring? Humph! Maybe you should pick up something less intellectually challenging. Shakespeare, for example," Barnes wrote. "In 'Hamlet,' for example, you already know in the first act that things are going to end badly for him. But the pleasure doesn't suffer from this—to the contrary. Anybody who finds excellence boring shouldn't follow sports where excellence is the goal but is seldom achieved."

The *Daily Telegraph* observed a certain affinity of character between Federer and the British. It stated in 2005 that "the fans not only admire his talent but also appreciate his personality. He's not a showman in the way that Becker, Connors or Agassi were. His modest, shy manner somehow appeals to the British character."

It took somewhat longer for the USA to accept Federer as an exceptional talent, which is not surprising considering his rather weak record there at the beginning of his career. When his winning streak also spilled into the big American tournaments, the reaction there was all the greater.

"In this age of nuclear equipment and supersized players, Federer plays with the deftness of long-ago men of modest size in long white slacks, rolled up shirtsleeves and wooden racquets," popular sports writer George Vecsey of the *New York Times* expressed admiringly.

The *New York Times* declared Federer to be the standard for everything at the US Open in 2005. "Who's No. 1? Federer, on and of the court," ran the headline in the trend-setting, august international publication. Federer was then compared to Lleyton Hewitt who, during his reign as top-ranked player, was known for his egoistical, imbalanced, and at times insulting comments, was locked in litigation with the ATP Tour and did little service to the sport. "Federer took his No. 1 ranking as a responsibility, not a perch of entitlement, maturing into a player of thought, action and social awareness," the *New York Times* wrote.

Bud Collins of the *Boston Globe,* probably the most widely-known American tennis reporter, presented Federer to his readers as "the Lone Roger," the lonesome cowboy whose cow is grazing on a mountain meadow, while he conquers the world. "No coach is in his stable these days. No agent. No propagandist. No valet, butler, footman, chauffer, sommelier. In short, no posse," Collins exaggerated. Federer's independence, as well as his extended solo stint without a coach and big agency, astounded observers nowhere as much as in the USA where every sports star who is worth anything has an entire entourage in tow. There wasn't a cliché Collins didn't use but his phrasing was very original. "As a veritable Swiss army knife in sneakers, Roger flashes numerous blades for cutting down rivals, and he does it with swings as sweet as Swiss chocolate, as impregnable as a Swiss bank account, as precise as a Swiss watch."

The *New York Post* meanwhile called out any critics who insisted that Federer's dominance of the sport could make tennis boring. The tabloid wrote in 2005 that "Roger Federer can win eight of the next 10 Slam finals, reach the semifinals of all the rest, and if Who and When at every tournament becomes inevitable, the How will remain captivating. We will watch it, in mesmerized fatalism." *Newsday*, the third largest newspaper in New York, demanded more respect for the "virtuoso" after Federer was forced to compete in his starting match at the US Open at 11 in the morning. He is, after all, "the tennis equivalent of Wayne Gretsky," drawing the comparison between Federer and the greatest hockey player in history. When *Sports Illustrated* chose Federer as its tennis player of the year in 2004, the magazine wrote that "were Federer from Milwaukee or Scranton or Fresno (not Basel, Switzerland), he would occupy a penthouse suite in the American sports pantheon."

Although the French Open turned out to be Federer's most difficult Grand Slam tournament and it proved to be a long road in realizing his potential in Paris, he was recognized and celebrated early on as a phenomenon in France. During this time, journalists constantly highlighted his human qualities, especially *L'Equipe* and its affiliated publications. The sports newspaper stated at the beginning of 2005 that "with Federer, there is no dramatization, no comedy, no exaggerated gestures or emotions, no tensing of his facial features when he plays. He doesn't seem to need anger or aggression to win like so many other champions do. The image that he prefers to cultivate is that of a simple man."

L'Equipe described Federer in terms of his friendliness and accessibility as "a No. 1 like nobody before him. Ivan Lendl was arrogant and overbearing, Andre Agassi was a virtually inaccessible star, Pete Sampras was cool as a cucumber, and John McEnroe was just McEnroe. But Federer is a unique and modest champion of unusual freshness and integrity." He appears almost surrealistic, as somebody from an era in which so many less talented colleagues puff themselves up at the slightest opportunity, the newspaper continued. "One can converse with complete freedom about God and the world, about everything or nothing with a champion of this caliber."

Even the most aggressive tabloids in the world have been generally unwilling to put Federer in the spotlight of scandals, as happened to John McEnroe and Boris Becker repeatedly. The role of genius has been reserved for him. He is Mr. Clean, the "silent killer with the ice-cold face of the future" (*Sydney Morning Herald*). "He couldn't place the balls more accurately if he walked over to the other side of the net and marked the desired spot," the *Daily Express* of Britain once exaggerated. The *Daily Mirror* described it as a "tyranny of beauty," writing that "in the era of Federer, elegance, power, and technique count more than toughness; variation defeats monotony."

In Germany, *Bild* described Federer during the German Open in 2004 as the "nicest No. 1 player of all times," and sighed "if only we had somebody like him! He doesn't curse, doesn't pull any dirty tricks, is always polite and courteous. Cheating is an abhorrence to him." German newspapers constantly lament that he wasn't born a few kilometers farther north in German territory.

Comments on Federer alone from experts, columnists, trainers and coaches could fill a nifty volume. Perhaps none were as euphoric as the American Nick Bollettieri in *The Independent* on July 4, 2005.

"Roger Federer is virtually indescribable," Bollettieri stated. "Whatever we say about him cannot express the jaw-dropping, breathtaking brilliance of his play. He moves like a whisper and executes like a wrecking ball. He is a genius, a magician. He is an athlete of such complete mental and physical power and calm combined that he is, I believe, unique in the history of tennis... Sampras was a wonderful champion, a great, no question. But he did have weaknesses, including a less than perfect return of serve on the backhand side sometimes. And great though his mobility was, Federer's is better. Borg was another true great, but he was a machine. He broke you down mentally. He did not overpower you in the way that Federer does. Federer's shots can be so blistering, so uncannily placed that they leave you nothing to say but, 'How?'" Bollettieri's conclusion, "Federer's talent is not of this planet. Whatever the future brings, we should just be glad we have seen him play."

On a Noble Mission

Roger Federer was in Sydney, Australia, when on December 26, 2004, a gigantic earthquake off the island of Sumatra in Indonesia created a tsunami that killed over 200,000 people in the region. Federer was deeply troubled by the tragedy. After flying over the catastrophic area en route to the Qatar Open in Doha only days later, he intensely followed the media coverage of the tsunami on television in his hotel.

"The whole thing really affected him like nothing else before," said girlfriend Mirka Vavrinec on the phone just days after the tragedy. The couple had finished a vacation in the Maldives only three weeks earlier where they flew out of Colombo, Sri Lanka, one of the most affected areas of the gigantic tidal waves. "We have close acquaintances there but we haven't been able to reach them for days now," said Mirka. Roger and Mirka were very connected to the region, having vacationed in the Thai island of Phuket and other areas in the region devastated by the tsunami. A few weeks before the tragedy, Federer won the Thailand Open in Bangkok. "It was a big shock for me," he wrote on his website. "It's hard to imagine what the people there are going through."

In an initial, spontaneous act, Federer transferred 20,000 Swiss francs ($16,000) to a Swiss relief organization. But he felt that he could do more and he wanted to do more. Back in Australia, he committed himself, along with other athletes, to a campaign at Melbourne's "Nike Town," where over 100,000 Swiss francs ($80,000) was raised. Nike matched this amount and contributed clothing for victims. On the eve of the Australian Open, Federer declared his willingness to "play any particular match to help the victims." It wasn't enough for him just to autograph racquets to be sold at auctions. He himself took the initiative and summoned his fellow players to conduct a unified campaign.

The result was a unique event in professional tennis. Before the tournament in Indian Wells, nine top players played an exhibition event on March 11 to raise money for tsunami victims. Top women players like Kim Clijsters, Elena Dementieva, Amelie Mauresmo and Daniela Hantuchova also participated. Players even collected contributions in cans from fans in the stands—resulting in $18,282.76 alone. The cash collected—as well as money raised from ticket sales for the event—was transferred to tsunami victims via UNICEF. A three-year children's relief program, the ACE (Assisting Children Everywhere), was also launched at the same event between UNICEF and the ATP. Later in the year before the US Open, Federer was recognized by UNICEF on behalf of the tennis tour for his charitable works. In April of 2006, UNICEF named Federer as a "Goodwill Ambassador" in a ceremony in New York.

What differentiates Federer from many other athletes who are willing to give back to people who are in need is the personal devotion. It's not enough for him just to send money. He is, as the campaign in Indian Wells demonstrated, also willing to get himself personally involved and invest his precious time to the project.

The Roger Federer Foundation—with headquarters in Bottmingen, Switzerland—was founded on December 24, 2003, shortly after he won his first Grand Slam title and before he was anywhere near financial security. The foundation's goals were to support needy children and to promote youth sports.

The foundation soon entered into a cooperative partnership with the Imbewu Organization, a South African relief organization with a branch in Switzerland committed to helping disadvantaged children and youth in the New Brighton Township in the South African city of Port Elizabeth. The township is among the poorest and most crowded slums in South Africa, where AIDS, violence and disease account for countless lives. Federer's foundation makes it possible for 30 children to attend classes in three different schools. The foundation picks up costs for meals, school uniforms and school materials and also finances three full-time social workers.

"I've already won so much in my short tennis career. I would like to give something back with my foundation, especially to those that have the least," Federer said at the time, explaining the purpose of his foundation. He hit upon the idea of South Africa, he said, "because my mother grew up in this country and I've always had a close tie to South Africa. South Africa for me is a model state that has overcome hatred and oppression."

The fact that for Federer, the foundation is a matter of cause and not effect became evident in the way he organized his first visit to the New Brighton Township in the early days of March, 2005. His communications advisor at the time, Thomas Werder, suggested he allow several media representatives to travel with them to events in the township and generate major publicity hits in numerous media outlets. Federer, however, refused. It wasn't a matter of achieving the greatest possible media coverage under the motto of "do good works and talk about them." The news of his visit to the township came as a surprise to most of the Swiss media. The small report ran on the visit late in the evening via the Swiss News Agency on March 2, 2005, when most newspapers had very little news space for the event and featured the story as only a news brief.

Accompanying Federer on his township visit was Mirka, his mother and Nicola Arzani of the ATP. "He didn't want to make a big deal out of it," Arzani recollected. "I convinced him to at least allow a photographer, a cameraman and a local journalist." Federer, he said, spent the entire day in New Brighton, played soccer and basketball with students, planted a tree and passed out 2,500 T-shirts with the saying "I'm Tomorrow's Future" on them. He also visited schools, infirmaries and a girl's home. Then he ate the traditional Xhosa meal of corn grits with beans with the children who sang and danced for him.

"I wasn't afraid at all," he later explained to Mark Mathabane, a South African living in the United States who wrote about the visit in *Deuce* magazine. "I wanted to see things for myself, to feel what it's like to live like that. I also wanted to find out how much difference my foundation was making in the lives of the people there." In November of 2005, Federer's parents presented the township with a multi-functional sports facility for basketball, netball and soccer.

In 2007, the Roger Federer Foundation was re-launched. New people came on board, like Christophe Schmocker, a very experienced man when it comes to foundations and charities. "The goal is to play in a higher league," Schmocker said. A new website and new projects were also launched, like

Federer's sponsorship of ten young Swiss athletes from different sports. One of the main goals of the foundation was "to help selected poor countries in the southern hemisphere," Schmocker explained. For example, the foundation sponsored a school in Ethiopia.

The Wimbledon champion quickly became aware that his position at the top of his sport would accord him the opportunity of becoming a role-model, to become an ambassador and to bring attention to matters that needed attention.

"If you ask me, he is the best tennis ambassador we've ever had," said Arzani. "He's so easy to work with because he understands perfectly the thing he is responsible for. He's completely dedicated to whatever it is he's doing. He does things not just because he has to. He always wants to know exactly why he is doing it, who will profit from it, why a tournament wants to do a particular thing, or why he should be doing a particular thing with the media. He's very committed to everything that he does."

"The enthusiasm he has for tennis is incredible," said Yves Allegro, one of his best friends. "There's nobody like him. This presents tennis—in fact the entire world—with a unique opportunity." John McEnroe made almost the same observation in 2005. "Roger cares about tennis. He embraces the responsibility of being ranked No. 1 in the world," he told *Newsday*.

When asked by Switzerland's special UN ambassador for sports, Adolf Ogi, if he was willing to help launch 2005 as the "International Year of Sports and Education" on behalf of the UN, Federer immediately agreed. Together with UN General Secretary Kofi Annan, Federer and Ogi announced this initiative at UN headquarters in New York on November 5, 2004. Almost a year later, Federer submitted an interim report on the project at the Palace of Nations in Geneva. He conducted both appearances with great enthusiasm.

"I am convinced that sports can help overcome disadvantages as well as build bridges between cultures and nations," Federer posted on his website. "If I can make my modest contribution to this, I certainly will. As ambassador for sport, making a contribution to help others is a very noble mission." Before Christmas of 2006, he took some time off to visit India in his role as UNICEF ambassador.

The role of ambassador appears to fit Federer well. Mark Miles, the former 16-year CEO of the ATP, couldn't believe his eyes when Federer and his girlfriend organized a media day in Hong Kong after the US Open in 2004—on their own initiative—to satisfy demands for Federer's time, as well as to promote the booming tennis movement in Asia.

Federer's willingness to help also created admiration with the organizers of the Tennis Masters Cup in Shanghai. They reservedly asked him if he would be willing to dedicate the new Qi Zhong Stadium in person as a lead-in to the 2005 Tennis Masters Cup. Federer willingly accepted. When he arrived in Shanghai for the one day visit after his win in Bangkok, he gave interview after interview and, instead of playing just one set of tennis with organizers and officials on the Centre Court at the facility, he played two sets. He also spent a great deal of time with the organizers, government officials, the media and fans. He even paid a visit to the kitchen after dinner to thank the cooks.

During the Tennis Masters Cup in Shanghai, reporters brought up his pre-event visit to christen the stadium and summarized that no other player would have done what Federer did to pre-promote the event, especially playing more tennis than was required. "My doubles partner wanted to play another set and I said, 'OK, no problem,'" he said. "We even won both sets. It was fun. It was fun to get a glimpse behind the scenes. In general, it's not every day that you can spend time with government officials, especially from China." He also observed that "tennis has given me so much that I'm convinced that I should give something in return. It's not a must for me but it makes me feel much better. I'm proud to support tennis or sports, and I hope the future No. 1 player will do this as well."

Lynette Federer enjoyed watching her son grow into his role as an ambassador and first noticed the great change within him when he first became the No. 1 player in the world in 2004. "Roger has become a perfectionist. He's very exact," she said in 2004. "It was completely different before. He didn't take things seriously and was always late. He's taking his role as No. 1 very seriously." She said that he stands for values like honesty, candidness, friendliness, team spirit, responsibility, loyalty and integrity.

Federer has been a role model for many fans and ambitious young tennis players for a long time. He has become somebody worth looking up to. He has probably signed more autographs and is more accessible than any No. 1 player ever before. "To make a dream come true for some people," Federer said once when asked why he was so patient when signing autographs. "When I was a ball boy, I also used to run after all the players in the hallways to get autographs. At home, I would then look the autographs as the catch of the day. I know how it is and I haven't forgotten that." One of his customs during tournaments is to invite unknown professionals or juniors to practice with him to give them an experience they'll never forget.

Federer knows that his opinion carries more weight than others and he uses it responsibly. He is not the type of person who spouts insipid clichés or promotes radical changes. He prefers supporting tennis traditions and conventional issues. He is against abolishing line judges in favor of electronic systems. He is against experiments with new scoring systems, as has been partially implemented in doubles events. He also was against the experiments with more round-robin tournaments, that promptly failed in early 2007. He also defended the rights of smaller tournaments to exist. "I think it's wrong if everything is just measured according to the Grand Slams because then other tournaments would also be basically meaningless," he said. But of course, he is aware of the fact that in the end, his own career will be primarily evaluated by how many Grand Slam titles he won and how many weeks he ranked No. 1 in the world.

Federer is not only an ambassador for sports, but also for Europe and especially Switzerland. Despite his close ties to South Africa, he consistently demonstrates how much Switzerland means to him. Representing Switzerland in Davis Cup play and the Olympics is very important to him, but unfortunately, his commitment to Davis Cup has sometimes been sacrificed to attend to priorities in his singles career. He described the moment he led the Swiss Olympic delegation as the flag-bearer at the Opening Ceremonies at the 2004 Olympic Games in Athens, Greece as one of the proudest of his life.

But above all, Roger Federer is a highly-talented, hard-working tennis ambassador who loves every facet of his sport. He is one who strives to promote his sport at any possible occasion and who knows that through tennis he can provide joy to a great number of people—and maybe make the world a little better place to live.

Roger Federer Career Timeline

August 8, 1981 Federer is born in Basel, Switzerland

July 15, 1996 Federer plays his first ITF world junior tournament in Davos, Switzerland at the age of 14 and defeats Lakas Rhomberg of Austria 6-1, 6-0 in the first round.

May 11, 1997 At the age of 15, Federer wins his first ITF world junior tournament in Prato, Italy, defeating Luka Kutanjac of Croatia 6-4, 6-0 in the final.

September 22, 1997 Federer, less than two months after turning 16, debuts on the ATP computer with a world ranking of No. 803.

July 5, 1998 A 16-year-old Federer defeats Irakli Labaze of the Republic of Georgia 6-4, 6-4 to win the Wimbledon junior singles title.

July 7, 1998 Federer plays his first ATP Tour match, losing to lucky-loser Lucas Arnold of Argentina 6-4, 6-4 in the first round of the Swiss Open in Gstaad.

September 30, 1998 Federer defeats Guillaume Raoux of France 6-2, 6-2 in the first round of Toulouse for his first ATP singles match victory.

December 20, 1998 Federer ends his career as a junior player by winning the prestigious singles title at the Orange Bowl in Key Biscayne, Fla., defeating Guillermo Coria of Argentina, 7-5, 6-3 in the final.

April 2, 1999 In the 100th year of Davis Cup, Federer makes his Davis Cup debut, defeating Davide Sanguinetti 6-4, 6-7 (3), 6-3, 6-4 in the opening day of play in Switzerland's defeat of Italy in Neuchatel. The match was the first for the 17-year-old Federer in a best-of-five-set match. "At first I was nervous but then I calmed down," said Federer. "I didn't do very well in the tie-break and took too many risks. But I think in the end taking a lot of risks combined with the public's support helped me win."

May 25, 1999 Ranked No. 111 in the world, 17-year-old Federer plays in his first main draw match at a Grand Slam tournament at the French Open, losing to two-time reigning US Open champion Patrick Rafter of Australia 5-7, 6-3, 6-0, 6-2.

June 22, 1999 Federer makes his main draw debut at Wimbledon and loses in the first round to Jiri Novak of the Czech Republic 6-3, 2-6, 4-6, 6-3, 6-4.

January 18, 2000 Federer plays and wins his first main draw match at the Australian Open, defeating Michael Chang 6-4, 6-4, 7-6 (5), en route to the third round.

February 13, 2000 Federer plays his first ATP Tour singles final but loses to countryman Marc Rosset 2-6, 6-3, 7-6 (5) in the final of the Marseille Open in France—the first ATP singles final played between two players from Switzerland.

June 2, 2000 Federer defeats fellow Swiss Michel Kratochvil 7-6 (5), 6-4, 2-6, 6-7 (4), 8-6 to reach the fourth round at Roland Garros—his first visit into the round of 16 at a Grand Slam tournament.

September 27, 2000 Federer loses the bronze medal match at the Olympic Games in Sydney, falling to France's Arnaud DiPasquale by a 7-6 (5), 6-7 (7), 6-3 margin.

February 4, 2001 Federer, at age 19, wins the first ATP title of his career, defeating Julien Boutter of France 6-4, 6-7 (7), 6-4 in Milan, Italy. "What a relief," he said after the match. "I'm really happy to have won my first title here in Milan. As a kid you always dream of winning your first title."

June 5, 2001 Federer advances to the quarterfinals of a Grand Slam event for the first time in his career, defeating Wayne Arthurs of Australia 3-6, 6-3, 6-4, 6-2 in the round of 16 at the French Open.

June 25, 2001 In his third appearance in the main draw at Wimbledon, Federer finally wins his first match in the gentlemen's singles competition, defeating Christophe Rochus of Belgium 6-2, 6-3, 6-2 in the first round.

July 2, 2001 Federer registers a stunning 7-6 (7), 5-7, 6-4, 6-7 (2), 7-5 Centre Court upset of seven-time Wimbledon champion Pete Sampras in the round of 16 at Wimbledon, ending the 31-match wining streak at the All England Club for Sampras as well as his quest for a record-tying fifth straight title.

May 19, 2002 Federer dominates Marat Safin to win his first Tennis Masters Series title at the German Open in Hamburg, defeating the Russian 6-1, 6-3, 6-4 in the final. Said Federer, "I played really well. It has been a wonderful tournament for me, really incredible. I have played well all week and it gives me great confidence going into the French Open." Federer cracks the top 10 in the rankings the next day by virtue of his effort.

June 25, 2002 Tagged as a pre-tournament dark horse favorite to win Wimbledon, Federer is beaten badly on Centre Court at the All England Club in the first round, losing to 18-year-old qualifier Mario Ancic of Croatia 6-3, 7-6 (2), 6-3.

July 6, 2003 Federer wins a Grand Slam tournament for the first time, defeating Mark Philippoussis 7-6 (5), 6-2, 7-6 (3) in the gentlemen's singles final at Wimbledon. The 21-year-old Federer becomes the first Swiss man in 117 editions of The Championships to win the title. Federer hits 21 aces and 50 winners against only nine unforced errors in the one hour and 56-minute final. "It's an absolute dream for me coming true," said Federer after the victory.

November 16, 2003 Federer routs Andre Agassi 6-3, 6-0, 6-4 to win the year-end Tennis Masters Cup for the first time in his career. Playing at the Westside Tennis Club in Houston, Texas, Federer fires 11 aces in the 88-minute match delayed two-and-a-half hours due to rain. "It was one of the best matches for me this season," said Federer. "I'm very happy how the whole year went, especially this tournament. I worked hard this year. You always have ups and downs but I feel this season has been complete."

February 1, 2004 Federer wins his first Australian Open crown and his second career Grand Slam singles title with a 7-6 (3), 6-4, 6-2 win over Marat Safin in the men's singles final. Federer's Australian Open result propels him into the No. 1 ranking the day after the final. "What a great start to the year for me, to win the Australian Open and become No. 1 in the world," Federer said. "To fulfill my dreams, it really means very much to me."

July 4, 2004 Federer wins Wimbledon for a second consecutive time, defeating first-time finalist Andy Roddick 4-6, 7-5, 7-6 (3), 6-4 in the men's singles final.

July 11, 2004 Federer wins his first pro singles title on Swiss soil at the Swiss Open in Gstaad, defeating Igor Andreev of Russia 6-2, 6-3, 5-7, 6-3 in the final.

August 1, 2004 On Switzerland's national holiday and on the second anniversary of the death of his coach Peter Carter, Federer defeats Andy Roddick 7-5, 6-3 in the final of the Canadian Open in Toronto. Federer also becomes the first player since Björn Borg in 1979 to win three consecutive tournaments on three different surfaces—grass, clay and hard courts. Said Federer, "I hope to be able to have coffee with Borg sometime and have a talk about these series."

August 17, 2004 In a self-described "terrible day," Federer's Olympic dreams come to an end in a matter of hours as he is eliminated from both the singles and doubles competitions at the Athens Olympics. In singles, Federer is dismissed in the second round by Tomas Berdych 4-6, 7-5, 7-5, then, with partner Yves Allegro, he loses to Mahesh Bhupathi and Leander Paes of India 6-2, 7-6 (7). "What can I say? It's a terrible day for me, losing singles and doubles," Federer said. "Obviously, I was aiming for a better result than this, but that's what I got. So I have to live with it."

September 12, 2004 A 23-year-old Federer wins the US Open for the first time, overwhelming Lleyton Hewitt 6-0, 7-6 (3), 6-0 in one hour and 51 minutes in the men's singles final. The US Open title adds to his Australian and Wimbledon titles also won in 2004 making Federer the first player since Mats Wilander in 1988 to win three Grand Slam tournament titles in the same year.

November 21, 2004 Roger Federer wins an Open Era record 13th singles final in a row, defeating Lleyton Hewitt 6-3, 6-2 in the final of the year-end Tennis

Masters Cup in Houston, Texas. The tournament victory, his 11th during the calendar year, caps a fantastic season for the Swiss world No. 1, who also won the Australian Open for the first time, Wimbledon for a second time and the US Open for a first time. Said Federer, "It's just an unbelievable end to a fantastic season for me."

January 27, 2005 Federer lets a match point slip away in his titanic 5-7, 6-4, 5-7, 7-6 (6), 9-7 loss to Marat Safin in the semifinals of the Australian Open.

February 27, 2005 Federer wins his 25th career singles title, defeating Ivan Ljubicic 6-1, 6-7 (6), 6-3 in the final of Dubai Open in the United Arab Emirates. The title is Federer's third in a row in the oil-rich middle eastern city. Said Federer, "To win three times here is fantastic. It's the first time to have achieved that anywhere."

April 3, 2005 Two points from defeat in the third-set tie-break, Federer rallies from two-sets-to-love down to defeat Spain's Rafael Nadal 2-6, 6-7 (4), 7-6 (5), 6-3, 6-1 in three hours and 43 minutes to win the NASDAQ-100 Open in Key Biscayne, Fla. Federer trails 4-2 in the third set and 5-3 in the third-set tie-break before rallying to win his 22nd consecutive match and his 18th consecutive final.

June 3, 2005 Rafael Nadal from Spain celebrates his 19th birthday and defeats Federer 6-3, 4-6, 6-4, 6-3 in the semifinals of the French Open. Said Nadal, "Federer, for me, is the best player wherever. Not only No. 1 for tennis, but the No. 1 for the person, and for sportsmanship."

July 3, 2005 Federer wins Wimbledon for a third straight year, defeating Andy Roddick, 6-2, 7-6 (2), 6-4 in the championship match. Says Roddick of the final in an entertaining post-match press conference, "I feel like I played decent, the statistics are decent and I got straight-setted. But I am not going to sit around and sulk and cry. I did everything I could. I tried playing different ways. I tried going to his forehand and coming in. He passed me. I tried to go to his backhand and coming in. He passed me. Tried staying back, he figured out a way to pass me, even though I was at the baseline. Hope he gets bored or something." Said Roddick of his personal feelings for Federer, "I have loads of respect for him as a person. I've told him before, 'I'd love to hate you, but you're really nice.'"

September 11, 2005 Andre Agassi calls Federer to best player he has ever faced in losing to Federer 6-3, 2-6, 7-6 (1), 6-1 in the final of the US Open. "Pete (Sampras) was great, no question," Agassi said. "But there was a place to get to with Pete. It could be on your terms. There's no such place with Roger. I think he's the best I've played against." Said Federer of Agassi's comments, "It's fantastic to be compared to all the players he's played throughout his career. We're talking about the best—some are the best in the world of all time. And it's still going and I still have chances to improve." The title is Federer's sixth Grand Slam tournament victory and second in Flushing Meadows.

November 20, 2005 David Nalbandian of Argentina stuns Federer 6-7 (4), 6-7 (11), 6-2, 6-1, 7-6 (3) in four hours and 33 minutes to win the year-end Tennis Masters Cup. Nalbandian's win snaps Federer's 35-match win streak and ends his streak of 24 straight victories in singles finals. Said Nalbandian to Federer in the post-match ceremony, "After knowing you a long time, don't worry, you'll win a lot more trophys. Let me keep this one." Federer finishes his 2005 season with an 81-4 record.

January 29, 2006 Federer gets emotional, cries and hugs all-time great Rod Laver during the post-match ceremony following his 5-7, 7-5, 6-0, 6-2 win over upstart Cypriot Marcos Baghdatis in the final of the Australian Open. Federer has difficulty putting to words the emotions he feels during the post-match ceremony and sobs after receiving the trophy from Laver. "I hope you know how much this means to me," he said as he wiped away tears. Federer becomes the first player to win three consecutive Grand Slam tournaments since Pete Sampras won at the 1994 Australian Open. The title is his seventh career Grand Slam title, tying him with John McEnroe, John Newcombe and Mats Wilander.

March 4, 2006 In a battle of the No. 1 and No. 2 players in the world, No. 2-ranked Rafael Nadal defeats world No. 1 Federer 2-6, 6-4, 6-4 in the final of the Dubai Open in the United Arab Emirates. Nadal's win ends Federer's 56-match hard court winning streak. Said Nadal, "I think it is unbelievable to win against the best player in the world — perhaps the best in history of the game."

May 14, 2006 In an epic match that officially cements the rivalry between Federer and Rafael Nadal as one of the greatest in the sport, Nadal defeats the man from Basel 6-7 (0), 7-6 (5), 6-4, 2-6, 7-6 (5) in five hours and six minutes in the final of the Italian Open in Rome. Federer leads by 4-1 in the fifth set and holds two match points, before he lets the 19-year-old from Mallorca back into the match to successfully defend his Italian title. Said Federer, "I'm on the right track, a step closer with this guy, just got caught at the finish line, but I should have won."

June 11, 2006 Federer fails in his quest to win a fourth consecutive Grand Slam title, losing to Rafael Nadal 1-6, 6-1, 6-4, 7-6 (4) in the final of the French Open. Federer, appearing in the French final for the first time in his career, nearly joins Don Budge and Rod Laver as the only men to hold all four Grand Slam titles at the same time. The loss also marked Federer's first defeat in eight career Grand Slam finals. Said Federer of his lost opportunity to win four straight majors, "Obviously, it's a pity, but it goes on, right?"

June 27, 2006 Federer wins his 42nd consecutive match on a grass court, defeating Richard Gasquet of France 6-3, 6-2, 6-2 in the first round of Wimbledon, breaking the record for consecutive match victories on grass courts held by Björn Borg.

July 9, 2006 Federer ends a five-match losing streak to Rafael Nadal, defeating his Spanish rival 6-0, 7-6 (5), 6-7 (2), 6-3 to win his fourth consecutive Wimbledon title, joining Björn Borg and Pete Sampras as the only men to win four straight men's singles titles at the All England Club. Said Federer, "I'm very well aware how important this match was for me. If I lose, it's a hard blow for me. It's important for me to win a final against him for a change and beat him for a change. Wimbledon I knew was going to be the place for me to do it the easiest way and it turned out to be tough."

August 13, 2006 Federer wins his 40th career title, defeating Richard Gasquet of France 2-6, 6-3, 6-2 in the final of the Canadian Open in Toronto. Said

Federer of his slow start against the Frenchman, "'I just always believe that I can turn any match around. That's what happened today. I know that once I turn it around, once I would take the lead then it would be very difficult for my opponent. That's what I always tell myself. Maybe it's an illusion sometimes, but it definitely works."

August 16, 2006 Federer's 55-match winning streak in North America comes to an end in a 7-5, 6-4 loss to Andy Murray of Britain in the second round of Cincinnati. "The streaks? I don't care about those now that they're over," said Federer, who had not lost in straight sets in his last 194 matches. "It's going to be a relief for everybody and now we can move on." Said Murray, "I know Federer didn't play his best match, but how many guys beat him when he's playing badly anyway?"

September 10, 2006 With golfing great Tiger Woods sitting in his box, Federer wins the US Open for a third consecutive year, defeating Andy Roddick 6-2, 4-6, 7-5, 6-1 in the final. "I can relate to what he's going through ... with the success I've had over the years now," Federer said of Woods. "I follow him a lot. I'm always happy when he wins...More and more often, over the last year or so, I've been kind of compared to Tiger. I asked him how it (is) for him (and) it's funny because many things (are) similar. He knew exactly how I kind of felt out on the court. That's something I haven't felt before, a guy who knows how it feels to be invincible at times, when you just have the feeling there's nothing going wrong any more. In the fourth set, for instance, it's I guess (like) him in the final round. He knows exactly how it feels."

January 28, 2007 Federer becomes the first man since Björn Borg at the 1980 French Open to win a Grand Slam title without losing a set with a 7-6 (2), 6-4, 6-4 win over Chilean Fernando Gonzalez in the final of the Australian Open. The title is Federer's 10th in a Grand Slam tournament.

February 26, 2007 Federer begins his 161st consecutive week as the No. 1 player in the world, breaking the all-time ATP record held by Jimmy Connors. Said Federer, "This record is something special to me. Even if I lost it tomorrow it would still take somebody more than three years to beat it."

Quotes On Roger Federer

"I am amazed, not only by the beauty of Roger's game, but also the consistency of his tournament wins. Even more amazing is the fact that he seems to love what he is doing and he handles the pressure so well. Roger is a great champion and ambassador for our sport."
—John McEnroe, 2007

"Roger's got too many shots, too much talent in one body. It's hardly fair that one person can do all this - his backhands, his forehands, volleys, serving, his court position ... the way he moves around the court, you feel like he's barely touching the ground, and that's the sign of a great champion. And his anticipation, I guess, is the one thing that we all admire."
—Rod Laver, 2007

"Well, I think when I look at Roger, I mean, I'm a fan. I'm a fan of how he plays, what he's about... he's a class guy on and off the court. He's fun to watch. Just his athletic ability, what he's able to do on the run. I think he can and will break every tennis record out there."
—Pete Sampras, 2006

"He simply does not have any more weaknesses left in him. It is such a pleasure to see him play. To me, Roger Federer is the right model for anyone aspiring to be a tennis player. It is such a pleasure to just watch him play. His shot-making has got better and I doubt there is any shot he cannot make in any part of the court...All records will tumble when it comes to Roger. He is such a complete player that I do not see anyone getting better than him for a long time from now."
—Björn Borg to *Gulf News* in 2007

"Roger is a complete player. What he has—and it's not luck—is the ability to change his game slightly as to what his opponent's doing to him...He's not known as a great aggressive player, but he's so good on the defense and so good at the return of serve that he's forcing the other player, mentally, to get a little bit of scaredness. 'I've got to serve a little better or Roger's going to knock it by me. ... I've got to make a better approach shot or he's going to pass me.' He's getting errors because of the threat of his skills. That's why he's the champ."
—Jack Kramer to the Associated Press, 2004

"Roger is like a good red wine, he's getting better with age. I think his best years are ahead of him. I think his big years will be when he is 26, 27, 28, as that is when he will be both mature and at his physical peak. I think he will become a better player in many respects. Roger hasn't even started to use a lot of his game. It's a challenge for all those trying to stop him. But they are playing against a man who will probably enter tennis history as the best ever. That should be motivation enough."
—Tony Roche to *The Age*, 2007

"[In the modern game], you're a clay court specialist, a grass court specialist or a hard court specialist ... or you're Roger Federer."
—Jimmy Connors to the BBC, 2006

"(Roger) has the potential to be the best ever. I wouldn't give it to him yet, but he is certainly on his way. I watch him and Tiger [Woods]. I feel very fortunate to be watching two who will probably be the best of all times. They are both phenomenal."
—Ivan Lendl to the *Sarasota Herald-Tribune*, 2007

"I'd like to be in his shoes for one day to know what it feels like to play that way."
—Mats Wilander to the Associated Press, 2004

"I've probably run out of adjectives to describe him on the court to talk about his excellence. He's just unbelievable."
—James Blake, 2006

"I really consider myself a top five player in the world, which it doesn't mean that I am close to Roger."
—**Ivan Ljubicic, 2006**

"He's a real person. He's not an enigma. Off the court he's not trying to be somebody. If you met him at McDonald's and you didn't know who he was, you would have no idea that he's one of the best athletes in the world."
—**Andy Roddick, 2005**

"The metaphysical explanation is that Roger Federer is one of those rare, preternatural athletes who appear to be exempt, at least in part, from certain physical laws. Good analogues here include Michael Jordan, who could not only jump inhumanly high but actually hang there a beat or two longer than gravity allows, and Muhammad Ali, who really could "float" across the canvas and land two or three jabs in the clock-time required for one. There are probably a half-dozen other examples since 1960. And Federer is of this type—a type that one could call genius, or mutant, or avatar. He is never hurried or off-balance. The approaching ball hangs, for him, a split-second longer than it ought to. His movements are lithe rather than athletic. Like Ali, Jordan, Maradona, and Gretzky, he seems both less and more substantial than the men he faces. Particularly in the all-white that Wimbledon enjoys getting away with still requiring, he looks like what he may well (I think) be: a creature whose body is both flesh and, somehow, light."
—**David Foster Wallace, *New York Times Magazine*, 2006**

"I've heard comparisons between what Federer is doing and what Tiger Woods is doing these days. But, here's the thing: Tiger doesn't do anything to you. Obviously, he's intimidating, but Tiger is playing the course, just like you. But Federer is playing you. And when he takes away the thing you do best, it just cripples you. He does what it takes to beat you, regardless of what kind of player you are."
—**Patrick McEnroe to the *St. Petersburg Times*, 2007**

"On Sunday night at Rod Laver Arena, Roger Federer took my breath away. I was mesmerized by the audacity of his stroke play. His sheer mastery of the art of tennis was pure genius and to bear witness was to evoke some sort of

spiritual experience that occurs only a handful of times in a lifetime—if you're lucky. To try to describe the way Federer plays tennis is like trying to describe how Rudolf Nureyev danced or Jascha Heifetz played the violin. Common words or images do none of them justice."
—Gareth Andrews of *The Age,* 2007

"Yes, I really hit with him when he was 15, during a tournament in Basel, and I knew then he would be good, but not this good. If he stays healthy, it will actually be a miracle if he doesn't win more Grand Slams than Pete [Sampras]. The way he picks his shots is unbelievable. He is fast, he has a great volley, a great serve, great backhand, great everything. If I was his coach, what can I tell him? He is a magician with a racquet. Even when he is playing badly, which is rarely, he can still do things with his racquet nobody else can do."
—Goran Ivanisevic to *The Independent,* 2004

"He's the most gifted player that I've ever seen in my life. I've seen a lot of people play. I've seen the Lavers, I played against some of the great players—the Samprases, Beckers, Connors, Borgs, you name it. This guy could be the greatest of all time. That, to me, says it all. He's probably the greatest player that ever lived. He can beat half the guys with his eyes closed!
—John McEnroe, 2004

"I've never enjoyed watching someone playing tennis as much as Federer. I'm just in awe. Pete Sampras was wonderful but he relied so much on his serve, whereas Roger has it all, he's just so graceful, elegant and fluid—a symphony in tennis whites. Roger can produce tennis shots that should be declared illegal."
—Tracy Austin, 2004

"The best way to beat him would be to hit him over the head with a racquet. Roger could win the Grand Slam if he keeps playing the way he is and, if he does that, it will equate to the two Grand Slams that I won because standards are much higher these days."
—Rod Laver, 2007

"I'm a fan of his game, his temperament, the way he handles himself on and off the court. I do picture myself how I would play him. Now that I'm sitting on my couch watching, I just kind of marvel at the things he's able to do. He's a great mover, does great things off both sides of the court, can come in when he has to, and has a pretty big first serve. He has the whole package. There's really nothing he can't do. I just love it. He just makes it look easy. He's smooth, a great athlete."
—**Pete Sampras, 2007**

"He's probably the most talented person to ever carry a racquet around—the shots that he can come up with, the way he's kind of become a totally complete player. But I think off the court, it's huge. There have been a lot of good champions, but he's just classy. He is never high and mighty in the locker room or anything like that."
—**Andy Roddick, 2005**

"You bring up tennis in this day and age and a lot of people roll their eyes, and they're not interested. But listen: if you're not paying attention to this guy, if you appreciate sports, you have to take a moment to appreciate this guy. It's like Tiger Woods. A lot of people are your meat-and-potatoes sports fans: I like football, I like basketball, I like baseball. If you don't appreciate golf, that's fine. You don't have to watch it, and you don't have to pay attention to it, but you have to appreciate the greatness of Tiger Woods. It's the same with tennis. You don't appreciate tennis? I'm not telling you that you have to. But, if you don't give Roger Federer his due, then you're just missing the boat. Roger Federer is the best player in any sport today, and it's not close. It's not close."...
—**Mike Greenberg of ESPN Radio's *Mike & Mike in the Morning,* 2006**

"What he's done in tennis, I think, is far greater than what I've done in golf. He's lost what ... five matches in three years? That's pretty good."
—**Tiger Woods to the Associated Press on Federer after Woods was told of his selection over Federer as AP Athlete of the Year, 2006**

Grand Slam Man

PERFORMED BY BINGE

Roger Federer, you're getting better-er
Every time I see you play
Roger Federer, that's what I said-er-er
(You're) gonna win it any way

He's your Grand Slam Man
He's your Grand Slam Man

He's from Switzerland, he's a wunderkind
But don't get in his way
You know he's hopin' to win the Open
He's got the opportunity

Roger Federer, you're a predator
He'll attack you from the start
Roger Federer, you're a shreader-er
He will tear you right apart

He's your Grand Slam Man
He's your Grand Slam Man
This one's for the fans

Roger Federer, you're getting better-er
I know you always steal the show
Roger Federer, put on your sweater-er
C'mon it's time to go

He's your Grand Slam Man
He's your Grand Slam Man
He's not just working on his tan...

He's your Grand Slam Man
He's your Grand Slam Man
He's not just working on his tan

He's even won in Rotterdam...
And they like him in Japan...
He's your Grand Slam Man

From The Publisher

There are many people to thank for their help with the English language publishing of this book. For starters, Emily Brackett with Visible Logic, who was the book's designer and a good friend of New Chapter Press, as well as Kyle and Petra Brown, who were the official translators of the book. Gisela Walker also assisted as a "pinch-hit" translator for certain sections of the book. Others to thank for their support and assistance include Bill Mountford, now with the LTA, and his wife Catherine O'Neal, Ben Sturner of Leverage Agency, Blair Cummins with DomainMinds and Sportsmates.com, Henry and Angela Doehla, John Macom and Joe Titone from "Binge" and www.tennistunes. com, Peter Balestrieri and staff at ASAP Sports, Arlen Kantarian and his staff at the USTA, in particular Chris Widmaier, Jeff Ryan, Tim Curry and Jean Daly, and Greg Sharko with the ATP. Last but not least, New Chapter Press wants to thank Rene Stauffer, who did a fantastic job chronicling the life of this international super star. His hard work under some tight deadlines to make this updated project work is greatly appreciated.

New Chapter Press
New York, NY, May 2007
www.newchapterpressonline.com

List Of Press Sources For Quotations

Page 6. "I considered myself not to be competent enough and he would have just upset me anyway."—Lynette Federer to *Basler Zeitung*

Page 6. "He would always come around shouting when I was with my friends or he would pick up the receiver when I was on the phone. He really was a little devil."—Diana Federer to *Replay—Roger Federer, His Story (DVD)*

Page 13. "When I first saw him, Roger hardly came up to the net. His talent was instantly visible. Roger could do a lot with the ball and the racquet at a very young age. He was playful and especially wanted to have his fun."—Peter Carter to *Basler Zeitung*

Page 19. "There was a new curtain at the tennis center..."—Roger Federer to *Replay—Roger Federer, His Story (DVD)*

Page 42. "He didn't kiss me until the last day of the Olympic Games."—Mirka Vavrinec to *Schweizer Illustrierte*

Page 43. "I don't think that this has to come out in public."—Roger Federer to *Facts*

Page 45. "Athletically, he had great shortcomings. There was enormous potential for improvement..."—Pierre Paganini to *Tages-Anzeiger Magazin*

Page 46. "He wants to work hard but he needs a lot of variety..."—Paganini to *Aargauer Zeitung*

Page 65. "South Africa is a haven for him away from the world of tennis...."—Lynnette Federer to *Neue Welt*

Page 68. "It was the first death Roger had to deal with it was a deep shock..."—Lynette Federer to *Replay - Roger Federer, His Story (DVD)*

Page 74. "He has an unbelievable repertoire..."—Peter Lundgren to *Swiss Sportsinformation*

Page 76. "The entire world keeps reminding me that I am supposed to win a Grand Slam..." - Roger Federer to *Journal du Dimanche*

Page 78. "I was simply not prepared mentally..."—Roger Federer to *Tennis Magazine* (Paris)

Page 90. "At the time, I was in a funk on the court, in kind of a trance that I could hardly remember...."—*Sport Magazin*

Page 109 – "It's a long way to No. 1. You have to overcome many obstacles to get there..."—*Tennis Magazine* (Paris)

Page 192. "Back then I wanted to show everybody what I was capable of, the difficult shots I had masters..."—Federer to *Le Figaro*

Page 193. "I was almost bored on the court..."—Federer to *Aargauer Zeitung*

Page 198. "He rose from being a world class player to rising to the caliber of a Grand Slam champion."—Boris Becker to *Tennis Magazin* Hamburg

Page 199. "I'd like to be in his shoes for one day to know what it feels to play that way." —Wilander to the Associated Press

Page 199. "He's head and shoulders above everyone else..."—Pete Sampras to *L'Equipe*

Page 188. "Mirka likes to cook and I like to eat..."—Federer to *Schweizer Illustrierte*

Page 188-189. "This is very private, it's something I don't discuss at all..."—Federer to *Sonntags Blick*

Page 229. "Roger has become a perfectionist..."—Lynette Federer to *Basler Zeitung*

Page 208. "One thing and another happened at IMG..."—Roger Federer to *Aargauer Zeitung*

Page 209. "We grew into the business"—Lynnette Federer to *Basler Zeitung*

Page 209. "I view myself as working in an advisory capacity..."—Robert Federer to *Facts*

Page 210. We were all taken by surprise..."—Roger Federer to *Sport Magazin*

Index

Acapulco 138
ACE (Assisting Children Everywhere) 226
Adams, Victoria 141
Agassi, Andre xv, 25, 37, 42,48,60, 62, 67, 72, 79, 81, 91, 96-99, 106, 119,120, 123,130, 134,137-139,150-153, 156, 161, 163,167, 197, 200, 201, 207, 211, 212, 218, 220, 222, 223, 235, 240
Alinghi 86
All England Club xiv, 54. 55, 78, 85, 86, 104, 105, 113, 115, 147,166,168, 215, 221, 232, 236
Allegro, Yves 39, 54, 55, 78, 85, 86, 104, 105, 113, 115, 147, 166, 168, 215, 221, 232
Allschwil 5, 8, 156
Ancic, Mario 147, 233
Andress, Ursi 220
Andreev, Igor 116, 233
Annan, Kofi 228
Arazi, Hicham 62, 68-69
Armstrong, Gerry 84
Armstrong, Lance 140
Arnold, Lucas 23
Arthur Ashe Stadium 151, 202
Arthurs, Wayne 38, 92
Arzani, Nicola vii, 210, 219
Aschwanden, Sergei 118
Ashe, Arthur 144
Athens 7, 116, 119, 140, 219, 230, 234
Austin, Tracy xvi, 242
Austria 3, 213, 231, 233
Australian Open 21, 35, 47, 60, 74, 75, 98, 102-108, 111, 122, 123, 133-136, 139, 142, 160, 167, 175-181, 210-213, 225, 232-237
Ayala, Luis 177

Babolat 206
Baghdatis, Marcos 161-163, 167, 177, 235
Ballesteros, Seve 140
Barcelona xviii, 139, 164
Barker, Sue 84
Barnes, Simon 220-221
Barossa Valley 12, 67
Basel xviii, 3-10, 18, 22-28, 44-49, 53, 58, 60, 67, 70, 83, 84, 101,104, 111, 116, 125, 127, 150, 152, 155, 156, 168, 173, 184, 200, 210, 220, 223, 231, 236, 241
Bastad, Sweden 150
Bastl, George 51
Beauty and The Beast 119
Beckenbauer, Franz 140
Becker, Boris xvi, 253, 147, 153, 169, 187, 188, 197, 198, 211, 217, 222, 224, 241
Beckham, David 141
Belarus 52
Bellinzona 11
Berdych, Tomas 7, 118
Bergelin, Lennart 87
Berneck, Switzerland 3,4
Bern 3, 38, 104, 208
Bertolucci, Paolo 32
Bhupathi, Mahesh 118, 234
Biel 18, 19, 46, 57
Bild 224
Bjorkman, Jonas 53
Blake, James 151, 170, 173, 177, 240, 242
Bojnice 40
Bollettieri, Nick 224
Bosch, Guenther 7
Borg, Björn v, xii, xv, xviii, 24, 25, 55, 77, 85, 87, 109, 117, 119, 126, 128, 134, 148, 166, 167, 168, 178, 180, 191, 207, 212, 220, 234, 236, 238

Boston Globe   xvi, 99, 222
Bottmingen   3, 104, 226
Bouin, Philippe   195
Boutter, Julien   47
Bouttier, Jean-Claude   165
Boy From Oz, The   119
Brennwald, Roger   24
British Daily Express   224
Bucharest   111
Budge, Don   122, 123, 142, 153, 163, 179, 236, 237
Burj al-Arab Hotel, Dubai   126
Burer, Stefan   72
Bush, Barbara   127
Bush, George H.W.   127

Cahill, Darren   xii, 67, 130
Calgary Sun   171
Capriati, Jennifer   xvi
Carlsen, Kenneth   193
Carter, Peter   12, 13, 17, 18, 21, 29, 34, 26, 52, 60, 65-69, 87, 117, 130, 178, 234
Cash, Pat   37, 63, 83, 85, 93, 106, 147
"CBS Early Show"   125
Chang, Michael   139, 144, 232
Chao Phraya River   125
Chiudinelli, Marco   8. 9, 11, 15, 137, 185
Christen, Bernhard   101
Christinet, Cornelia   14-16
Christinet, Vincent   14-16
Ciba   3, 5, 8, 20, 209
Cincinnati   150, 169, 176, 237
Clement, Arnaud   35, 47, 50-51, 112
Clijsters, Kim   226
Cochet, Henri   48
Coe, Sebastian   140
Cohn, Arthur   125
"Cold Pizza"   124
Collins, Bud   xvi, xvii, 73, 95, 99, 222
Cologne   37
Concordia Club   6
Connolly, Maureen   123
Connors, Jimmy   xviii, 25, 109, 122, 143, 155, 176, 178, 199, 211, 222, 237
Copperfield, David   125
Coria, Guillermo   139, 140, 186, 217, 231
Corretja, Alex   38-39
Costa, Albert   71-72
Costa do Sauipe   138

Courier, Jim   25, 77, 109, 139, 172
Court, Margaret Smith   123
Crawford, John Herbert   153, 177

Daily Express   224
Daily Mirror   88, 224
Daily News of Los Angeles   171
Daily Telegraph   82, 88, 171, 220, 221
Danzig, Allison   123
Davenport, Lindsay   212
Davis Cup   ix, xii, xv, xiii, 23, 24, 28, 31-35, 38, 47-52, 60, 65-68, 77, 92, 93, 98, 106, 110, 112, 119, 131, 132, 137, 143, 155, 163, 173, 175, 186, 230-232
Davydenko, Nikolay   112, 144, 156, 161, 170
Dedman, Robert   183
Dementieva, Elena   42, 226
Deuce   227
De Vito, Danny   125
DiPasquale, Arnaud   42, 47, 118
Djokovic, Novak   173
Doha, Qatar   175, 225
Doherty, Laurie   48
Douglas, Kirk   125
Dubach, Arthur   65
Dubai   75, 95, 111, 116, 126, 132, 137, 138, 150, 163, 164, 166, 168, 175, 214, 234
Duke of Kent   84
Durand, Lynette   3, 4
Dusseldorf   210

Eagle, Joshua   66
Ecublens   xi, 13-18, 45
Edberg, Stefan   25, 54, 77, 85, 109, 153, 211, 220
El Aynaoui, Younes   68-69
El Guerrouj, Hicham   140
Emerson, Roy   22, 178
Escude, Nicolas   50-51
Evert, Chris   211

FC Basel   186
Federer, Diana   4, 6, 7
Federer, Heinrich   4
Federer, Lynette (Durand)   5, 6, 15, 18, 712, 86, 147, 178, 204, 205, 209, 229

Federer, Robert 3, 4, 6, 18, 20, 63, 147, 148, 149, 178, 205, 209, 210
Fernandez, Mary Joe 212
Ferreira, Wayne 66
Ferrero, Juan-Carlos 72, 81, 89, 92-94, 99, 106, 107, 110, 146
Fittipaldi, Emerson 140
Flushing Meadows 150-151, 153, 185, 235
Forbes 212
Forstmann, Ted 213
Fracassi, Nohuel ix
Franklin, Benjamin 218
French Open xv, xvi, xviii, 30, 31, 38, 53. 62, 75-81, 91, 112, 117, 126, 132, 137, 140-145, 155, 158, 166,174, 178, 198, 223, 231-235, 240
Freyss, Christophe 13
Fromberg, Richard 24

Gabriel, Craig 131
Gambill, Jan-Michael 47-48
Gasquet, Richard 139, 140, 166, 236, 237
Gaudenzi, Andrea 60
Gaudio, Gaston 127, 158, 200
Gilbert, Brad 114
Gillette 213
Gimelstob, Justin 48
Ginepri, Robby 151
Gloucester Hotel Casino xv
Godsick, Tony 169, 212
Gonzalez, Fernando 23, 146, 173, 177-178, 237
Gooding, Cuba 141
Goteborg 37
Gottfried, Brian 122
Graf, Simon 215
Graf, Steffi xv, 123, 211
Gretsky, Wayne 223
Grone Tennis Club 185
Groneveld, Sven 37
Grosjean, Sebastian 81
Gross, Christian 186
Gstaad 21, 22, 33, 57, 63, 86, 88, 89, 116, 117, 195, 231
Guggach ix
Gullikson, Tom 32
Gulyas, Istvan 131

Günthardt, Heinz x, xviii, 21, 72, 116, 162, 191, 192, 206
Gurler, Murat 41

Haas, Tommy 22-23, 42, 60, 70, 161, 177
Hagler, Marvin 165
Halle, Germany 79, 95, 113, 146, 166
Hamburg 38, 61, 62, 68, 77, 110, 112, 134, 140, 143, 151, 164, 172, 233
Hantuchova, Daniela 226
Hermenjat, Jacques "Kobi" 21, 22, 89
Henin-Hardenne, Justine 43
Henman, Tim 94, 11, 120, 173, 200
Henry, Thierry 213
Hering Schuppener 210
Hewitt, Leyton xi, xiii, 17, 35, 44-45, 58, 60, 62-63, 70-77, 80- 81, 92-94, 98, 105-109, 113, 120-122, 128, 130, 135, 138-140, 143, 145-147, 151, 156, 177, 200-201, 222, 234,
Hingis, Martina x, xvi, xvii, 40, 43, 47, 57, 123, 299, 205
Hippo Company 208
Hlasek, Jakob x, xiii, 49-52, 70, 189, 206
Hoffman, Dustin 151
Hofsaess, Klaus xiv
Hong Kong 229
Hopman Cup 43
Horna, Luis 76
Hotel Bellagio 125
Hotel Bellevue 89
Hotel du Crillon, Paris 126
Houston 127, 129, 134, 157, 201, 202, 218, 233
Hrbaty, Dominik 117
Huggel, Benjamin 186
IMG xvi, 205, 208, 210, 212, 213

The Independent 88, 165, 221, 224, 241
Indian Wells 75, 95, 111, 119, 120, 137-139, 151, 163, 172, 213, 226
Ivanisevic, Goran 25, 56, 63, 128, 147, 153, 241

Jaeger, Andrea xvi
Johnson, Michael 140
Jordan, Michael 140
Juan Carlos, King of Spain 141

Kacovsky, Adolf "Seppli" 9, 10, 12, 88
Kafelnikov, Yevgeny 31, 39, 47, 48, 60, 110
Kalwa, Jurgen   vii
Kempton Park 3
Kendrick, Robert 167
Kent, Duke of 184
Key Biscayne 95, 112, 138, 139, 151, 163,
    193, 231, 235
Kiefer, Nicolas 79, 146, 161
Kipling, Rudyard 104
Klaus-Peter "KP" see Witt
Kooyong Classic 106, 134, 175, 176
Kournikova, Anna xvi
Kovac, Pavel   75, 79, 84, 113, 148
Krajicek, Richard 54
Kratochvil, Michel 38, 68
Kreuzlingen, Switzerland   40
Kuerten, Gustavo 61, 156

Labadze, Irakli   21
Lacoste, Rene 162
Lacroix, Maurice 207, 210, 213
Lake Constance xvii, 3, 40
Lake Geneva xi, xvii, 13, 14
Lammer, Michael xvii, 11, 56-58, 156, 185
Lapentti, Nicolas 61
Laureus Award 140, 141, 164
Lausanne 112
Laver, Rod v, 93, 122-123, 131, 134, 142,
    147, 163, 178-180, 190, 236
Lendl, Ivan xv, 24, 25, 37,109, 132-134,
    143, 147, 151, 177, 190, 199, 200, 211,
    223, 239
Leonard, Sugar Ray   165
L'Equipe 192, 195, 223
Letterman, David   154
Lewis, Chris   132, 147
Limpopo   66
"Live with Regis and Kelly" 124
Ljubicic, Ivan 134, 138, 157, 161, 194, 234
London 21, 22, 30, 35, 55, 62, 82, 91,
    104, 106, 200, 220
Lopez, Feliciano 26, 80, 88, 111
Lundgren, Julia   103
Lundgren, Lukas 103
Lundgren, Peter   18, 36-38, 45, 46, 47,
    50, 54, 55, 61, 62, 64, 67-69, 74, 76, 79,
    82, 84, 86, 87, 96, 100, 101, 103-107,
    117, 128, 134,

Madrid   126, 135, 155, 156, 173, 184
Maldive Islands 175, 225
Malisse, Xavier 32, 53
Marcolli, Chris 193
Maribor 41
Marseille 31, 35
Martin, David 17
Martin, Todd 47
Massu, Nicolas 164
Mathabane, Mark 227
Mauresmo, Amelie 226
Mauritius 101
McCormack, Mark xvi, 212
McEnroe, John xii, xv, 25, 44, 109, 124,
    126, 128, 133, 140, 143, 147, 153, 158-
    159, 162, 180, 187, 198, 208, 211, 217,
    223-224, 228, 234, 236, 238, 241
McEnroe, Patrick 48, 54, 62, 246
McIngvale, Jim 97-99, 127
Medvedev, Andrei 142
Melbourne 20, 30, 60, 92, 106, 109,
    111,130, 131, 137, 161-163, 175, 178,
    225
Melbourne Age 162
Mercedes 99
Mezzadri, Claudio 32
Mickelson, Phil 76
Milan 47, 60, 232
Miles, Mark 229
Mills, Alan 84
Mirnyi, Max 61
Monte Carlo 33-34, 38, 53, 60, 139, 155,
    163-166
Montreal 57, 91, 92, 150, 156
Morocco 68
Moses, Edwin 140
Moya, Carlos 69
Munchenstein 8
Murray, Andy 155, 168, 237
Muster, Thomas 49, 109, 110, 126

Nadal, Rafael 112, 122, 138-139, 144-145,
    150-151, 155-156, 161, 164-168, 173-
    174, 177, 184, 200, 234-235
Nalbandian, David 24, 27, 60, 63, 70, 75,
    91-98, 106, 151, 157, 158-161, 164, 200,
    217, 235
Nastase, Ilie 22, 140, 178, 211
Navratilova, Martina 41, 86, 140, 141,
    153, 211

Nestor, Daniel 128
Neuchatel 50
Neue Zurcher Zeitung 101-102, 189
New Brighton 227
Newcombe, John 22, 131, 143, 163, 236
Newsday 223, 228
New York Post 223
New York Times 194, 222, 240
Nicklaus, Jack 140, 169. 179
Nike 25, 112, 146, 197, 206, 225,
Noah, Yannick 25, 143
Novak, Jiri 33, 89
Nuriootpa 12

Oberer, Stephane 23, 31
Oberwil 104
Obwalden 105
Octagon 212
Ogi, Adolf 228
Old Boys Tennis Club 8, 9, 12, 17, 88
O'Neal, Tatum 211
Oriental Hotel 125

Pacific Life Open 119
Paes, Leander 86, 118
Paganini, Pierre 13, 45-47, 58-59
Panatta, Adriano 112
Paris 21, 30, 31, 38, 62, 67, 70, 76, 78, 94,
    126, 131, 142-145, 155, 156, 164-168,
    178, 198, 218, 223
Parsons, John 220
Pavel, Andrei 111
Peninsula Hotel, NY 126, 153
Perry, Fred 142, 168
Phelps, Michael 140
Philippoussis, Mark 35, 81-84, 105
Phillips, Tim 104
Phukat, Thailand 73, 225
Pioline, Cedric 33, 51
Port Elizabeth 226
Portland 112
"Prix Orange" 219
Puerta, Mariano 144-145

Qi Zhong Stadium 157

Rafter, Pat 32-33, 54, 56, 82, 130, 133-
    134, 143, 147
Ramirez, Raul 48
Raoux, Guillame 44, 231

Renshaw, William 162
RF Cosmetic Company 210
Rios, Marcelo 37, 110, 139, 177
Roberts, John 221
Roche, Tony 22, 126, 131, 134, 136, 144,
    146-151, 163-165, 173, 175, 180, 190,
    191, 199
Rochus, Christopher 53
Rochus, Olivier 21, 53
Roddick, Andy 27, 70, 79, 81-83, 91-93,
    97-99, 107, 109, 113-117, 120, 124-128,
    147-151, 156, 161, 170, 173, 176, 177,
    184, 193, 200, 201, 215, 221, 233
Roland Garros xv, 41, 32, 76, 78, 112,
    122, 131, 142-144, 163, 164,
Rolex 207, 213
Rome 38, 60, 139, 155, 163-164, 166, 236
Rose, Charlie 124
Rosewall, Ken 22, 131, 178
Rosset, Marc x, xiii, xix, 23, 25, 32-35, 46,
    49-51, 75, 91-92, 170, 205, 206, 232
Ruf, Walter 41
Rye Brook, NY 37

Safin, Marat 42, 53, 60-62, 69, 75, 77,
    103, 107, 109, 128, 134-136, 139, 142-
    144, 156, 161, 233, 234
St. Jakobshalle Hall 24, 25, 173
St. Polten 38
"Sala Polivalenta" 111
Sampras, Pete v, xii, xv, xvii, 13, 23, 25,
    37, 42, 48, 53, 54-58, 62, 77, 80, 132,
    134, 139, 143, 148, 152-153, 168-169,
    171, 172-179, 197, 202, 206, 211, 220,
    223-224, 232, 235
Sanguinetti, Davide 32, 60, 231
Santoro, Fabrice 51
Savoy Hotel 86
Schmidt, Caius 68
Schmocker, Christophe 227, 228
Schnyder, Dany xvii, 10
Schnyder, Patty 10
Schuettler, Rainer 75, 99
Schumacher, Michael 140
Schweizer Illustriere 206
Sears, Richard 153, 162
Sedgman, Frank 48, 232
SFX 212
Shanghai 7, 15, 69 71, 95, 96, 155-159,
    173-176, 183, 229

Shanghai Daily   159
Sharapova, Maria   xvi, 146, 212
Sheshan Golf Club   173
Shields, Brooke   211
Smash   10
Smythe, Patty   211
Soderling, Robin   165
Sonnstags Zeitung   vii, 192, 215
Sports Illustrated   223
Squillari, Franco   61, 74
Stammbach, Rene   50
Stadler, Roland   49
Staubli, Reto   27, 113, 215
Steinberg, Mark   169
Stern   220
Stolle, Sandon   66
Suddeutsche Zeitung   220
Swiss News Agency   227
Sydney   20, 39-42, 47, 50, 58, 60, 74, 118, 130-133
Sydney Morning Herald   224

Tages-Anzeiger   vii, 245
Tennis Masters Cup   15, 58, 69-74, 95-102, 108, 119, 124, 127, 128, 155, 156-161, 173, 186, 200, 201, 210, 218, 229, 233-235
Thailand Open   125-126
The Sun   148
Tilden, Bill   153, 178
Tipsarevic, Janko   173
Toronto   66, 67, 117, 168, 234, 237
Toulouse   24, 24, 28, 29, 75, 112, 231
Trifu, Gabriel   111
Trump, Donald   151
Turramurra   132

Ubolratana, Rajakanya (Thai Princess)   126
Ulihrach, Bohdan   61
Ungricht, Christine   68, 93
UNICEF   175, 226
US Open   x, xviii, 24, 27, 28, 31-33, 39-43, 58, 63, 68, 91, 92, 95, 108, 119-122, 126-128, 131, 135, 143, 145, 151, 153, 158, 170-179, 194-196, 198, 200, 210, 212, 223, 226, 229, 231-237

Vavrinec, Drahomira   40
Vavrinec, Mirka   40-43, 58, 71, 79, 84-87, 102, 104, 112, 117, 118, 125, 129, 147, 155, 173-176, 187, 188, 209, 215, 227,
Vavrinec, Miroslav   40
Van Garsse, Christophe 32
Vienna   33, 47, 69, 70, 93, 95, 233
Vilas, Guillermo   122, 158, 165
Vinceguerra, Andreas   21
Voinea, Adrian   61

Wagga Wagga   130
Wallis   185
Washington, MaliVai   62
Wawrinka, Stanislas   137
Weber, Gerry   70
Werder, Thomas   210, 227
Wilander, Mats   xv, 37, 122, 143, 162, 180, 198, 234, 236, 239
Wilding, Tony   153
Willenborg, Blaine   xiv
Williams, Robbie   187
Williams, Robin   151
Williams, Serena   xvi, 86, 163, 199
Williams, Venus   xvi
Wilson   25, 54, 61, 197, 206, 208, 213
Wimbledon   v, x, xiv, xvi, xvii, 8, 15, 21-25, 30-33, 39, 53-63, 67, 77-92, 97, 101-117, 122,123, 131, 41, 153, 184, 185 1978, 200, 201, 210-215, 220, 221, 228, 231-236
Wintour, Anna   187
Witt, Klaus-Peter "KP"   xiv, xv, xvi
Woodbridge, Todd   92
Woods, Tiger   vii, 140, 169, 173, 179, 198, 199, 212, 213, 241, 243

Xhosa meal   227
Yakin, Murat   186